XAML

IN A NUTSHELL

Other resources from O'Reilly

Related titles

Programming Windows Presentation Foundation
Programming C#
C# Cookbook™
Programming Visual Basic 2005
Visual Basic 2005 in a Nutshell
Programming ASP.NET
ASP.NET 2.0 Cookbook™
XML in a Nutshell
HTML & XHTML: The Definitive Guide

oreilly.com

oreilly.com is more than a complete catalog of O'Reilly books. You'll also find links to news, events, articles, weblogs, sample chapters, and code examples.

oreillynet.com is the essential portal for developers interested in open and emerging technologies, including new platforms, programming languages, and operating systems.

Conferences

O'Reilly brings diverse innovators together to nurture the ideas that spark revolutionary industries. We specialize in documenting the latest tools and systems, translating the innovator's knowledge into useful skills for those in the trenches. Visit *conferences.oreilly.com* for our upcoming events.

Safari Bookshelf (*safari.oreilly.com*) is the premier online reference library for programmers and IT professionals. Conduct searches across more than 1,000 books. Subscribers can zero in on answers to time-critical questions in a matter of seconds. Read the books on your Bookshelf from cover to cover or simply flip to the page you need. Try it today for free.

XAML

IN A NUTSHELL

Lori A. MacVittie

O'REILLY®

Beijing • Cambridge • Farnham • Köln • Paris • Sebastopol • Taipei • Tokyo

XAML in a Nutshell
by Lori A. MacVittie

Published by O'Reilly Media, Inc., 1005 Gravenstein Highway North, Sebastopol, CA 95472.

O'Reilly books may be purchased for educational, business, or sales promotional use. Online editions are also available for most titles (*safari.oreilly.com*). For more information, contact our corporate/institutional sales department: (800) 998-9938 or *corporate@oreilly.com*.

Editor: Jeff Pepper
Production Editor: Matt Hutchinson
Copyeditor: Rachel Monaghan
Proofreader: Matt Hutchinson
Indexer: Ellen Troutman
Cover Designer: Karen Montgomery
Interior Designer: David Futato
Illustrators: Robert Romano, Jessamyn Read, and Lesley Borash

Printing History:

March 2006: First Edition.

This book uses RepKover™, a durable and flexible lay-flat binding.

ISBN: 0-596-52673-3
[M]

Table of Contents

Part IV. Appendixes

Preface

Windows Vista is on its way, and with it comes a brand-new mechanism for defining user interfaces. XAML is one of many new technologies appearing in Windows Vista and promises to be a pervasive part of core Windows programming across a variety of yet-to-be-introduced Windows frameworks. XAML completely removes the need for user-interface designers to understand code. Third-party visual layout applications can now generate valid XAML for use in building sophisticated Windows Vista applications.

The Windows Presentation Foundation (WPF), and therefore XAML, offer many sophisticated user-interface features that are not available in other declarative markup languages such as HTML or XUL. Scaling and rotation of both text and graphics, animation, and extensibility are all core parts of WPF and accessible to XAML developers. While HTML was developed primarily for displaying text and graphics on the Web, XAML's primary target is native Windows applications (although it can also target web-based deployments).

The close relationship between runtime objects and the elements in a XAML file make XAML an easy choice for user-interface design on the Windows platform. It offers the means to create rich, or "smart," clients that act more like a full-featured interface than a web-based application.

XAML can be used to design user interfaces without the need for code, or it can be used in conjunction with supported .NET languages such as C# and VB.NET. XAML is the preferred method of developing interfaces for applications on the Windows Vista platform because its powerful features allow developers to create interfaces that go above and beyond traditional interface design. XAML and the WPF open up endless possibilities for exciting new user interfaces, and this book will provide an understanding of the language and the framework upon which those interfaces are developed.

Who Should Read This Book

This book is intended for both .NET developers and user-interface designers familiar with HTML and the basics of XML. Developers intending to write full applications should have a good understanding of an existing .NET language such as C# or Visual Basic, as application logic requires development of code in a .NET-supported language.

Familiarity with other declarative markup languages such as HTML or XUL will help you quickly grasp the concepts and user-interface elements used to design interfaces with XAML.

Even if you are not familiar with a .NET language or other declarative markup languages, this book will be invaluable in providing you with an understanding of XAML.

What This Book Covers

This book covers XAML as it exists in the WinFX SDK (Community Technology Preview, October 2005). It covers core XAML constructs and discusses syntax as it relates to interfacing with the WinFX runtime—the WPF. The book provides examples and documentation of all core components and presents detailed discussions on features such as animation, resources, and layout that will jump-start you on your way to becoming a XAML developer.

There are already several flavors of XAML, each created to enable the design of user interfaces for a specific Windows API, such as Windows Workflow Foundation. This book focuses on the core XAML language as intended for use in building user interfaces for Avalon and will not explore API-specific subsets.

Organization

This book is organized into four sections. Each section focuses on a particular set of topics that are grouped together logically.

Part I, Introducing XAML

This part of the book introduces the basics of XAML. It details the prerequisites necessary to begin building user interfaces in XAML and introduces MSBuild, Microsoft's new unified build system.

Because XAML supports many new features such as animation and resources, Part II has been devoted to covering these unique concepts. The basics will be covered here, but new concepts such as animation and transformations are given in-depth attention later on.

Chapter 1, *Introducing XAML*
: This chapter provides you with a quick introduction to XAML and includes a list of references to tools available for developing XAML applications.

Chapter 2, *Getting Started with XAML*
: This chapter details the system prerequisites and basics necessary to begin developing and building XAML applications. It introduces Microsoft's new unified build system, MSBuild, and describes how to use it to build XAML applications. The chapter also walks you through an example of using Microsoft's Visual Studio tools to create and build an application.

Part II, XAML Concepts

This part of the book delves into the details of XAML. You'll learn about elements, controls, styles, and animations, and how to use them to create your own user interface.

There are many specific elements not discussed directly in other sections of this book. These elements, in conjunction with all core XAML elements, are detailed here for quick and easy access.

Chapter 3, *The Basics of XAML*
: This chapter describes the core XAML syntax and delves into the types of elements used to create XAML applications. Attributes, attached properties, and event handler coding techniques are explained and accompanied by examples of how to use them.

Chapter 4, *Layout and Positioning*
: This chapter details how to position individual elements using a variety of techniques, including panels and absolute positioning.

Chapter 5, *Resources*
: This chapter provides an overview of resources, focusing on the use of global resources to create a customized look and feel for your interface. It describes how to define and reference resources and details the use of triggers to apply styles based on events.

Chapter 6, *Storyboards and Animations*
: This chapter details the mechanisms available for animating XAML elements. It includes examples of animating properties, such as position and size of elements.

Part III, Core XAML Reference

This part of the book details syntax rules and attributes for XAML in a series of quick-reference chapters. This section divides XAML elements into logical categories of elements, controls, shapes and geometry, layout, animations, and transformations.

Chapter 7, *Elements*
: This reference chapter details and provides examples for the basic elements used within XAML, including `Brush` and `Pen`, `ListItem`, and elements used for text decoration, such as `Inline`, `Bold`, and `Italic`.

Chapter 8, *Controls*
: This reference chapter details the control elements available within XAML, such as `Button`, `CheckBox`, `ImageViewer`, and `Expander`. It also contains a reference to common events.

Chapter 9, *Shapes and Geometry*
: This reference chapter explains the differences between shape and geometry classes and details the `Shape` and `Geometry` elements available within XAML.

Chapter 10, *Layout*
: This reference chapter details the XAML elements used to lay out user interfaces such as `Grid` and `Panel`, and describes supporting elements such as `Trigger`, `Style`, and `Border`.

Chapter 11, *Animations and Transformations*
: This reference chapter details the types of animations and transformations available to XAML elements.

Chapter 12, *Events*
: This reference chapter explains the WPF event system and details the events available to XAML elements.

Part IV, Appendixes

The appendixes detail the CLR classes in the WinFX runtime that are available through XAML, list all of the predefined `Color` values supported by XAML, and present a complete code-only example of building a XAML application.

Appendix A, *System.Windows.Controls*
: Lists the elements found in the `System.Windows.Control` namespace

Appendix B, *System.Windows.Documents*
: Lists the elements found in the `System.Windows.Documents` namespace

Appendix C, *System.Windows.Shapes*
: Lists the elements found in the `System.Windows.Shapes` namespace

Appendix D, *System.Windows*
: Lists the elements found in the `System.Windows` namespace

Appendix E, *System.Windows.Media*
: Lists the elements found in the `System.Windows.Media` namespace

Appendix F, *System.Windows.Input.ApplicationCommands*
: Lists the elements found in the `System.Windows.Input.ApplicationCommands` namespace

Appendix G, *Predefined Colors*
: Lists the available predefined colors supported by XAML

Appendix H, *XAML Interface in Code*
: Contains a XAML declaration used to build a simple application

Conventions Used in This Book

The following list details the font conventions used in the book:

`Constant width`
: Indicates anything that might appear in a XAML document, including element names, tags, attribute values, and entity references, or anything that might appear in a program, including keywords, operators, method names, class names, and literals.

`Constant width bold`
: Indicates user input or emphasis in code examples and fragments.

`Constant width italic`
: Denotes replaceable elements in code statements.

Italic
: Indicates emphasis in body text, new terms when they are defined, pathnames, filenames, program names, and host and domain names.

This icon signifies a tip, suggestion, or general note.

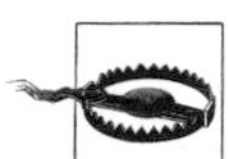

This icon indicates a warning or caution.

Significant code fragments, complete applications, and documents generally appear in a separate paragraph, like this:

```
<Page xmlns="http://schemas.microsoft.com/winfx/avalon/2005"
      xmlns:x="http://schemas.microsoft.com/winfx/xaml/2005">
  <StackPanel>
     <TextBlock>Hello World</TextBlock>
  </StackPanel>
</Page>
```

When a property has a fixed set of values from which to choose, those choices will be displayed as a pipe-separated list:

```
SelectionMode="Single|Multiple|Extended" >
```

XAML, like XML, is case-sensitive. The `Page` element is not the same as the `PAGE` or `page` element. Both are also character-encoding-sensitive, and the smart quotes found in a Microsoft Word document or in the help files accompanying the WinFX SDK are not considered the same as the double quotes produced by applications such as Microsoft's Visual Studio or Notepad. Smart quotes are not valid within a XAML document, so it is important that you use the "Copy code" option in the WinFX SDK help system or turn off smart quotes in Microsoft Word if you wish to use either program to create XAML applications.

Using Code Examples

Most of the examples in this book have very little real-world value and are unlikely to be reused, although they work well as templates to get you started in designing your own user interfaces with XAML. In general, you may use the code in this book in your programs and documentation. Permission is not required unless you're reproducing a significant portion of the code. For example, writing a program that uses several blocks of code from this book does not require permission. Selling or distributing a CD-ROM of examples from O'Reilly books *does* require permission. Answering a question by citing this book and quoting example code does not require permission. Incorporating a significant amount of example code from this book into your product's documentation *does* require permission.

Attribution is appreciated, but not required. An attribution usually includes the title, author, publisher, and ISBN. For example: "*XAML in a Nutshell,* by Lori A. MacVittie. Copyright 2006 O'Reilly Media, Inc., 0-596-52673-3."

If you feel your use of code examples falls outside fair use or the permission given above, feel free to contact us at *permissions@oreilly.com*.

Comments and Questions

Please address comments and questions concerning this book to the publisher:

O'Reilly Media, Inc.
1005 Gravenstein Highway North
Sebastopol, CA 95472
(800) 998-9938 (in the U.S. or Canada)
(707) 829-0515 (international/local)
(707) 829-0104 (fax)

There is a web page for this book that lists errata, examples, or any additional information. You can access this page at:

http://www.oreilly.com/catalog/xamlian

To comment or ask technical questions about this book, send email to:

bookquestions@oreilly.com

For more information about books, conferences, Resource Centers, and the O'Reilly Network, see the O'Reilly web site at:

http://www.oreilly.com

Safari® Enabled

When you see a Safari® Enabled icon on the cover of your favorite technology book, that means the book is available online through the O'Reilly Network Safari Bookshelf.

Safari offers a solution that's better than e-books: it's a virtual library that lets you easily search thousands of top tech books, cut and paste code samples, download chapters, and find quick answers when you need the most accurate, current information. Try it for free at *http://safari.oreilly.com*.

Acknowledgments

Jeff Pepper, the editor who proposed the book and got things rolling.

Brad Shimmin, for bringing the opportunity to my attention in the first place.

My husband, Don, for encouraging me to agree to this undertaking and putting up with long hours spent staring at the screen trying to figure out why something wasn't working the right way, and for a second set of technically minded eyes.

The reviewers of early versions of the manuscript were invaluable in this effort. Thanks especially to Tim Patrick and Filipe Fortes for their thorough reviews and helpful comments.

I

Introducing XAML

1
Introducing XAML

XAML (pronounced "Zamel") stands for e*X*tensible *A*pplication *M*arkup *L*anguage. It is Microsoft's new declarative language for defining application user interfaces. XAML provides an easily extensible and localizable syntax for defining user interfaces separated from application logic, similar to the object-oriented technique for developing *n*-tier applications with a MVC (Model-View-Controller) architecture.

XAML was created by Microsoft expressly for the purpose of interfacing with its .NET Framework on its Windows Vista (formerly codenamed "Longhorn") operating system through the WinFX (codename "Avalon") presentation subsystem runtime environment. XAML gives developers the ability to control the layout of all .NET user-interface elements such as text, buttons, graphics, and listboxes, using XML. Because XAML is XML-based, your code must be well-formed XML. Every XAML tag corresponds directly to a .NET Framework class whose properties are controlled through the use of XML attributes. For example, the `<Button>` tag corresponds directly to the `System.Windows.Controls.Button` class. XAML elements represent a Common Language Runtime (CLR) class, the runtime engine for Microsoft's .NET framework. The CLR is similar to the Java Virtual Machine (JVM), except that the JVM can only run Java language programs, while the CLR can run applications written in a number of .NET languages, such as C#, J#, and VB.NET.

Because XAML elements represent CLR objects (this book focuses on those in the Windows Presentation Foundation [WPF]), anything that can be done with XAML can also be accomplished with procedural code. There are some things, however, that can be done by manipulating the object model programmatically that are not accessible through XAML. Properties that are read only are not exposed through XAML; only those properties that are public and have both a get and a set method are accessible to XAML developers.

Events and handlers can also be specified by XAML attributes, and the necessary code behind the handlers, `codebehind`, can be written in .NET-supported languages—currently C# and VB.NET. This code can be inlined in the XAML file or placed in the `codebehind` file, similar to what is done with ASP.NET code. If procedural code is embedded in a XAML page, you must compile the application before you can run it; if there is no procedural code in the XAML page, you can display it on a Windows Vista system by double-clicking the page file (just as you would with HTML pages). On Windows XP, however, the XAML pages must be "compiled" into an executable application before they can be displayed or loaded into a browser.

XAML is similar to other markup languages designed for rendering in web browsers, such as XHTML and HTML, and uses mechanisms similar to Cascading Style Sheets (CSS) for designating properties of XAML elements. Just as HTML objects are parsed to build out a Document Object Model (DOM) tree, XAML elements are parsed to build out an `ElementTree`.

XAML is inherently object-oriented since its elements represent CLR classes. This means that an element derived from another XAML element inherits the attributes of its parent. For example, a `System.Windows.Controls.Button` derives from `System.Windows.Controls.ButtonBase`, which derives from `System.Windows.Controls.ContentControl`, which derives from `System.Windows.FrameworkElement`, which derives from `System.Windows.UIElement`. Therefore, the `Button` element has very few attributes of its own but still boasts a lengthy list of attributes that it has inherited from classes above it in the hierarchy, such as `Width` and `Height`. It is necessary to understand the nature of inheritance in order to take advantage of XAML and its ability to be extended. Custom controls can be created for XAML by creating subclasses in one of the supported .NET languages (C# or VB.NET), for example, and then exposing the class to XAML developers for use in user-interface design.

Some XAML elements require children and attributes to be of a specific type, usually one of the base classes. Because of the nature of object-oriented programming, any element requiring that its children be of type `UIElement` can be declared as an element derived from `UIElement`. The `Brush` object is a very common attribute type for XAML elements, yet an instance of `Brush` is rarely used as an attribute. Instead, one of `Brush`'s subclasses, such as `SolidColorBrush` or `LinearGradientBrush`, is often used. The nature of object-oriented programming allows an attribute to be broadly defined as a base class and lets the designer choose which specialized subclass will be used.

Because of XAML's object-oriented nature, not all attributes will be listed with the element. It is necessary to understand an element's hierarchy to fully understand all of the attributes available to describe the element. In Part III, I have included each element's hierarchy—as well as a description of abstract elements—to facilitate this understanding. While abstract elements are rarely, if ever, declared in XAML, their description and attributes are used by derived classes and will therefore be fully described.

The Benefits of XAML

XAML offers similar benefits to other markup-based application interface mechanisms such as XUL (e*X*tensible *U*ser-interface *L*anguage), HTML (*H*yper*T*ext

Markup Language), and Flex. Markup-based interfaces are quick to build and easily modifiable. They require less code than traditional structured programming. For example, creating and defining the properties of a Button with XAML requires just one line of syntax, as opposed to multiple lines in C# or VB.NET:


```
<Button Click="OnClickHandler" Background="Green" Content="Submit" />
```

The same Button object created using C# requires four lines:

```
Button myBtn = new Button( );
myBtn.Background = Brushes.Green;
myBtn.Text="Submit";
myBtn.Click += new System.EventHandler(OnClickHandler);
```

While HTML has limited programmatic functionality and control, XAML and other new-generation declarative markup languages offer back-end scripting language support to circumvent this limitation. While XAML separates the user interface from application logic, it still provides a mechanism by which the two can easily interact. This separation offers several benefits, including easily localized user interfaces and the ability for developers to modify application logic without affecting the user interface, and vice versa.

XAML also opens up user-interface design to a wider group of developers, namely graphic designers and markup developers. Anyone with experience using HTML or other web-oriented markup languages will find XAML to be intuitive; they will be able to jump in and begin developing user interfaces in a short period of time. This alleviates the burden placed on .NET developers and allows them to focus on developing application logic, while others determine the look and feel of the user interface.

XAML is toolable, which offers third-party developers opportunities to create applications that support it. Several third-party applications already exist that offer visual environments for developing XAML. Additional products are expected as Windows Vista begins to be generally deployed.

XAML is extensible, as its name implies. XAML can easily be extended by developers creating custom controls, elements, and functionality. Because XAML is essentially the XML representation of objects defined by the WPF, XAML elements can easily be extended by developers using object-oriented programming techniques. Custom controls and composite elements can be developed and exposed to user-interface designers or shared with other developers.

Finally, by using XAML, Windows applications can be delivered unchanged via the Web to Windows clients. *Smart clients*, Microsoft's term for rich user interfaces with full Windows functionality, can be delivered to any connected Windows machine over the Internet through a web browser without requiring the overhead of a managed desktop to deploy full-featured thick-client applications.

What XAML Is Not

XAML is purely a markup language designed for describing user-interface components and arranging them on the screen. Though there are components of XAML that appear to be programmatic in nature, such as the Trigger and Transform elements, XAML is not a procedural programming language and is not designed to execute application logic.

XAML is interpreted, not compiled—though it can be compiled. Microsoft recommends that XAML be compiled by compacting it into Binary Application Markup Language (BAML). Both XAML and BAML are interpreted by the WPF and then rendered on the screen in a manner similar to HTML. Unlike HTML, however, XAML is strongly typed. HTML defaults to ignoring tags and attributes it doesn't understand, while XAML requires that every tag and attribute be understood, including the typing of attributes. Although all attributes initially appear to be strings, don't let that fool you. The string represents an object, and because those objects must be understood by WPF, XAML is strongly typed.

Finally, XAML is not HTML. Although there are similarities in the declaration of elements, application of styles, and assignment of event handlers, XAML is an XML-based interface to the Windows Presentation Framework, while HTML is a markup language that is rendered within the context of the browser and operating system in which it is loaded. XAML is far more than a mechanism for displaying information and soliciting basic user input. It is a complete user-interface design and development markup language that reaches beyond the scope of simple HTML elements by including advanced features such as 3-D element rendering and rich vector-based drawing capabilities.

XAML Development Resources

XAML can be developed in myriad ways. XAML can be written in any text editor. For example, all the code included in this book was written in Notepad and then compiled using MSBuild.

There are much easier ways to develop a XAML user interface, however, and most of them involve a visual layout tool. There are several third-party tools, as well as tools from Microsoft that support XAML. Some are focused on only one aspect of XAML, such as development of 3-D interfaces, while others are more generally applicable. Some popular tools available as of this writing include:

Electric Rain ZAM D XAML Tool (*http://www.erain.com/products/zam3d/*)
: A tool that supports visual development of 3-D interface elements for XAML.

Xamlon Pro and XAML Converter (*http://www.xamlon.com/*)
: Xamlon Pro supports development of XAML user interfaces in a visual environment. XAML Converter converts other formats to XAML.

MyXAML (*http://www.myxaml.com/*)
: An open source project dedicated to XAML development. Includes a mailing list and forums focused on discussion of XAML and the sharing of tips, tricks, and techniques.

Mobiform Aurora XAML Editor (*http://www.mobiform.com/2005/XAML/xamlhome.htm*)
: A visual editor for XAML from Mobiform.

XamlViewer (*http://weblogs.asp.net/gmilano/archive/2004/11/24/269082.aspx*)
: A visual editor for XAML that integrates into Visual Studio 2005.

XamlPad
: A simple, real-time visual editor for XAML. XamlPad does not support visual layout of elements, but it does offer a visual representation, in real time, of XAML elements. XamlPad is included in the WinFX SDK.

Microsoft's Visual Studio 2005 Extensions for WinFX
: Tools that include XAML Intellisense support through schema extensions for the editor and project templates for the WPF, the Windows Communication Foundation (formerly known as "Indigo"), and WinFX SDK documentation integration. These tools do not include a graphical design surface for either the WPF or the Windows Communication Foundation.

Microsoft Expression Interactive Designer (formerly "Sparkle") (http://www.microsoft.com/products/expression/en/interactive_designer/default.aspx)
: A forthcoming Microsoft visual-design tool for developing WinFX applications.

2 Getting Started with XAML

As with most development-oriented tools, it's important to have the proper environment before you can start developing user interfaces with XAML. This chapter discusses the prerequisites necessary to define and run XAML applications and later details the basic structure of a XAML project, as well as how to compile and run that application.

This chapter assumes that you have a working knowledge of XML and are at least somewhat familiar with other user-interface markup languages, such as ASP.NET and HTML.

XAML Prerequisites

Although XAML is designed specifically for Windows Vista, it's also available on Windows XP and Windows Server 2003, given that certain system requirements are met. This makes it possible for developers to become familiar with XAML and the WinFX SDK before Windows Vista is officially available.

XAML can be used to develop applications on the following operating systems:

- Windows XP SP2
- Windows Server 2003 SP1
- Windows Vista

On Windows XP SP2 and Windows Server 2003 SP1, you will first need to install the WinFX runtime, which contains, among other things, the Windows Presentation Foundation (Avalon). Regardless of the operating system you choose, you'll need to install the WinFX SDK. The SDK contains the libraries, build tools, and documentation necessary to begin developing user interfaces with XAML. Depending on the operating system you choose, the WinFX SDK may also have prerequisites that must be met.

If you plan on using the WinFX Extensions to Visual Studio 2005, you *must* install Visual Studio 2005 before installing the WinFX SDK.

Defining XAML Applications

Getting Started

A XAML application comprises two types of elements: an application element and the set elements that make up the user interface. The XAML files contain the user-interface definition for your application. The `codebehind` files will contain the application logic and the code that handles event processing. XAML does not provide a mechanism for handling events, but it can direct the runtime engine to call event handlers written in C# or VB.NET. If you're a developer, you'll code the event handlers and application logic just as you always have, but because the user-interface code is separate, you'll have to pay a bit more attention to the names of the handlers and elements you reference because you don't define them—they're declared and named in the XAML file.

You can define XAML applications completely using C# or VB.NET. The CLR classes represented by XAML are all accessible through code, and you can write applications just as you always have, if you so desire. XAML offers you the ability to completely separate the presentation layer (user interface) from the application logic, thus making it easier to split up development responsibilities and isolate UI changes from the code. Appendix H provides an example of an application declared in XAML, as well as entirely in C#.

The most common application element is of type `NavigationApplication`. `NavigationApplication` defines an application that behaves like a web application or wizard in that it consists of pages between which a user navigates using hyperlinks and forward and back buttons.

The application definition is generally declared in its own file. It requires two properties to be set, the namespace and the startup URI, which is the URI of the first page that should be loaded when the application starts. For our purposes in this chapter, the application definition file will be called *MyApp.xaml*. It is detailed in Example 2-1.

Example 2-1. MyApp.xaml

```
<NavigationWindow
    xmlns="http://schemas.microsoft.com/winfx/avalon/2005"
    StartupUri="Page1.xaml" />
```

In XAML, element names correspond to CLR object names, and attributes represent properties. The exception to this rule is with standard XML elements, such as `xmlns`, which is used to declare the namespace used within the XML file. The namespace used here is the default namespace for the application and identifies the Avalon types. If we did not specify the Avalon namespace as the default, all core XAML elements would need to include a reference to it. That's a lot of extra typing. It is much easier to use the Avalon namespace as the default, unless you will be primarily using custom elements defined in your own namespace, in which case, it is probably easier to specify your own namespace as the default and explicitly identify XAML elements instead. All the examples in this book will declare the Avalon namespace as the default. Every XAML element requires either explicit references to the namespace on a per-element basis or the declaration of the Avalon namespace as the default of the root element. Of course the latter is recommended, as it will alleviate the requirement to explicitly reference the namespace for every XAML element in the file.

The first element declared in any XAML file is called the *root element*. The root element must contain a reference to the namespace in which it is defined. For XAML elements, the namespace is `http://schemas.microsoft.com/winfx/avalon/2005`.

The default namespace will change when WPF officially ships.

Root elements are containers that hold other XAML elements. The most common root element for the application definition is `NavigationWindow`. The most common root elements for a page definition are `Panel` and its subclasses, `DockPanel` and `StackPanel`, and `Page`. `Window` is also used, though less often than the aforementioned elements.

In Example 2-1, the `StartupUri` attribute of the `NavigationWindow` specifies the XAML page that will be loaded when the application starts, in this case *Page1.xaml*. Additional attributes of `NavigationWindow` can be specified. For a complete description of `NavigationWindow`, see Chapter 8.

Page1.xaml will contain the actual definition for the user interface. Any subsequent pages will be referenced through allowable mechanisms, such as the `HyperLink` element. Like all XAML files, *Page1.xaml* requires a root element. The file is shown in Example 2-2.

Example 2-2. Page1.xaml

```
<StackPanel xmlns="http://schemas.microsoft.com/winfx/avalon/2005">
   <TextBlock>Hello World</TextBlock>
   <Button Width="100">Click Me</Button>
</StackPanel>
```

`StackPanel` is fully described in Chapter 7. Like `DockPanel`, it is used to hold elements, and that is all you need to know for now. The `TextBlock` element holds text, and the `Button` element represents a standard user-interface button. Interpreting the code in XamlPad produces the output shown in Figure 2-1.

This is an extremely simple example of a XAML application with absolutely no attention paid to style, layout, or usefulness. Refining these aspects of user-interface design is a subject for subsequent chapters. For now, it is only important that the file declares the minimum requirements for a XAML application. With a successfully defined application definition (*MyApp.xaml*) and a page definition (*Page1.xaml*), it's time to build the application into a Windows executable.

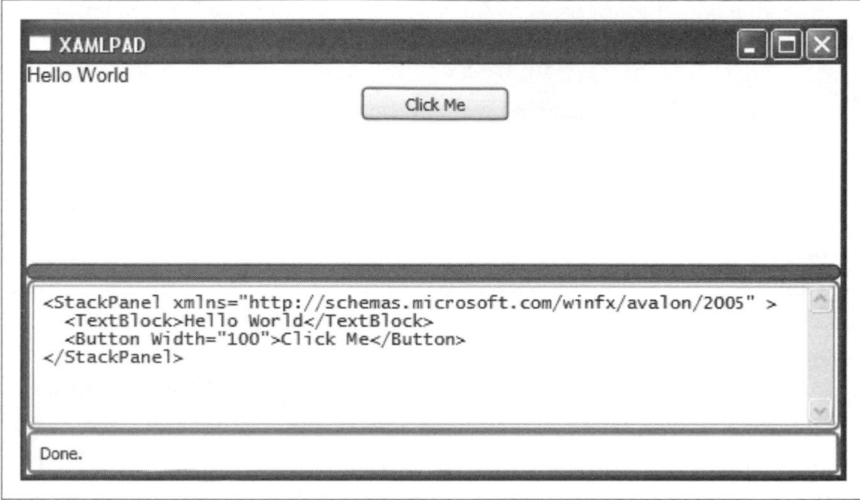

Figure 2-1. A simple XAML page previewed in XamlPad

Building XAML Applications

While XAML can be used to create libraries and modules that can be shared and used to build other applications (in the same way that C# or VB.NET can be used to build DLLs or shared assemblies), it is more likely that you will use XAML to generate an application. There are two types of XAML applications: express and installed. *Express applications* are hosted in a web browser. *Installed applications* are traditional desktop applications and can be either Windows applications or console applications. The type of application generated is determined by a property value in the project file MSBuild uses to assemble the application.

MSBuild is one of the new features in Windows Vista and Visual Studio 2005. With the release of Visual Studio 2005, Microsoft has moved to a unified build environment. All projects now use MSBuild facilities to generate CLR assemblies. The most exciting, and beneficial, aspect of this change is that Visual Studio is no longer required to compile and build applications; builds can be completely automated without it. MSBuild is distributed with the WinFX SDK.

> If you're using Visual Studio to edit XAML and associated `codebehind` files, don't worry about the details of MSBuild. The relevant files are generated automatically by Visual Studio.

MSBuild is similar to ANT and Unix/Linux *make* facilities. MSBuild reads in XML-based project files, conventionally named with a *.proj* extension, and executes the tasks contained in the project file to produce the desired target.

There are a number of XML elements that can be used in a project file. This discussion covers only the basic elements and the typical ways that they are used to create an Avalon project file. The following list describes the key elements in an Avalon project file:

`Project`
: Functions as the root element for all project files

`PropertyGroup`
: Contains project property settings, such as the build configuration setting (`Debug` or `Release`)

`ItemGroup`
: Contains the list of items, such as source or resource files, that make up the project

`Import`
: Allows you to import other project files, such as target files, into your project

There are a multitude of options that can be configured with MSBuild. It is a very rich schema designed to handle building targets in a dynamic environment. The following code illustrates the minimum requirements for a project file:

```
<Project
    xmlns="http://schemas.microsoft.com/developer/msbuild/2003">
    <PropertyGroup>
        <AssemblyName>MyFirstApplication</AssemblyName>
        <TargetType>winexe|exe|library|module</TargetType>
        <OutputPath>.\</OutputPath>
    </PropertyGroup>
    <Import Project="$(MSBuildBinPath)\Microsoft.CSharp.targets" />
    <Import Project="$(MSBuildBinPath)\Microsoft.WinFX.targets" />
    <ItemGroup>
        <ApplicationDefinition Include="MyApp.xaml" />
        <Page Include="Page1.xaml" />
    </ItemGroup>
    <ItemGroup>
    <Reference Include="System">
          <Private>false</Private>
    </Reference>
    <Reference Include="System.Xml">
          <Private>false</Private>
    </Reference>
    <Reference Include="System.Data">
          <Private>false</Private>
    </Reference>
    <Reference Include="WindowsBase">
          <Private>false</Private>
    </Reference>
    <Reference Include="PresentationCore">
          <Private>false</Private>
    </Reference>
    <Reference Include="PresentationFramework">
          <Private>false</Private>
    </Reference>
    <Reference Include="WindowsUIAutomation">
          <Private>false</Private>
    </Reference>
```

```
      <Reference Include="UIAutomationProvider">
          <Private>false</Private>
      </Reference>
    </ItemGroup>
  </Project>
```


The most important piece of the project file is the `ItemGroup`, which specifies the inclusion of the XAML files that make up your project. You'll need one `ApplicationDefinition` file, identified by the `<ApplicationDefinition .../>` element, and one or more page definition files, included through the use of the `<Page .../>` element.

You can set a few optional attributes in the `PropertyGroup` element:

`HostInBrowser`
: This `Boolean` value is set to `true` to generate express applications or `false` to generate an installed application. The default value is `false`.

`Install`
: This `Boolean` value determines the type of deployment file to generate. When set to `true`, a deployment file for an installed application is generated. When set to `false`, a deployment file for an express application is created. If `HostInBrowser` is set to `true`, the default value for this property is `false`. If `HostInBrowser` is `false`, the default value for this property is `true`.

`Configuration`
: This `String`-based value determines the type of configuration to build: `Debug` or `Release`. The default is `Release`.

MSBuild relies on a number of environment variables related to the location of libraries and the identification of the .NET Framework version used to build the application. The WinFX SDK includes a batch file to appropriately set these environment variables. The necessary variables are:

```
SET FrameworkVersion=v2.0.50215
SET FrameworkDir=%windir%\Microsoft.NET\Framework
SET WinFX=%ProgramFiles%\Reference Assemblies\Microsoft\WinFX\
%FrameworkVersion%
SET URT=%FrameworkDir%\%FrameworkVersion%
SET WinFXSDK=C:\Program Files\Microsoft SDKs\WinFX
SET FrameworkSDKDir=%WinFXSDK%\
SET WinFXSDKTOOLPATH=%WinFXSDK%\bin
SET PATH=%URT%;%WinFXSDKTOOLPATH%;%WinFXSDK%\vc\bin;%path%;
SET INCLUDE=%WinFXSDK%\Include;%WinFXSDK%\vc\Include;
SET LIB=%WinFXSDK%\Lib;%WinFXSDK%\vc\Lib;
```

After the environment variables have been set and the project file is appropriately configured for your application target, execute MSBuild on the command line to generate your application. When completed, you will see several files:

MyFirstApplication.exe
: The executable application. This file is always generated.

MyFirstApplication.xbap
: The express application. This file is recognized by the Windows IE browser and can be run by opening the file within IE. This file is generated only when

HostInBrowser is set to true. (This file extension was *.xapp* in previous CTP releases.)

MyFirstApplication.exe.manifest
: This file is always generated.

MyFirstApplication.pdb
: The program database file, used for debugging and incremental build purposes. This file is always generated.

MyFirstApplication.application
: The deployment file for the application. This file is generated only when Install is explicitly set to true or when HostInBrowser is set to false.

When you run MSBuild, the files are parsed into two corresponding files: a C# generated file, identified by the extension *.g.cs* (the g stands for generated, the *cs* for C#), and a BAML file, identified by the *.baml* extension. These files are automatically placed into a created subdirectory that is named according to the Configuration property located in the PropertyGroup section of the project file. For a release configuration, the subdirectory is called *obj\Release*. Similarly, the *obj\Debug* hierarchy is used for a Debug configuration.

The class files generated from markup are partial class files. A class file containing the implementation of event handlers and other application logic will be merged with the generated partial class file during compilation.

You must compile an Avalon application before running it, even if the pages contain only markup.

The C# files are then compiled into an assembly. The assembly is named according to the AssemblyName attribute and placed into the location referenced by the OutputPath attribute. All that remains of the markup is the BAML, which is deserialized into CLR objects at runtime by the System.Windows.Serialization.Parser class. This class can be used to (de)serialize any BAML or XAML at runtime.

If you generated a Windows executable, you can now double-click on the name of the file or run it from the command line. If you specified the creation of a hosted application, you'll need to load the *.xbap* file from Microsoft Internet Explorer, which will launch the presentation manager and run the application.

Running the Windows executable defined in the previous section generates the application in Figure 2-2.

You'll note that there are similarities and differences between the preview shown in Figure 2-1 and the application shown in Figure 2-2. XamlPad, one of the tools installed with XAML, is an excellent real-time What You See Is What You Get (WYSIWYG) environment for playing around with XAML, but it does not support the full definition of an application. Because NavigationWindow is used as the root element for this application, the application automatically inherits a navigation "chrome" at the top of the application, with forward and back buttons similar to those used in Internet Explorer to navigate through web pages. Aside from this difference, the resulting page appears the same.

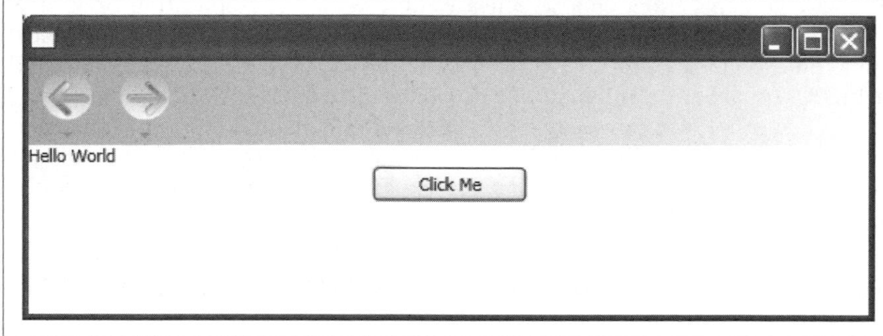

Figure 2-2. MyFirstApplication

XAML Applications and Visual Studio

Working in Visual Studio, you'll be able to select a number of WinFX Applications, and the project files and application manifest will be generated automatically. You can choose to create a WinFX Windows executable, a WinFX WebBrowser application, a WinFX Service Library (which creates a WinFX library comprising the definition and implementation of a WinFX Service), or a WinFX Custom Control Library (for extending WinFX controls). However, you'll still have to edit both the XAML and associated C# or VB.NET `codebehind` files manually.

If you've downloaded and installed the WinFX extensions for Visual Studio 2005, fire up the IDE. Choose Create Project and you'll be presented with a list of options, as illustrated in Figure 2-3.

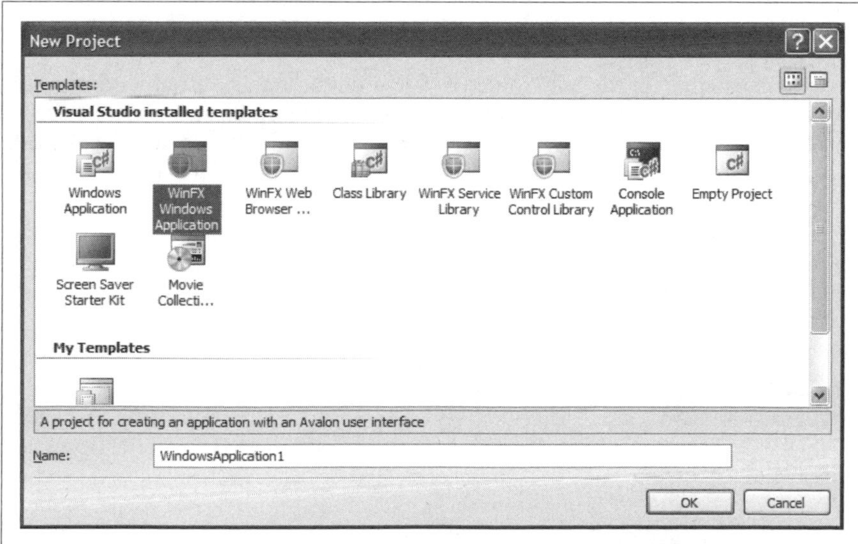

Figure 2-3. WinFX application options in Visual Studio 2005

To create an application, choose either WinFX Windows Application or WinFX WebBrowser Application, depending on whether you want to deploy the application as an executable or for use within a web browser. Give the project a name and click OK. Visual Studio automatically generates the default XAML and `codebehind` files. In Figure 2-4, you can see that it has generated *Windows1.xaml* (Example 2-5) and *Windows1.xaml.cs* (Example 2-6). The language of the `codebehind` file depends on your choice of .NET-supported languages. I have chosen C#, so the generated files will reflect that choice.

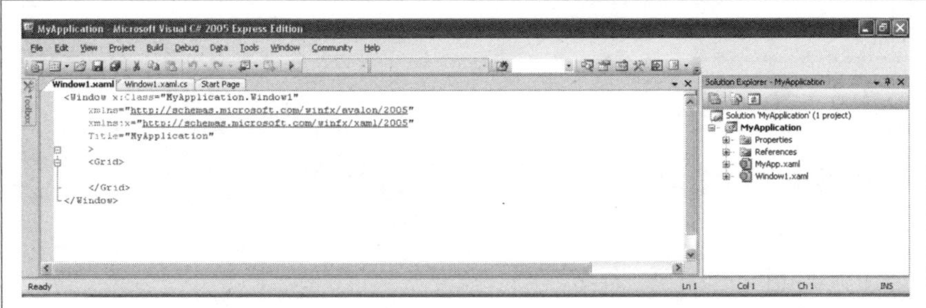

Figure 2-4. Default files generated by Visual C# 2005 Express Edition

There are some minor differences between creating a WinFX WebBrowser and WinFX Windows application that occur whether or not you use Visual Studio. In a WebBrowser application, the default start page's root element is `Page`. In a WinFX Windows application, the default start page's root element is `Window`. The `Window` class will not work in a WebBrowser application by design because Avalon applications running in the browser are sandboxed and don't have the appropriate permissions to open new windows.

If you look carefully in the SolutionExplorer, you'll note that Visual Studio generates additional XAML and C# files to represent the application. Because you normally won't be working with the application-level files and instead will work on individual pages, Visual Studio will only display the first `Window` and its `codebehind` file after generating the appropriate code. You can see the relationship between the two files in Examples 2-3 and 2-4. The `StartupUri` value for the `Application` element is `Window1.xaml`, which is the XAML file that automatically opens for editing after Visual Studio generates the files for the application.

Example 2-3. Default C# code generated for the application

```
using System;
using System.Windows;
using System.Data;
using System.Xml;
using System.Configuration;

namespace MyApplication
{
```

Example 2-3. Default C# code generated for the application (continued)

```
    /// <summary>
    /// Interaction logic for MyApp.xaml
    /// </summary>

    public partial class MyApp : Application
    {

    }
}
```

Getting Started

Example 2-4. Default XAML code generated for the application

```
<Application x:Class="MyApplication.MyApp"
    xmlns="http://schemas.microsoft.com/winfx/avalon/2005"
    xmlns:x="http://schemas.microsoft.com/winfx/xaml/2005"
    StartupUri="Window1.xaml"
    >
    <Application.Resources>

    </Application.Resources>
</Application>
```

The automatically generated XAML (Example 2-5) and codebehind file (Example 2-6) contain the shell of a XAML definition and include, by default, the root `Window` element and an instance of the `Panel`-derived `Grid` element. Microsoft is encouraging developers to use `Grid` for base user-interface design, primarily for its flexibility in positioning elements on the page.

Example 2-5. Default XAML code generated by Visual Studio 2005

```
<Window x:Class="MyApplication.Window1"
    xmlns="http://schemas.microsoft.com/winfx/avalon/2005"
    xmlns:x="http://schemas.microsoft.com/winfx/xaml/2005"
    Title="MyApplication" >
    <Grid>

    </Grid>
</Window>
```

Example 2-6. Default C# code generated by Visual Studio 2005

```
using System;
using System.Windows;
using System.Windows.Controls;
using System.Windows.Data;
using System.Windows.Documents;
using System.Windows.Media;
using System.Windows.Shapes;


namespace MyApplication
{
```

Example 2-6. Default C# code generated by Visual Studio 2005 (continued)

```
    /// <summary>
    /// Interaction logic for Window1.xaml
    /// </summary>

    public partial class Window1 : Window
    {

        public Window1( )
        {
            InitializeComponent( );
        }

    }
}
```

First, add a Button element with the name MyButton and a Click handler called ChangeMe to *Window1.xaml*. Your code should look something like Example 2-7 when you have finished.

Example 2-7. Adding a Button with a handler to Window1.xaml

```
<Window x:Class="MyApplication.Window1"
    xmlns="http://schemas.microsoft.com/winfx/avalon/2005"
    xmlns:x="http://schemas.microsoft.com/winfx/xaml/2005"
    Title="MyApplication"
    >
    <Grid>
        <Button
             Grid.Row="0"
             Grid.Column="0"
             Background="Aqua"
             Content="This is a test"
             Name="MyButton"
             Click="ChangeMe"/>
    </Grid>
</Window>
```

Next, open *Window1.xaml.cs*. Inside the partial class definition for Window1, you'll need to add an event handler for the button you just added to the XAML file. Add the following code:

```
    void ChangeMe(object sender, RoutedEventArgs eventArgs)
      {
          count++;
          MyButton.Content = "You have clicked " + count + " times!";
      }
```

Don't forget to add the variable count as a member of the class. Your code should look something like Example 2-8 when you have finished. When you reference the Button in *Window1.xaml* in code, make sure that you use the Name you assigned to the Button in the XAML file (MyButton in this example). There is no need to declare the element again; it already exists in the partial class generated when the

XAML file is "compiled." It will be joined with the partial class defined in the codebehind file when the solution is built to form a cohesive class. This is why you can reference elements by the Name with which they are declared in the XAML file within the codebehind file as well.

Example 2-8. Adding an event handler to Window1.xaml.cs

```
using System;
using System.Windows;
using System.Windows.Controls;
using System.Windows.Data;
using System.Windows.Documents;
using System.Windows.Media;
using System.Windows.Shapes;


namespace MyApplication
{
    /// <summary>
    /// Interaction logic for Window1.xaml
    /// </summary>

    public partial class Window1 : Window
    {
        int count = 0;
        public Window1( )
        {
            InitializeComponent( );
        }

        void ChangeMe(object sender, RoutedEventArgs eventArgs)
        {
            count++;
            MyButton.Content = "You have clicked " + count + " times!";
        }

    }
}
```

After adding elements and the appropriate handlers, logic, etc., you'll build the solution the same way you've always built applications using Visual Studio. Choose Build, then Build Solution (or just hit F6), and wait for the application to compile. You can then test, debug (Figure 2-5), and deploy the application just as you would any other application created using Visual Studio.

Save the changes to the files and build the solution, then run the application. The application will appear as an aqua button filling the entire application (Figure 2-5). The text will initially read "This is a test." Click on the button. You'll notice that the handler you implemented (ChangeMe) executed and replaced the text with "You have clicked 5 times!".

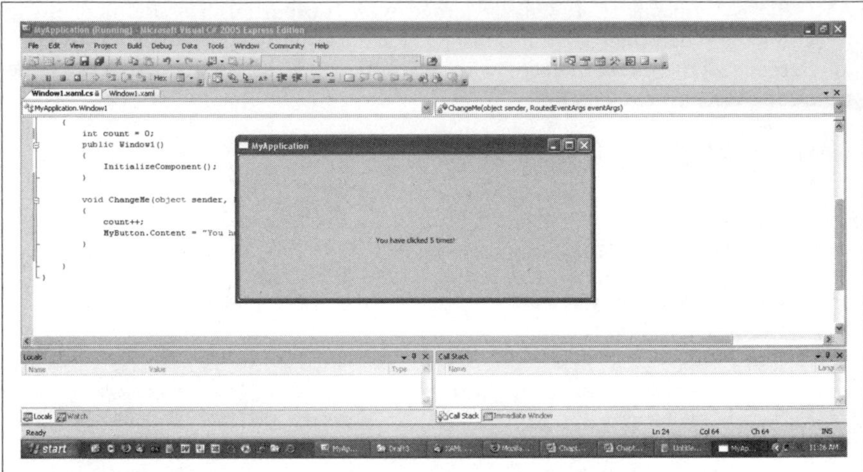

Figure 2-5. Debugging a XAML application within Visual Studio

This process should be familiar to .NET developers. The XAML file is akin to the visual representation of a page or Windows application, and the `codebehind` file is the equivalent of the server-side code necessary to handle events and process requests from users. The difference between developing .NET applications and XAML applications is that at this time, there is no visual mechanism for designing XAML applications. The XAML file is similar to the source view of a .NET page.

As mentioned earlier, when using Visual Studio, it is not necessary to generate the project files or understand how the new unified build system operates. The necessary files are all generated automatically for you by Visual Studio.

Now that you know how to define and build a basic XAML application, it's time to move on to something a bit more interesting. The next chapter dives into the mechanics of XAML and explains more about the language.

XAML Concepts

3
The Basics of XAML

XAML is an XML-based markup language. Given that, it shares many properties with other XML documents, such as case sensitivity and having to be well-formed. XAML has some specific syntax peculiarities designed for easing the declaration of specific types of elements. It provides abbreviated markup syntax for specific types of elements that take advantage of the underlying Common Language Runtime (CLR) class constructors.

This chapter will examine the core XAML syntax, as well as some of the peculiarities of its abbreviated markup syntax, in preparation for understanding more complex concepts in later chapters.

Core XAML Syntax

XAML generally follows XML syntax rules, just as any other XML-based markup language does. Each XAML element has a name and one or more attributes. Attributes correspond directly to object properties, and the name of the XAML element exactly matches the name of a CLR class definition.

XAML is pure markup, which means that while the names of event handlers are specified as attributes, you must implement the actual logic of the event handler in code. If you're familiar with ASP.NET programming techniques, then you'll be familiar with the term `codebehind`, which refers to the code "behind" a XAML interface element that is responsible for providing application logic such as event handlers. It can be implemented in either C# or VB.NET. In both cases, the code can be placed inline in the XAML file, although this contradicts best practices in separating the presentation and application logic layers.

How does this work? Every event in XAML can be assigned to a `codebehind` handler, which is implemented in a supported .NET language. For example, it's a common task to do something when a `Button` is clicked. So, first a `Button` is declared with the XAML code shown in Example 3-1.

Example 3-1. XAML Button declaration

```
<Button
    OnClick="ButtonClickedHandler"
    Name="MyButton"
    Width="50"
    Content="Click Me!" />
```

Then, a corresponding codebehind handler is declared, and, when the Button is clicked, the handler is automatically executed (Examples 3-2 and 3-3).

Example 3-2. Button OnClick handler in C#

```
void ButtonClickedHandler(object sender, RoutedEventArgs eventArgs)
{
      MyButton.Width = 100;
      MyButton.Content = "Thank you!";
}
```

Example 3-3. Button OnClick handler in VB.NET

```
Sub ButtonClickedHandler(ByVal sender As Object,
                         ByVal eventArgs as RoutedEventArgs)
    MyButton.Width = 100
    MyButton.Content = "Thank you!"
End Sub
```

In both Examples 3-2 and 3-3, the handler will change the width of the Button from 50 to 100 and change the text displayed on it from "Click Me!" to "Thank you!". All XAML attributes can be manipulated within code because they are simply XML representations of actual CLR class attributes. You could just as easily change the button's background color, height, and even its position in code, just as you could in a traditional Windows application.

It is also acceptable to inline code in the XAML file by specifying the <x:Code> element. All inline code must be enclosed in the <CDATA[...]]> tag to ensure that the parser does not try to interpret the code. The XAML code from Example 3-1 and the C# code from Example 3-2 yield Example 3-4.

Example 3-4. Inlining code within a XAML file

```
<Button
    OnClick="ButtonClickedHandler"
    Name="MyButton"
    Width="50"
    Content="Click Me!" />

<x:Code>
  <![CDATA
    void ButtonClickedHandler(object sender, RoutedEventArgs eventArgs)
    {
      MyButton.Width = 100;
      MyButton.Content = "Thank you!";
    }
```

Example 3-4. Inlining code within a XAML file (continued)

```
    ]]>
</x:Code>
```

Application developers familiar with C# or VB.NET will immediately grasp the concept of `codebehind` and inline code and will be able to apply their existing skills to develop the code that drives the application.

XAML developers need to be aware that in order for application logic developers to access specific XAML elements, the elements must be named using either the `Name` or `ID` attribute. Developers will use one of these attributes to reference and manipulate the element directly from code. In Example 3-1, the `Button`'s `Name` attribute was declared as `MyButton`. The same name was then used in both code examples to reference and directly access the object.

There are three basic rules to follow when declaring XAML elements:

- XAML is case-sensitive. Element and attribute names must be properly cased.
- All attribute values, regardless of data type, must be enclosed in double quotes.
- The resulting XML must be well-formed.

The basic syntax for declaring XAML elements and attributes is:

```
<ElementName AttributeName="Value" AttributeName="Value" ... />
```

A simple login user interface, as shown in Figure 3-1, could be described with the code in Example 3-5, which illustrates these basic rules. Note the careful attention to case in declaring elements and attributes, the enclosure of all attribute values (regardless of underlying data type) in double quotes, and the fact that all elements are well-formed and closed with an end tag.

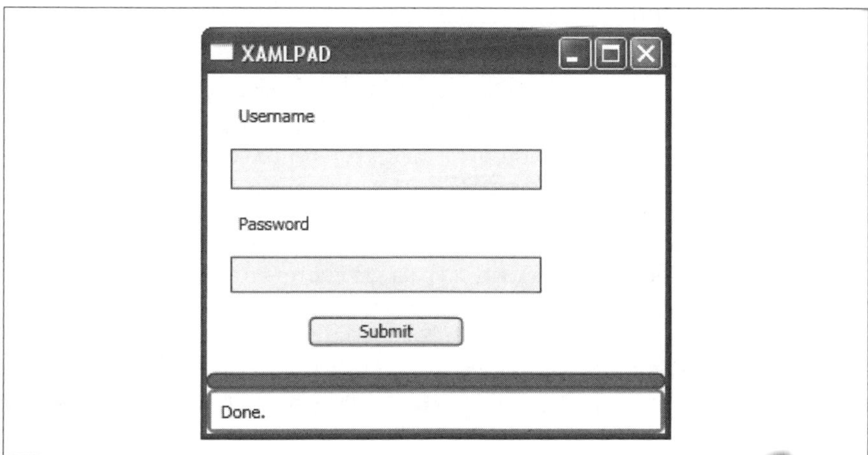

Figure 3-1. A simple user login XAML page

Example 3-5. A simple login user interface

```
<StackPanel
    xmlns="http://schemas.microsoft.com/winfx/avalon/2005"
    HorizontalAlignment="Left"
    Margin="10">
    <Label
        Margin="5"
        Content="Username" />
    <TextBox
        Margin="5"
        BorderBrush="Blue"
        BorderThickness="1"
        Background="AliceBlue"
        Foreground="Black"
        Width="200"/>
    <Label
        Margin="5"
        Content="Password" />
    <PasswordBox
        Margin="5"
        BorderBrush="Blue"
        BorderThickness="1"
        Background="AliceBlue"
        Foreground="Black"
        Width="200" />
    <Button
        Margin="10"
        Background="AliceBlue"
        Foreground="Black"
        Width="100"
        Height="20"
        Content="Submit" />
</StackPanel>
```

Formatting is a matter of style and corporate standards. The format for the examples in this book was chosen because it is readable and clearly displays the nesting of elements in more complex markup. Elements can be declared all on one line, or attribute declarations can be split across lines; formatting is completely up to you. Because XAML is compiled into BAML before deployment, the amount of space taken up by elements in a XAML file is irrelevant. There are no advantages to using less space by declaring elements on a single line and no disadvantages to the formatting used in this book. The elements will become binary representations before deployment, and the whitespace will have no impact on the footprint of finished applications.

Clearly, XAML is comprised of elements and their attributes. The rest of this chapter will examine each of these concepts in depth.

Elements

All XAML elements are an XML representation of CLR classes, but not all CLR classes are represented in XAML. Most of those represented are user-interface elements and are ultimately derived from `System.Windows.UIElement`, which provides basic visual user-interface properties that are shared by most XAML elements. A `System.Windows.UIElement` can render itself, receive input via the keyboard and mouse, visually size and position its child elements, and raise events.

Not all XAML elements are derived from `System.Windows.UIElement`. Some, such as `LineBreak`, `TableColumn`, and `Document`, are derived from `System.Windows.FrameworkContentElement`. `System.Windows.FrameworkContentElement` elements cannot render themselves but are instead rendered by another class, usually the container in which they have been placed.

Most XAML elements can be organized into five basic categories:

- Root elements
- Control elements
- Panel elements
- Shape and geometric elements
- Document elements

Root Elements

Root elements function as the page's base container for all user-interface elements. A page is required to have one root element. The most commonly used root elements are the panel elements—`StackPanel`, `DockPanel`, `Canvas`, and `Grid`—and `Page`, a root element that allows you to declaratively control a number of the properties of the window containing the XAML page. To be considered a root element, the element must be a container for at least one other element. (When displaying XAML output in XamlPad, you don't have to include a root element because XamlPad provides it on your behalf.) You can create custom root elements by deriving new classes from `Page` or `Window` and exposing them as XAML elements.

The root element must contain a reference to the appropriate namespace (in most cases, the default Avalon namespace, `http://schemas.microsoft.com/winfx/avalon/2005`). As with all XML documents, unless otherwise specified, it is assumed that all elements in the page are associated with the default namespace declared on the root element. The declaration in XAML is the same as in any XML document.

```
<Page xmlns="http://schemas.microsoft.com/winfx/avalon/2005" .../>
```

Control Elements

Control elements handle user interaction. Controls are interactive and allow the user to enter data, make choices, and perform other interactive tasks. They can be broken up into five categories: *simple controls*, *content controls*, *item controls*, *header item controls*, and *header content controls*. They are differentiated by the attributes they support, namely Content, Headers, and Items. Attribute support is determined by the underlying CLR class represented by the XAML element. Even if you don't use the Header attribute supported by a header item control, it doesn't become an item control because the CLR class it represents still has a Header whether or not you assign it a value. Table 3-1 summarizes this information neatly.

Simple controls
: Derive directly from the System.Windows.Control class and do not have Content, Items, or Header attributes. Examples of simple controls are HorizontalScrollBar, VerticalScrollBar, Frame, TextBox, and RichTextBox.

Content controls
: Have a Content attribute, but no Items or Header attributes. Content controls are restricted to only one element as its content, though that content may be an element (such as a Panel) that can contain more than one element. Examples of content controls are Button, RepeatButton, Label, RadioButton, CheckBox, ListBoxItem, GroupItem, StatusBarItem, ToolTip, ScrollViewer, and Window.

Item controls
: Have an Items attribute, but no Header or Content attributes. Item controls expose a list of elements, usually offering you a choice. Item controls include ListBox, ComboBox, Menu, ContextMenu, RadioButtonList, and TabControl.

Header item controls
: Have an Items attribute and a Header attribute but no Content attribute. The Header attribute determines the label for the Items, and the Items attribute contains child elements. The Items attribute is implicitly declared as a sequence of child elements that are not assigned to it. The following declaration of a MenuItem shows how this works:

```
<MenuItem Header="First Menu Item">
      <MenuItem Header="First Child Item" />
      <MenuItem Header="Second Child Item" />
</MenuItem>
```

Header item controls include MenuItem and ToolBar.

Header content controls
: Have a Header attribute and a Content attribute, but no Items attribute. Like a content control, the header content control may contain only one child element in its Content attribute. Header content controls include Expander and TabItem.

Table 3-1. Attributes supported by control type

	Content	Header	Items
Simple	N	N	N
Content	Y	N	N
Item	N	N	Y
Header item	N	Y	Y
Header content	Y	Y	N

Panel Elements

Panel elements handle page layout and act as containers for elements, such as controls or other panels. Some panel-derived elements are used as root elements, but the primary purpose of the panel is to provide support for layout and placement of elements on the page. Some panel classes are intended for designing the user interface, while others are special panels designed specifically for special layout scenarios. An example is the bullet panel, which is used specifically to display only two child elements (usually a text element and a glyph representing a checkbox or a radio button), and is used as a component of other elements such as `RadioButton` and `CheckBox`. When you declare a `RadioButton`, a `BulletPanel` is one of the underlying components that is rendered on the screen.

The panel elements designed for user-interface design are `DockPanel`, `StackPanel`, `Canvas`, `WrapPanel`, and `Grid`.

Shape and Geometric Elements

Shape and geometric elements represent 2-D vector graphics. Shapes derive from the `Shape` class and represent predefined geometric shapes. WPF shapes available for use with XAML are `Ellipse`, `Line`, `Path`, `Polygon`, `Polyline`, and `Rectangle`. Shapes are a type of `UIElement`, which means they can be used inside panels and most other controls.

Geometric elements, while also representing 2-D vector graphics, are more flexible than shape elements and can also be used for hit-testing and clipping purposes. Geometry elements can be simple vector graphics such as circles or polygons, or more complex elements comprised of Bezier lines and arcs. Geometries cannot render themselves. They must be drawn by another element, such as `Drawing` or `Path`. The attributes common to shape—`Fill`, `Stroke`, and `StrokeThickness`—are attached to the element that draws the geometries rather than the geometry element itself. Geometry elements are `CombinedGeometry`, `LineGeometry`, `EllipseGeometry`, `GeometryGroup`, `PathGeometry`, `RectangleGeometry`, `PathSegment`, `ArcSegment`, `LineSegment`, `BezierSegment`, `QuadraticBezierSegment`, `PolyQuadraticBezierSegment`, `PolyLineSegment`, `PolyBezierSegment`, `StartSegment`, and `CloseSegment`.

There are some similarities between respective shape and geometric entities. For example, `Ellipse` and `EllipseGeometry` provide the same basic functionality, i.e., both declare an ellipse. However, the way in which these elements are interpreted differs. An `Ellipse` is a standalone element. Its attributes provide all the information necessary to render a complete ellipse. `EllipseGeometry`, however, does not. Because it is designed to be a part of an ordered collection of geometric types, `EllipseGeometry` relies on attributes defined on the element appearing before it in the collection. Similarly, attributes assigned to `EllipseGeometry` will be used to render the next geometry instance in the collection. This trait is shared by all the geometry objects and differentiates them from their `Shape`-based counterparts.

Document Elements

Document elements handle document presentation. Documents are categorized as either flow or fixed. The `FixedDocument` element is designed to be What You See Is What You Get (WYSIWYG) and is intended to appear in all formats (print, browser, application) with exactly the same layout.

A `FlowDocument` element provides more flexibility in appearance to enhance readability. Flow documents dynamically reformat content based on a variety of factors, including screen and page size, font size, and optional user preferences. Flow documents are comprised of one or more elements derived from `Block` or `Inline`. Block elements such as `Block`, `Figure`, `Floater`, `List`, `ListItem`, `Paragraph`, `Section`, `Table`, and `TableCell` are used to organize and format blocks of text. Inline elements are used to format text within a block. Inline elements are `Bold`, `AccessKey`, `LineBreak`, `Hyperlink`, `Italic`, `Subscript`, `Superscript`, and `Underline`.

Some of these elements might look familiar, such as `Paragraph`, `Table`, and `Italic`. Similar formatting elements exist in other user-interface markup languages, such as `<p>`, `<table>`, and `<i>`, respectively, in HTML. These elements are virtually identical in execution but have structural differences as well as an abundance of attributes in XAML that do not exist in their HTML counterparts.

While the core syntax of XAML is very similar to markup languages such as HTML, XAML user-interface elements are not restricted to containing traditional content. For example, a `Button` is not required, nor restricted, to present text-based content as a prompt. The flexibility of XAML and its object-oriented nature offer unlimited possibilities. You can just as easily decorate the face of a `Button` with any `UIElement`-derived element. Example 3-6 declares three circles—defined by an `Ellipse` element with equivalent x- and y-axis radii—as the content element of a `Button`. While content control-derived classes may only have one child element, that child element may contain additional elements, such as the `DockPanel` or `StackPanel`.

Example 3-6. Using alternate elements as the content of a Button

```
<StackPanel xmlns="http://schemas.microsoft.com/winfx/avalon/2005"
    HorizontalAlignment="Center"
    Margin="10">
    <Button
        Width="50"
        Height="100">
        <DockPanel>
            <Ellipse Margin="5"
                 DockPanel.Dock="Top"
                 Stroke="Black"
                 RadiusX="10"
                 RadiusY="10"
                 Fill="Red" />
            <Ellipse Margin="5"
                 DockPanel.Dock="Top"
                 Stroke="Black"
                 RadiusX="10"
                 RadiusY="10"
```

Example 3-6. Using alternate elements as the content of a Button (continued)

```
                Fill="Yellow" />
          <Ellipse Margin="5"
                DockPanel.Dock="Top"
                Stroke="Black"
                RadiusX="10"
                RadiusY="10"
                Fill="Green" />
      </DockPanel>
   </Button>
</StackPanel>
```

The result of evaluating Example 3-6 is shown in Figure 3-2.

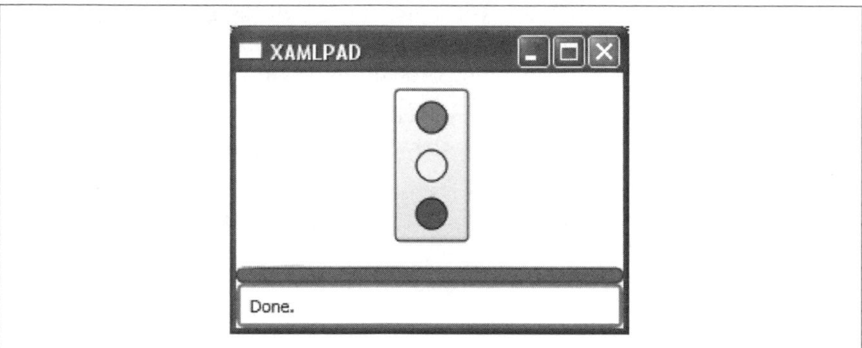

Figure 3-2. Defining a content control with multiple child elements

Attributes

Attributes are the XML representation of the properties of an element's corresponding CLR class. The `Width` attribute of the XAML `Button` element corresponds directly to the `Width` property of the `System.Windows.Button` class. To show the correlation between XAML and CLR classes, Examples 3-7 and 3-8 declare a `Button` instance and its attributes in both XAML and C#.

Example 3-7. Button declared in XAML

```
<Button
     Width="100"
     Name="myButton"
     Height="20"
     Content="This is my button" />
```

Example 3-8. Button declared in C#

```
Button myButton;
myButton.Width=100;
myButton.Height=20;
myButton.Content = "This is my button";
```

As with the XAML tags for elements, attributes are spelled exactly the same as their corresponding CLR class properties. (`Width` = `Width`, `Content` = `Content`... You get the picture.)

There are two types of XAML attributes. The first, *dependency properties*, are public static read-only fields on CLR classes that are derived from `DependencyProperty` and have declared CLR accessor methods. In other words, the value of dependency properties can be dependent on (hence the name) other variables in CLR classes and, therefore, can only be accessed with a public get or set accessor method to be evaluated properly.

Dependency properties are like stock certificates. The stock certificate represents a value (money), but the actual amount of money it is worth (its value) is determined by external calculations and can change at nearly any time. To determine the value of your stock certificate, you must consult the stock exchange and do some multiplication. Dependency properties can also be based on external resources and often rely on calculations to determine their value.

Dependency property values are determined from a number of different places. The WPF property system searches for the value from the following places in this order:

- Storyboards or event triggers that start an animation; property values set by an animation override even local values
- Local value (i.e., `<Object Property="`*`value`*`">`)
- Property triggers
- `TemplatedParent`'s template (i.e., that template includes `<Setter>`)
- `Style` property
- `ThemeStyle`
- Inheritance (from your parent element, not your superclass)
- `DefaultValue` specified when you registered the property (or override metadata)

These attributes provide support for value expressions, property invalidation, default values, inheritance, data binding, animation, and styling. The property system is complex, so WPF provides simple get and set accessor methods to manipulate these attributes.

The second type of attribute supported in XAML is the common language runtime property. *Common language runtime properties* are standard read/write CLR class properties that can be accessed directly and do not require get or set accessor methods, although they generally have them.

Both dependency properties and common runtime properties are accessed in XAML using the same techniques. The difference between them is important only when you are using more advanced techniques, such as defining styles or triggers that act upon a specific attribute. Some attributes of elements *must* reference a dependency property, so you need to know which attributes are dependency properties and which are not.

Regardless of their underlying types, all XAML attributes can be assigned in one of two ways. They can be assigned inline, as part of the element declaration, or they can be explicitly declared as nested elements within the element being described. As a general rule, complex attributes must be declared explicitly, while simple attributes can be defined inline, as shown in Example 3-9. Simple attributes are those whose data types are primitives, such as `String`, `Integer`, and `Double`. Enumerations are also declared inline, using a `String` representation of the name of the enumerated value. All inline attribute declarations must be enclosed in double quotes, regardless of the underlying data type of the property being described. You don't have to enclose attributes of type `String` in two sets of quotes. `String` is sort of the exception to the rule, because it is, after all, already a `String`.

Example 3-9. Inline declaration of a simple attribute

```
<Button
    Content="Click Me" />
```


Complex attributes are defined as a CLR class or are of type `struct`. They are declared explicitly, as shown in Example 3-10. In this example, `GeometryDrawing` has two complex attributes: `Pen` and `Geometry`. Neither attribute can be specified using abbreviated syntax, so it is necessary to explicitly declare them. The exception to this rule is the specification of child elements, which are declared by using standard XML mechanisms without the name of the attribute. This is illustrated in Example 3-10, in which two instances of `EllipseGeometry` are implicitly declared as children of `GeometryGroup`. It is not necessary to specify child elements as a complex attribute by name. Elements nested between the opening and closing tags of an element are assumed to be the children of that element and are automatically added to the appropriate container property according to the CLR class, usually the `Children` or `InternalChildren` property of the parent element.

Example 3-10. Explicit declaration of a complex attribute

```
<GeometryDrawing
    Brush="Blue" >
    <GeometryDrawing.Pen>
        <Pen
            Thickness="1"
            Brush="Black" />
    </GeometryDrawing.Pen>
    <GeometryDrawing.Geometry>
        <GeometryGroup>
            <EllipseGeometry
                RadiusX="0.2"
                RadiusY="0.45"
                Center="0.5,0.5" />
            <EllipseGeometry
                RadiusX="0.45"
                RadiusY="0.2"
                Center="0.5,0.5" />
        </GeometryGroup>
    </GeometryDrawing.Geometry>
</GeometryDrawing>
```

Abbreviated syntax must sound like jabberwocky at this point, but it's really a pretty neat concept. It uses a predefined format, such as CSV (comma-separated values), to essentially declare the arguments that will be passed to the appropriate class constructor beneath the covers. You can think of the `String` definition as the list of arguments you'd normally pass to a constructor, except that sometimes you don't need a comma to separate the arguments.

Example 3-11 first creates an `EllipseGeometry` in C# and then assigns a `Point` to be its `Center` property by instantiating a new `Point` and passing the appropriate values to its constructor. The XAML code in the same example creates an `EllipseGeometry` and then assigns a `Point` to be its `Center` attribute using abbreviated syntax. The `0.5, 0.5` is parsed by the WPF engine, and the values are passed to a `Point` constructor as its arguments.

Example 3-11. Abbreviated syntax and arguments in C#

```
C#
EllipseGeometry ellipse;
ellipse.Center=new Point(0.5, 0.5);

XAML
<EllipseGeometry
    Center="0.5,0.5" />
```

A very common example of using abbreviated syntax to declare attribute values is the assignment of predefined color names to an attribute declared as type `Brush`, such as the `Background` attribute. Rather than forcing you to go through all the typing required to explicitly declare a `Brush` and set its color, XAML allows you to just declare the attribute as `Red` or `Green` instead.

Figure 3-3 shows the result of declaring a `Red` `SolidColorBrush` as the background `Brush` for a `Button` using both abbreviated markup and by explicitly declaring the complex attribute. Example 3-12 shows the code used to declare both elements.

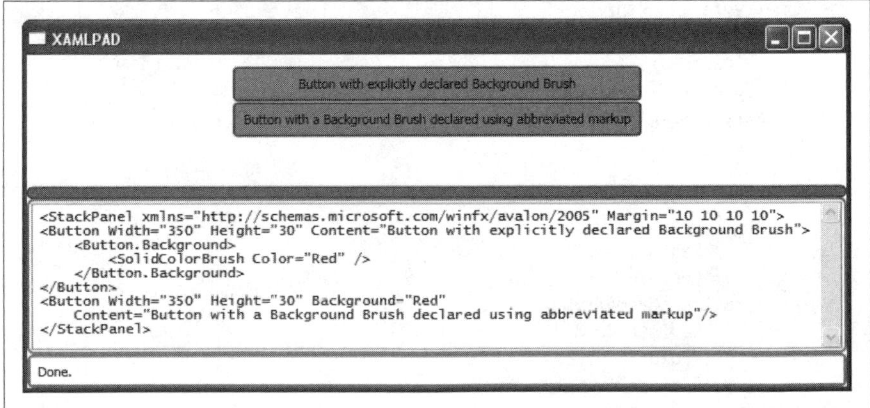

Figure 3-3. Result of explicit declaration and abbreviated markup declaration of a Brush attribute on a Button

Example 3-12. Explicit declaration of a Brush versus abbreviated markup

```
<StackPanel
    xmlns="http://schemas.microsoft.com/winfx/avalon/2005"
    Margin="10 10 10 10">
    <Button
        Width="350"
        Height="30"
        Content="Button with explicitly declared Background Brush">
        <Button.Background>
            <SolidColorBrush Color="Red" />
        </Button.Background>
    </Button>
    <Button
        Width="350"
        Height="30"
        Background="Red"
        Content="Button with a Background Brush declared using abbreviated
                markup"/>
</StackPanel>
```

As you can see in Figure 3-3, both buttons are painted with the same background, regardless of the method used to declare the Brush. Abbreviated syntax is typically used because it requires less typing. There are no advantages to using explicit syntax in most cases where abbreviated syntax is available, and it's less typing for you.

A more complex example is the common use of abbreviated markup syntax to declare elements of the type Point. Point is a common, complex attribute that is used in the declaration of almost every geometric XAML element. You can use the abbreviated markup syntax for a Point element wherever an element of type Point is declared. You'll notice in Example 3-13 that EllipseGeometry has several attributes. While RadiusX and RadiusY are Double values, the Center attribute for an EllipseGeometry is actually a complex attribute of type Point. In its abbreviated syntax, Point accepts two comma-separated values representing the X and Y positions, respectively. Example 3-13 shows different ways of using Point (in this case, it is used through the Center attribute).

Example 3-13. Example of abbreviated markup versus explicit syntax

```
<GeometryGroup>
    <EllipseGeometry
        RadiusX="0.45"
        RadiusY="0.2"
        Center="0.5,0.5" />
    <EllipseGeometry
        RadiusX="0.2"
        RadiusY="0.45">
        <EllipseGeometry.Center>
            <Point
                Y="0.5"
                Y="0.5" />
```

Example 3-13. Example of abbreviated markup versus explicit syntax (continued)

```
        </EllipseGeometry.Center>
    </EllipseGeometry>
</GeometryGroup>
```

Elements that can be declared using abbreviated markup syntax are specifically noted in Part III.

Attached Properties

A few XAML elements have attributes that are declared in other elements rather than in the element itself. These attributes are called attached properties. *Attached properties* are generally used to position elements within a parent element. Two elements with attached properties are `Grid` and `DockPanel`. `Grid` uses attached properties to describe the row and column in which an element should be contained. `DockPanel` uses attached properties to describe the location within the panel where an element should be placed.

Attached properties can be set on any element that derives from `DependencyObject`. `UIElement` derives from `DependencyObject`, so the requirement is met by most XAML elements.

Attached properties are declared in an element by using a reference to the element and the attribute being declared in the following manner: `AttachPropertyProvider.PropertyName`. For example, `Grid` has two attached properties: `Row` and `Column`. An element contained within a specific row/column combination in a grid would specify the row as an attribute with the name `Grid.Row` and the column similarly as `Grid.Column`. Example 3-14 describes the use of these attached properties.

Example 3-14. Using the attached properties of Grid

```
<Grid
    ShowGridLines="true">
    <ColumnDefinition
         Width="50"/>
    <ColumnDefinition
         Width="50"/>
    <RowDefinition
         Height="100" />
    <RowDefinition
         Height="25" />
    <RowDefinition
         Height="25" />
    <TextBlock
         Grid.Column="0"
         Grid.Row="0">Col 0, Row 0
    </TextBlock>
    <TextBlock
         Grid.Column="1"
         Grid.Row="0">Col 1, Row 0
    </TextBlock>
```

Example 3-14. Using the attached properties of Grid (continued)

```
    <TextBlock
         Grid.Column="0"
         Grid.Row="1">Col 0, Row 1
    </TextBlock>
    <TextBlock
         Grid.Column="1"
         Grid.Row="1">Col 1, Row 1
    </TextBlock>
</Grid>
```

Binding Properties

Another mechanism in XAML that can be used to declare the value of attributes is a bind declaration. A *bind declaration* allows you to set an attribute's value by referencing the value of another element. Bind declarations must be attached to a specific dependency property of a target element. Remember that dependency properties are static read-only properties of a CLR class that are exposed only through get and set accessor methods to support concepts such as binding. Properties are bound together in a bind declaration using the `Binding` element.

`Binding` elements are used to bind the source to target elements. If the dependency properties in the source elements change when the application runs, the dependency properties in the target elements will change as well. Basically, you're telling an attribute that its value should always be determined by evaluating some other attribute or data source. It's like assigning a value to one variable by assigning it to another, as shown in the following example:

```
int a = 1;
int b;
b = a;
```

The difference between code-based variable assignments and XAML binding is that in XAML, the association is permanent. The assignment of `b = a` in the code example happens only once, and, if `a` changes later, `b` doesn't follow suit. In XAML, the `Binding` keyword ties the values together permanently.

The syntax for a `Binding` element is as follows:

```
<ElementName Attribute="{Binding Path=SimpleProperty, Mode=OneTime} />
```

The curly braces are a general indicator to the parser that the value contained in the braces is not a simple value. Instead, the first keyword within the braces indicates the type of special handling needed. The `Binding` statement at the beginning of the string indicates a binding declaration.

An example of how binding works is when you are tying together the content of two different elements, such as a `Button` and a `TextBlock`. In Example 3-15, every time the `Button` is clicked, the C# code (Example 3-16) in its codebehind handler will increment a static counter and change the content of the `Button` to include that count. The `TextBlock` will bind its own content attribute to the content attribute of the `Button`, so every time the `Button` is clicked, it too will change its content—automagically through the use of the `Binding` element.

Example 3-15. Binding attributes: XAML

```
<Page
    xmlns="http://schemas.microsoft.com/winfx/avalon/2005"
    xmlns:x="http://schemas.microsoft.com/winfx/xaml/2005"
    x:Class="BindExample.Page1">
    <StackPanel >
        <Button
            Width="150"
            Content="You have clicked 0 times!"
            Name="MyButton"
            Click="ButtonClicked"/>
        <TextBlock>
            <TextBlock.TextContent>
                <Binding
                    ElementName="MyButton"
                    Path="Content"/>
            </TextBlock.TextContent>
        </TextBlock>
    </StackPanel>
</Page>
```

Example 3-16. Binding attributes: C#

```
using System;
using System.Windows;
using System.Windows.Controls;
using System.Windows.Navigation;
using System.ComponentModel;

namespace BindExample
{
    public partial class Page1 : Page
    {
        static int clickCount = 0;
        void ButtonClicked(object sender, RoutedEventArgs e)
        {
            MyButton.Content="You have clicked " + ++clickCount + " times!";
        }
      }
}
```

After compiling the application and running it, the content of MyButton is appropriately, "You have clicked 0 times!" (Figure 3-4).

Clicking on the Button executes the ButtonClicked handler detailed in Example 3-16. The counter increments and the Content of the Button is changed to include the count. Notice that nowhere in the code do you touch the TextBlock declared in Example 3-15. The Content of that TextBlock is bound to the Button's Content attribute by the Binding element, and whenever it changes, so will the content of the TextBlock. Clicking on the Button a few more times results in Figure 3-5.

You might think that this isn't very useful. Binding content attributes of one element to another isn't something you'll do very often, but the Binding element

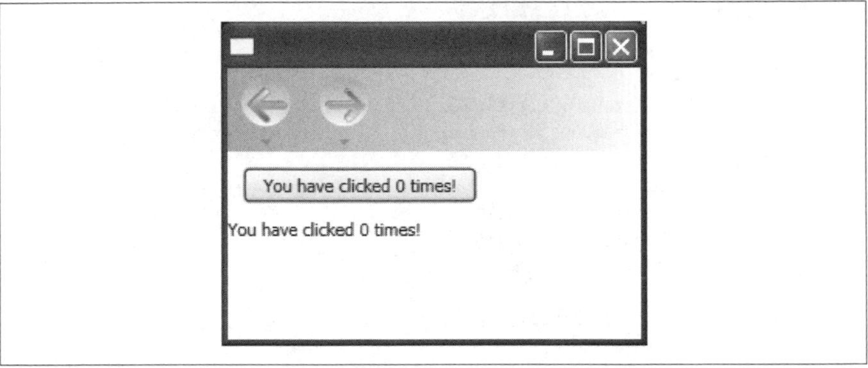

Figure 3-4. Binding example on initial run

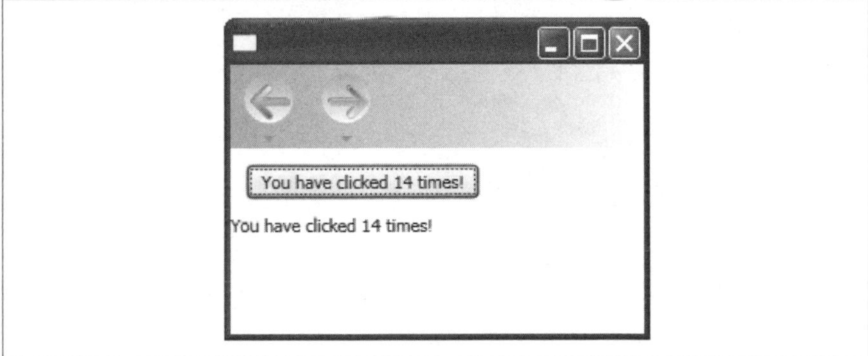

Figure 3-5. Binding example after a few clicks

can also be used for more common scenarios, such as binding a `ListBox` to an XML data source and then binding the attribute of a `TextBlock` to the selected value in the `ListBox`. Example 3-17 demonstrates binding an element to an XML data source.

Example 3-17. Binding to an XML data source

```
<Page xmlns="http://schemas.microsoft.com/winfx/avalon/2005"
      xmlns:x="http://schemas.microsoft.com/winfx/xaml/2005">
    <StackPanel >
        <StackPanel.Resources>
        <XmlDataSource
            x:Key="UserData"
            XPath="/Users">
            <Users xmlns="">
                <User ID="1">
                    <Title>CEO</Title>
                    <Name>Elisabeth</Name>
                </User>
                <User ID="2">
                    <Title>CTO</Title>
                    <Name>Galina</Name>
```

Example 3-17. Binding to an XML data source (continued)

```
                </User>
                <User ID="3">
                    <Title>CSO</Title>
                    <Name>Donald</Name>
                </User>
                <User ID="4">
                    <Title>CFO</Title>
                    <Name>Victoria</Name>
                </User>
                <User ID="5">
                    <Title>CIO</Title>
                    <Name>Korey</Name>
                </User>
            </Users>
            </XmlDataSource>
            <DataTemplate x:Key="UserDataTemplate">
                 <TextBlock FontSize="Small" Foreground="Red">
                    <TextBlock.TextContent>
                       <Binding XPath="Title"/>
                    </TextBlock.TextContent>
                 </TextBlock>
            </DataTemplate>
        </StackPanel.Resources>
        <ListBox
            HorizontalAlignment="Left"
            Margin="10"
            Width="100"
            Height="100"
            Name="MyListBox"
            SelectedValuePath="Name"
            ItemsSource="{Binding Source={StaticResource UserData}, XPath=User}"
            ItemTemplate="{StaticResource UserDataTemplate}"/>
        <TextBlock
            HorizontalAlignment="Left"
            Margin="10">
            <TextBlock.TextContent>
                <Binding ElementName="MyListBox" Path="SelectedValue" />
            </TextBlock.TextContent>
        </TextBlock>
    </StackPanel>
</Page>
```

In Example 3-17, there are three uses of the `Binding` element. It is first used as the value of the `ListBox`'s `ItemsSource` attribute. This declaration tells the `ListBox` that it should get its items from the `StaticResource UserData` and to use the `XPath` *`User`* to determine what an item consists of. The second use of the `Binding` element, the `ItemTemplate` value, tells the `ListBox` how to display the data. The `UserDataTemplate` tells the `ListBox` that each item should be displayed as a text block with a small, red font and that the value shown is the `User` attribute *`Title`* (specified by the `XPath="`*`Title`*`"` declaration).

The final use of the `Binding` attribute appears within the `TextBlock` declaration. It binds the content of the `TextBlock` to the *`SelectedValue`* attribute of *`MyListBox`*. The great thing about this particular use of the `Binding` attribute is that there's no code necessary. When a `User` is selected from the `ListBox`, the `TextBlock Content` will automatically update to reflect that user's `Name` (Figure 3-6). The `SelectedValuePath` in the `ListBox` determines what value is displayed in the `TextBlock` when the selection changes.

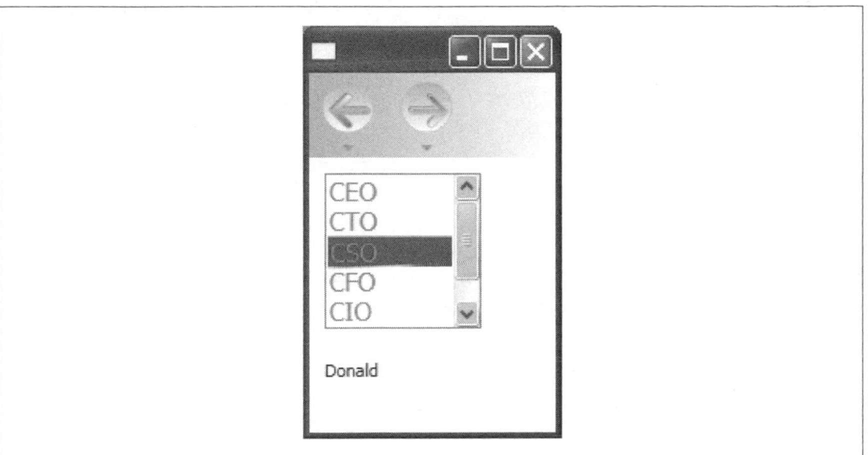

Figure 3-6. Result of evaluating Example 3-17 in XamlPad

Basically, the ability to bind the attributes of an element to other elements and even data sources provides a non-coding method of manipulating data and display.

codebehind

The concept of `codebehind` has been mentioned but not fully explored yet. You've already noted that event handlers can be assigned to elements and implemented in code and that the attribute name *must exactly* match the handler name in code. The event handlers specified by name as attributes for controls are associated with the `codebehind` in a C# or VB.NET file during the compilation process. The compiler generates a partial class for XAML and then assembles it with the code, which defines the rest of the class in a `codebehind` file. This allows the two pieces to be tied together when the code is interpreted within the runtime engine.

But there are other things that can be accomplished in code besides handling events. Many applications require initialization of data sources, or automatically adding fields to the user interface depending on the user's role. These things cannot be done in XAML; they must be done programmatically.

Every XAML application represents the declaration of a partial CLR class. Part of the class is declared using XAML, and the rest of it can be declared in a `codebehind` file using C# or Visual Basic. The implementation can then programmatically modify the user interface or interact with other systems such as a database or remote application to accomplish the application's designated task.

As with event handlers, the name of the class assigned as the implementation class for a XAML application *must exactly* match, including the namespace. For example, the XAML class declaration in Example 3-18 referencing the `StartPage` class with a namespace of `MyNameSpace` exactly matches the name of the class in Example 3-19. Note that the `Page` element in the XAML file has no other elements. The `TextBlock` and `Button` seen in Figure 3-7 are the result of programmatically adding the two elements to the `Page` in the C# `codebehind` implementation.

Example 3-18. XAML declaration of StartPage.xaml

```
<Page xmlns="http://schemas.microsoft.com/winfx/avalon/2005"
      xmlns:x="http://schemas.microsoft.com/winfx/xaml/2005"
      x:Class="MyNameSpace.StartPage"
      Loaded="Init" />
```

Example 3-19. C# implementation of StartPage class within StartPage.xaml.cs

```
using System;
using System.Windows;
using System.Windows.Controls;
using System.Windows.Navigation;

namespace MyNameSpace
{
   public partial class StartPage : Page
   {
       TextBlock txtElement;
       StackPanel rootPanel;
       Button aButton;
       void Init(object sender, EventArgs args)
       {
                 rootPanel = new StackPanel( );
                 txtElement = new TextBlock( );
                 aButton = new Button( );
                 txtElement.TextContent = "Some Text";
                 aButton.Content = "Press me";
                 Child = rootPanel;
                 rootPanel.Children.Add(txtElement);
                 rootPanel.Children.Add(aButton);
       }
   }
}
```

In Example 3-19, you can see that a `StackPanel` is declared as `rootPanel`, indicating that it will be the first (and only) child of `Page`. `Page` is only allowed a single child of type `UIElement`, so all other elements to be displayed on the page will have to be added to the `StackPanel`. The C# code in this example is equivalent to the XAML code in Example 3-20.

Figure 3-7. Programmatic creation of a XAML application

Example 3-20. XAML declaration to produce Figure 3-7

```
<Page xmlns="http://schemas.microsoft.com/winfx/avalon/2005"
      xmlns:x=http://schemas.microsoft.com/winfx/xaml/2005 >
    <StackPanel>
        <TextBlock>Some Text</TextBlock>
        <Button Content="Press me" />
    </StackPanel>
</Page>
```

If it can be done in XAML, it can be done programmatically. Every XAML element is accessible from C# or Visual Basic and can be manipulated within event handlers or from within the class's implementation. This provides you with the means to add or remove elements from the user interface, allows for localization, and offers the ability to dynamically build a user interface based on data-driven principles.

While XAML was designed to separate the presentation layer from the application logic, its representative CLR classes are available to the programmer and can be used to build an application in the same way traditional Windows Forms or .NET applications are built.

4

Layout and Positioning

One of the most important facets of user-interface design is the layout and positioning of elements on the page. The user interface must be pleasing to the eye without being cluttered, and it must enhance productivity through ease of use. Elements should be paired with visual clues such that their use is intuitive, which reduces the amount of learning time required.

One of the primary mechanisms for building an intuitive, usable user interface is layout elements. Layout elements position elements on the screen and insure that they are grouped together in a way that enhances readability. XAML offers a plethora of options for page layout and user-interface construction. Margins, padding, and panels provide basic layout capabilities that can be combined to position elements exactly where you want them on the page.

The largest hurdle to building a user-interface layout is the variation in screen resolution and size among end users. This is especially true for applications loaded in a web browser. There are several mechanisms available through scripting and CSS to counter the layout problems inherent in serving a wide variety of screen resolutions and sizes.

XAML addresses these issues by dynamically sizing elements relative to the size of the page in which they are placed. All XAML elements will stretch to fit their entire container, unless you indicate otherwise. If the default container is a page 800 pixels wide, then all elements added to the page will size themselves to be 800 pixels wide. Similarly, if the page is resized, the elements will dynamically resize themselves to fit the page.

While this resizing behavior is needed to handle varying window sizes, it isn't necessary for elements to take up the entire screen. This chapter examines the XAML elements and attributes that control the layout and size of elements on the page while maintaining the flexibility that dynamic sizing offers.

StackPanel and DockPanel

The two most commonly used `Panel` subclasses are `StackPanel` and `DockPanel`. Both are used for relative positioning of elements and automatically handle placement of elements based on the order in which they are declared.

The differences between the two types of `Panel` can be summed up as follows:

`StackPanel`
: Defaults to automatically rendering elements in the order in which they are declared in the XAML file, from top to bottom.

`DockPanel`
: Defaults to automatically rendering elements in the order in which they are declared in the XAML file, from left to right.

: The attached attributes of `DockPanel` can be used to alter the relative positioning of child elements.

The concept is best illustrated by recreating the user login interface (from Chapter 3) using both types of panels. The result is shown in Figure 4-1. The elements of this user login interface are each added in the following order:

1. The Username `Label` element
2. The username `TextBox`
3. The Password `Label` element
4. The password `PasswordBox`
5. The Submit `Button` element

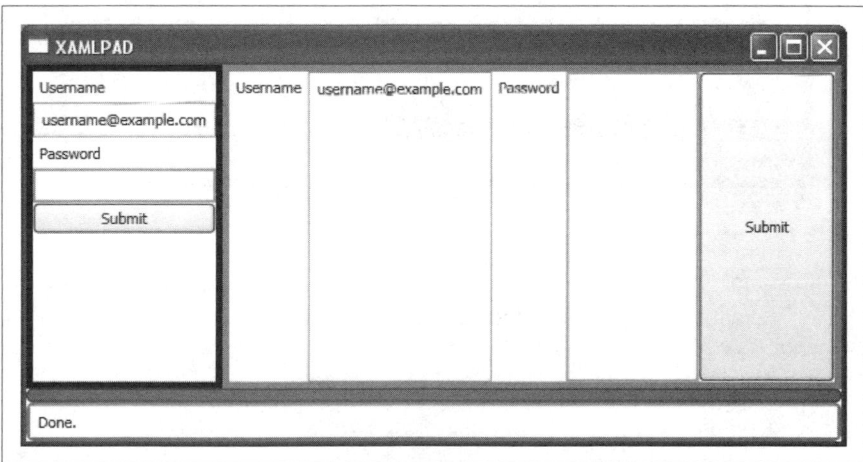

Figure 4-1. Positioning elements with StackPanel and DockPanel

The `StackPanel`, indicated by the black-bordered area in Figure 4-1, stacks elements from top to bottom as they are added. The `DockPanel`, indicated by the lighter-bordered area in Figure 4-1, positions them from left to right as they are added. There is no additional formatting nor any positioning attributes specified, so the default values are active, which gives the interface a very strange look (especially in the DockPanel).

The default Orientation for StackPanel is Vertical, but it can be set to Horizontal. Changing the Orientation of the StackPanel to Horizontal will cause the elements to be stacked from left to right rather than from top to bottom.

DockPanel can be further manipulated in terms of the way elements are stacked within the Panel. For example, elements can be "docked" at the top, which will cause them to expand horizontally to fill the width of the DockPanel. Elements can be docked at the left or right, which will cause them to expand vertically to fill their allocated space and align either their left or right edges with the DockPanel. Elements can also be docked at the bottom, which will cause them to align their bottom edges with the bottom of the DockPanel and expand horizontally to fill their allocated space. Elements use the attached property DockPanel.Dock to determine where they will be docked.

Because elements are rendered in the order in which they are added, using the positioning of DockPanel's properties makes the values relative to the last element added. For example, if the first element added specifies a DockPanel.Dock attribute as Top and the second also declares Top, the second element docks itself at the bottom edge of the first element because that is the top of the layout for the second element. Figure 4-2 illustrates this concept.

Figure 4-2. Effects of specifying DockPanel.Dock="Top"

As you might expect, changing the value of DockPanel.Dock from Top to Bottom for all four elements in Figure 4-2 does not change much but the order. When all elements specify DockPanel.Dock="*Bottom*", Element #1 appears on the bottom, Element #2 above it, and so on. You can probably guess what happens if all elements specify Left for DockPanel.Dock, as well as Right. Elements are rendered in order from left to right and right to left, respectively.

The real fun begins when you start mixing and matching all four values to rearrange your user interface. For example, specifying Left, Right, Top, and Bottom as DockPanel.Dock values for each of the four elements—in order—results in a fairly orderly interface, shown in Figure 4-3.

While it's orderly, it may be somewhat of a surprise to see that Element #3 is docked at the top of the screen and does not appear to be docked relative to

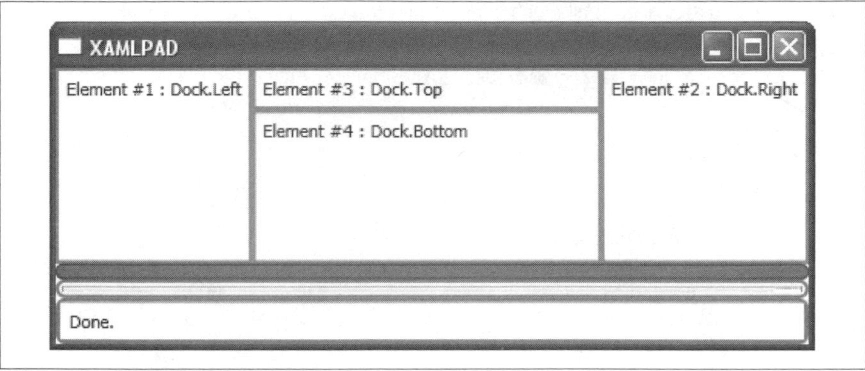

Figure 4-3. Mixing and matching DockPanel.Dock values

Element #1. It actually is relative to Element #1 and Element #2, but both these elements have taken up all the layout space on the left and right edges, according to their `DockPanel.Dock` values. That leaves only the area between the two elements for Element #3 and Element #4 to occupy.

If the values of `DockPanel.Dock` are reversed so that Element #1 specifies `Top` and Element #2 specifies `Bottom`, then Element #3 declaring `Left` will touch the left side of the panel but between Element #1 and Element #2. This leaves Element #4 to declare `Right`, which positions it against the right edge of the panel, but like Element #3, between Elements #1 and #2. Figure 4-4 shows the results of switching the values.

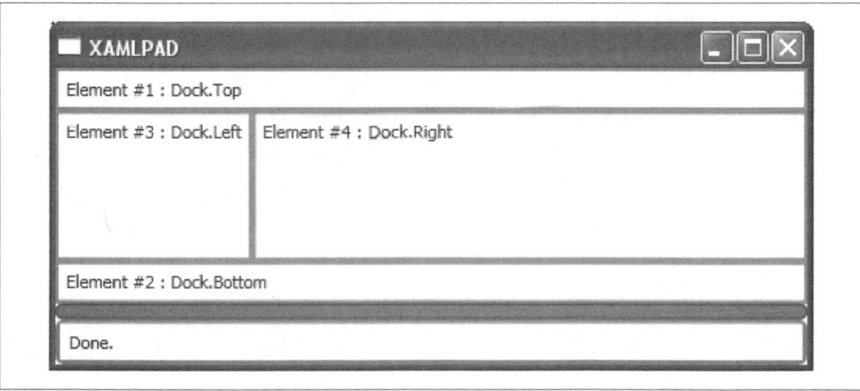

Figure 4-4. Mixing and matching DockPanel.Dock values again

The last element added will occupy whatever space remains; that's why Element #4 always appears bigger than Element #3, even though intuitively it seems that they should be the same size.

Example 4-1 uses `Border` elements around the user-login interface elements to illustrate the effects of specifying the attached attribute `DockPanel.Dock` on elements added to the `DockPanel`. Figure 4-5 shows the result of evaluating Example 4-1 with XamlPad.

Example 4-1. Using DockPanel.Dock to position elements

```
<Page
    xmlns="http://schemas.microsoft.com/winfx/avalon/2005">
    <Border
        BorderBrush="Black"
        BorderThickness="1">
        <DockPanel>
            <Border
                DockPanel.Dock="Top"
                BorderBrush="Red"
                BorderThickness="1">
                <Label>Username Label</Label>
            </Border>
            <Border
                DockPanel.Dock="Right"
                BorderBrush="Red"
                BorderThickness="1">
                <TextBox>username@example.com</TextBox>
            </Border>
            <Border
                DockPanel.Dock="Left"
                BorderBrush="Red"
                BorderThickness="1">
               <Label>Password Label</Label>
            </Border>
            <Border
                DockPanel.Dock="Top"
                BorderBrush="Red"
                BorderThickness="1">
                <TextBox>This is the password box</TextBox>
            </Border>
            <Border
                DockPanel.Dock="Bottom"
                BorderBrush="Red"
                BorderThickness="1">
                <Button
                    Content="Submit" />
            </Border>
        </DockPanel>
    </Border>
</Page>
```

This user-login interface isn't looking quite like it should, however, even when using a DockPanel to position elements. StackPanel and DockPanel are useful for the general positioning of elements, but to fine-tune the layout of a user interface, you must specify additional attributes such as Width and Alignment.

Using Width and Alignment

By default, XAML renders elements on the screen in the order in which they are defined within the XAML file. If the TextBox in Example 4-2 is added to the StackPanel before the first Label, then it will appear as the first element and the

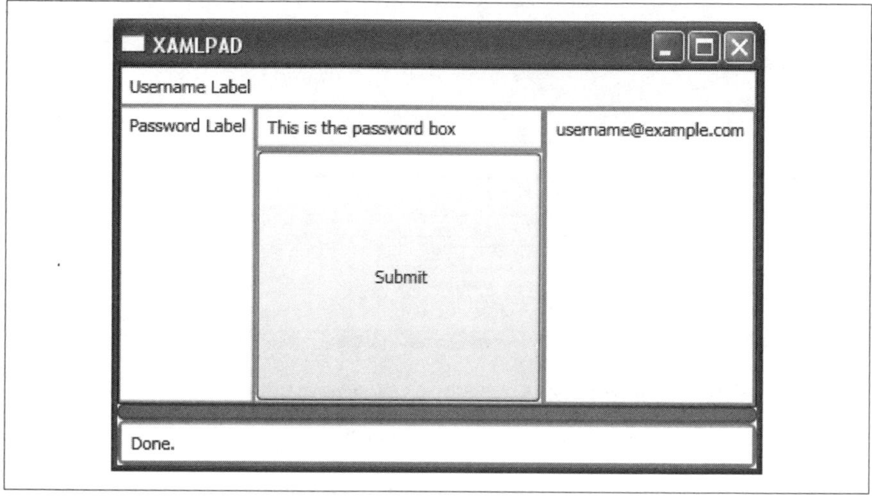

Figure 4-5. Using DockPanel.Dock to position elements

`Label` will appear after it. By default, all elements have a width equal to the container element of which they are children. Using the login page example from Chapter 3 without specifying any kind of formatting or layout restrictions yields the user interface in Figure 4-6.

Example 4-2. Example code for user login screen with no layout or formatting

```
<Page
    xmlns="http://schemas.microsoft.com/winfx/avalon/2005">
    <StackPanel>
        <Label>Username</Label>
        <TextBox>username@example.com</TextBox>
        <Label>Password</Label>
        <PasswordBox></PasswordBox>
        <Button Content="Submit" />
    </StackPanel>
</Page>
```

This is neither aesthetically pleasing nor is it particularly usable. There is no clear delineation between elements, and it is hard on the eyes. The first thing to do is limit the width of the elements to make them easier to read. There are three options to accomplish this: define the `Width` attribute on all the elements added to the `StackPanel`, limit the width of the `StackPanel` itself, or change the `HorizontalAlignment` of the `StackPanel`. The second option will force all the elements in the `StackPanel` to be the same width. While this is a viable option, it may not be appropriate for every situation, especially if you don't want all the elements to be the same width as the `TextBox`. The best option in this case is to limit the width of each individual element. Note that specifying the `Width` of an element will change its resizing behavior. When a width is set, the element no longer automatically resizes when its container changes size. Example 4-3 shows how to use `Width` to constrain the size of an element.

Figure 4-6. User login screen with no layout or formatting

Example 4-3. Using Width to constrain the size of elements

```
<Page
    xmlns="http://schemas.microsoft.com/winfx/avalon/2005">
    <StackPanel>
        <Label
            Width="100">Username</Label>
        <TextBox
            Width="150">username@example.com</TextBox>
        <Label
            Width="100">Password</Label>
        <PasswordBox
            Width="150"></PasswordBox>
        <Button
            Width="100"
            Content="Submit" />
    </StackPanel>
</Page>
```

As you can see from Figure 4-7, it is now possible to clearly delineate between elements, but the result is still not acceptable. The elements are centered on the page when they really should be left-justified. That's easy enough—you can align elements within a container using the `HorizontalAlignment` and `VerticalAlignment` attributes.

Alignment can be a tricky subject because there's more than just left, right, and center, and alignment interacts with width in strange and mysterious ways. Traditional alignment values act as you'd expect. `StackPanel` will align elements on its left edge, its right edge, or centered, based on the value of `HorizontalAlignment`. The default value for `HorizontalAlignment` is `Stretch`. This forces all contained elements to stretch themselves (appropriate, isn't it?) to fill the entire width of the panel.

Using a `HorizontalAlignment` of `Stretch` and specifying widths on individual elements has interesting effects. In Figure 4-8, the first element added is a border

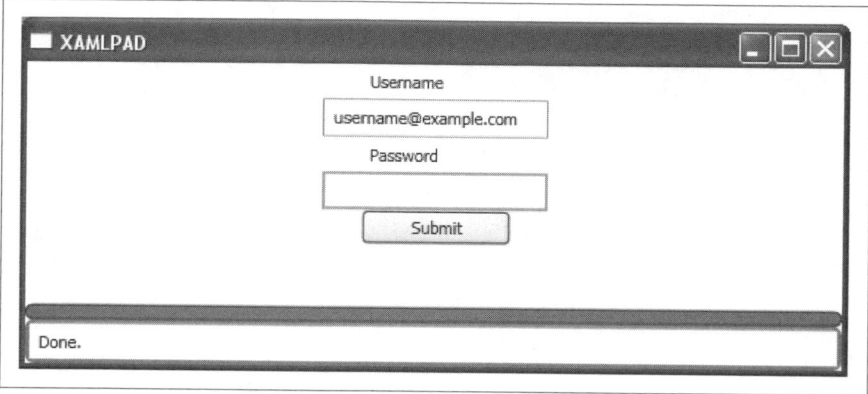

Figure 4-7. Result of using Width to constrain element sizes

with a width of 200 and a `TextBlock`. The element's width has been rendered correctly, but it is centered in the panel. Elements in a `StackPanel` using `Stretch` as its `HorizontalAlignment` are positioned centrally in the panel and then stretched equally to the left and right according to their width. In the third element ("I have no width"), you can see that if no width is specified, the element stretches to fill the entire panel.

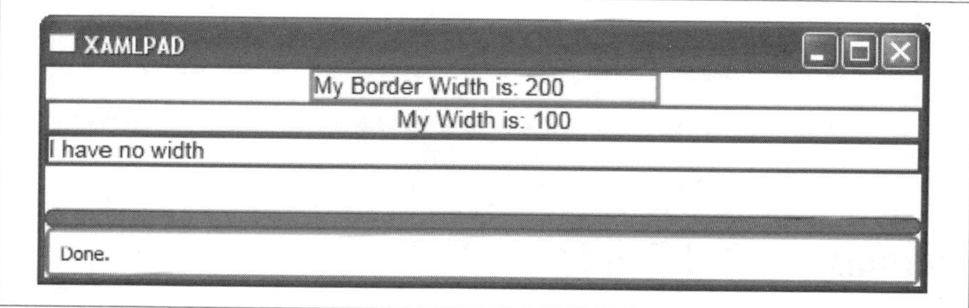

Figure 4-8. Specifying widths and HorizontalAlignment=Stretch

The second element added is a `Border` with no width, so it appropriately fills the width of the panel, but the `TextBlock` contained *within* the `Border` element has a set width of 100. The `TextBlock` is therefore centered and stretched equally to the left and right to fill the specified width of 100. When using `Stretch`, remember that elements are stretched from a center point in the `StackPanel`, not anchored to the left and stretched across the width of the panel.

There are also some odd effects when specifying a width for only one element using alignments other than `Stretch`. Elements with no width will automatically size themselves to their content or to the size of the element with a specified width, whichever is larger.

The `Height` and `Width` of an element take precedence over `HorizontalAlignment` and `VerticalAlignment`. For example, explicitly setting the `Width` of an element in conjunction with `Stretch` as its `HorizontalAlignment` will result in the `Stretch` value being ignored.

Returning to the example interface and applying a `Left` `HorizontalAlignment`, as well as specifying widths for the elements, produces Figure 4-9. While this is certainly closer to the original, the elements are still bumping up against one another, and the `TextBox` and `PasswordBox` are too close to the left edge of the page. To fine-tune this interface further, you must use the `Margin` and `Padding` attributes.

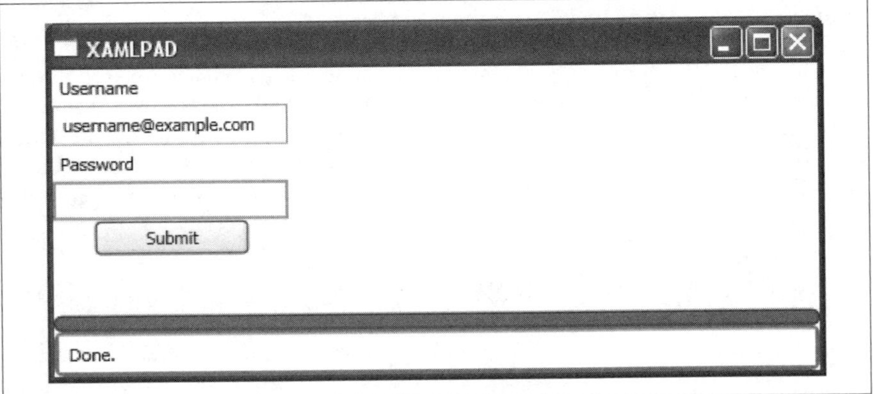

Figure 4-9. Result of setting HorizontalAlignment to Left

Margins and Padding

If you're familiar at all with CSS, then you're familiar with the concept of padding and margins. Padding and margins assist user-interface designers in positioning elements and content in elements. The two attributes are both described by a `Thickness` element but serve different purposes in layout.

`Margin` describes the distance between the element and its children or peers. It is used to position elements relative to other elements. Using abbreviated markup syntax, you can specify its thickness as a uniform distance around the element, e.g., `Margin="20"`, or as the distance in each individual direction in terms of left, top, right, and bottom (in that order), e.g., `Margin="20, 10, 20, 10"`.

`Margin` is one of the elements that does not require commas in its abbreviated markup. It can be described using either comma- or space-separated values.

Specifying a `Margin` value on the `StackPanel` in our user-login example will only change the distance between the `StackPanel` and the edges of the `Page`. To illustrate the concept of Margin, examine Figure 4-10. A second StackPanel has been added, containing the same elements for the user-login interface as well as borders to illustrate the Margin property at work. (In order to produce a side-by-side comparison of two StackPanel elements, both were enclosed in a DockPanel.) The black-bordered StackPanel has no Margin at all, while the lighter-bordered StackPanel has a uniform Margin of 20 device-independent pixels. You can see the difference in the positioning of the elements in relation to their children. The Margin of 20 has offset all the elements by 20 pixels, moving them away from the edge of the StackPanel.

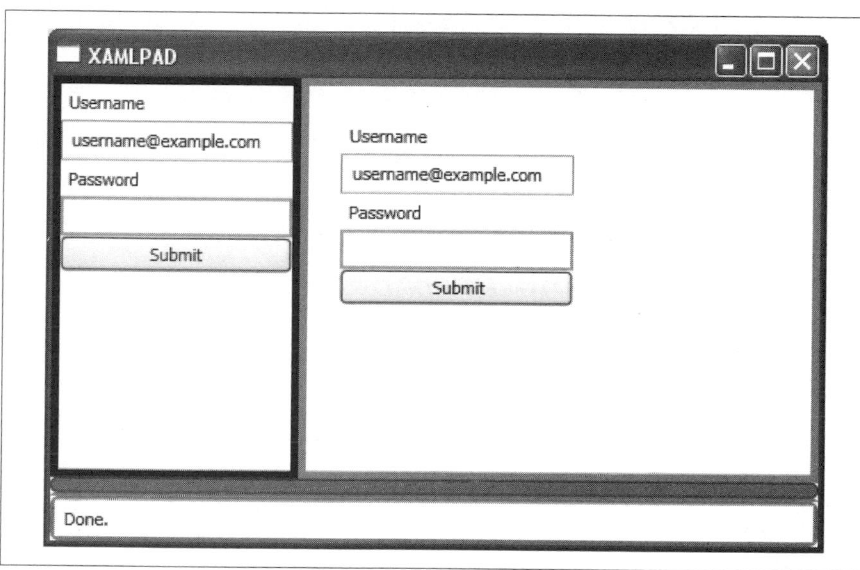

Figure 4-10. Using Margin versus no Margin to lay out elements

Example 4-4 shows the code used to produce Figure 4-10.

Example 4-4. Using Margin to position elements

```
<Page
    xmlns="http://schemas.microsoft.com/winfx/avalon/2005">
    <DockPanel>
        <Border
            BorderBrush="Black"
            BorderThickness="5">
            <StackPanel
                HorizontalAlignment="Left">
                <Label
                    HorizontalAlignment="Left"
                    Width="100">Username</Label>
                <TextBox
                    Width="150">username@example.com</TextBox>
                <Label
                    HorizontalAlignment="Left"
                    Width="100">Password</Label>
                <PasswordBox
```

Example 4-4. Using Margin to position elements (continued)

```
                    Width="150"></PasswordBox>
                <Button
                    Content="Submit" />
            </StackPanel>
        </Border>
        <Border
            BorderBrush="Red"
            BorderThickness="5">
            <StackPanel
                HorizontalAlignment="Left"
                Margin="20">
                <Label
                    HorizontalAlignment="Left"
                    Width="100">Username</Label>
                <TextBox
                    Margin="0 0 0 10"
                    Width="150">username@example.com</TextBox>
                <Label
                    HorizontalAlignment="Left"
                    Width="100">Password</Label>
                <PasswordBox
                    Margin="0 0 0 10"
                    Width="150"></PasswordBox>
                <Button
                    Margin="0 0 0 10"
                    Content="Submit" />
            </StackPanel>
        </Border>
    </DockPanel>
</Page>
```

Setting the Margin on the StackPanel did nothing for the crowded appearance of its child elements. That's because the margin of the StackPanel only affects the StackPanel itself, not elements contained within it. The Margin must be set on every element you wish to reposition in order to achieve a less-crowded appearance (Figure 4-11).

The disadvantage of specifying a Width for elements is that it can be detrimental to localization efforts. The word "submit" in English is fairly short, but in another language it may consist of several words or a much longer string. Specifying a Width means that the Button will likely need to be sized according to the longest possible content it will contain; it may look awkward when using other languages with shorter or longer content strings.

Padding is similar to Margin in most respects, except that it is only exposed on three elements: Block, Border, and Control. Since Control is the base class for almost all user-input elements, it can be used on most user-interface elements. The Padding attribute determines the distance between the outer edge of the control and its child elements. Like Margin, Padding is defined as a Thickness and

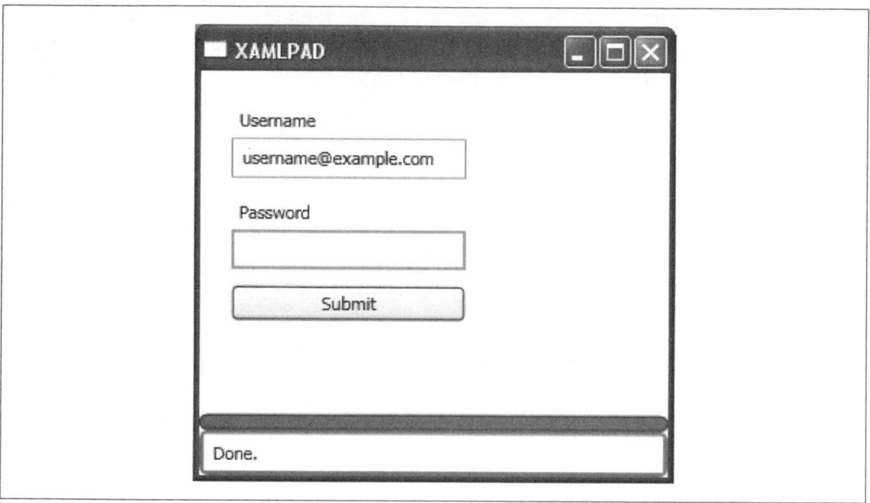

Figure 4-11. User-login page after applying a Margin to input elements

can be declared using abbreviated markup syntax. Setting the `Padding` attribute effectively changes the element's size to accommodate the additional space separating the edge of the element and its content.

Figure 4-12 duplicates the user-login panel and uses a border to accentuate the difference between the elements on the left, which have no `Padding` attribute specified, and the elements on the right, which do. The `Padding` for the elements on the first `Label`, `TextBox`, and `Button` has been specified as a uniform thickness of 10 (`Padding="10"`).

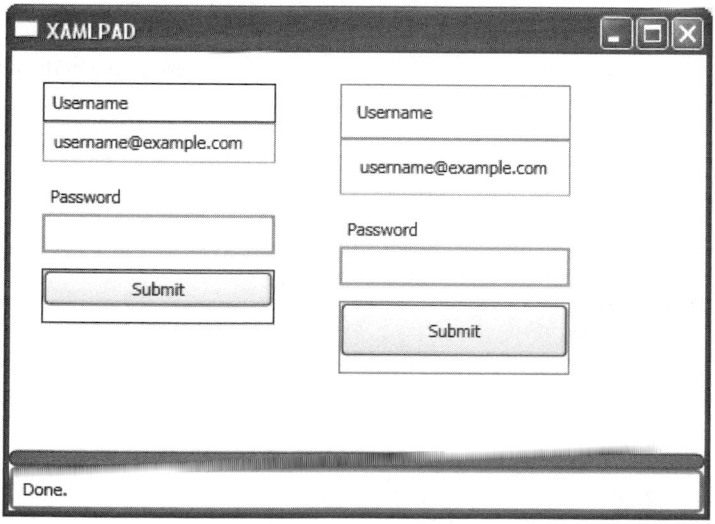

Figure 4-12. Applying the Padding attribute to the user-login page

The Padding attribute increases the size of the elements on the right to accommodate a 10-pixel distance between the outer edge of the elements and their content.

Grid

The Grid element is useful for relative, automatic positioning strategies in which some control over element placement is required. Grid is similar to Table (just like the HTML Table) and provides individual cells in which elements can be positioned. Grid is more complex than Table, however, and should not be treated as a simple Table element. Grid cell sizes can be explicitly declared as a number of device-independent pixels, as a percentage of the overall available Width and Height, or as auto-size factors based on their content by using the enumeration Auto.

Grid, like DockPanel, uses attached attributes to position child elements. Grid uses two attached attributes, Row and Column, to determine placement of child elements within its cells.

Grid uses zero-based indexing when specifying Row and Column placement.

A sample Grid might appear as follows:

Column 0, Row 0	Column 1, Row 0	Column 2, Row 0
Column 0, Row 1	Column 1, Row 1	Column 2, Row 1

To add elements to the Grid, specify which row and column the element is being added to. For example, to add an element to the cell in Column 1, Row 1, you would declare the element like this: <*ElementName* Grid.Column="1" Grid.Row="1" .../>. Example 4-5 shows the positioning of elements in our user-login interface using a Grid.

Example 4-5. Positioning elements using a Grid

```
<Page
    xmlns="http://schemas.microsoft.com/winfx/avalon/2005">
    <Grid
        ShowGridLines="true" >
        <ColumnDefinition
            Width="Auto" />
        <RowDefinition
            Height="Auto" />
        <RowDefinition
            Height="Auto" />
        <RowDefinition
            Height="Auto" />
        <RowDefinition
            Height="Auto" />
        <RowDefinition
```

Example 4-5. Positioning elements using a Grid (continued)

```
            Height="Auto" />
        <RowDefinition
            Height="Auto" />
        <Label
            Grid.Row="0"
            Grid.Column="0"
            Width="100">Username</Label>
        <TextBox
            Grid.Row="1"
            Grid.Column="0"
            Width="150">username@example.com</TextBox>
        <Label
            Grid.Row="2"
            Grid.Column="0"
            Width="100">Password</Label>
        <PasswordBox
            Grid.Row="3"
            Grid.Column="0"
            Width="150"></PasswordBox>
        <Button
            Grid.Row="4"
            Grid.Column="0"
            Width="100"
            Content="Submit" />
    </Grid>
</Page>
```


It's not a very exciting layout because there aren't many child elements, but you can see how to specify the attached attributes of a Grid, Row, and Column to position elements within a Grid. There is no need to declare specific cells within the Grid, but elements contained in the Grid must be declared within the opening and closing tags for the Grid element. Though the elements have been declared in order here, there is actually no need to do so. The elements are added based on the declaration of the Grid's Row and Column attached attributes.

Absolute Positioning

Thus far, StackPanel, DockPanel, and Grid elements have been used to position elements on the Page. Positioning with these Panel elements is a purely relative positioning strategy and offers no control over the x- and y-coordinate values of the element's position. Like CSS, relative positioning is used to allow elements to flow and reposition in the event that the page size changes. There are times, however, when absolute positioning is desired. XAML supports absolute positioning through the use of the Canvas element.

All elements on a Canvas element must be absolutely positioned or they will stack on top of one another. Absolute positioning is accomplished using the attached attributes of Canvas, namely Top, Left, Bottom, and Right.

If specified, the attached attributes Top or Left take priority over Bottom or Right.

The coordinate system used to position elements places 0,0 in the upper-left corner of the Canvas. Values specified for Top, Left, Bottom, and Right are relative to the Canvas, not the Page. If the Page contains only a single Canvas, then the value is relative to both, but only because the Canvas ends up positioned with 0,0 in the same place as 0,0 on the Page.

So, absolute positioning is actually relative, in an absolute kind of way. An example is probably in order after that mouthful. Figure 4-13 shows the relativity of absolute positioning. A Canvas has been added to a Canvas, specifying Top and Left values of 100 and 200, respectively. The unboxed coordinates are Label elements added to the parent Canvas, while the boxed coordinates are those added to the second Canvas. The Labels were added with the same Top and Left coordinates, but you can see that the Labels added to the second (the child) Canvas are offset. The code producing Figure 4-13 is shown in Example 4-6.

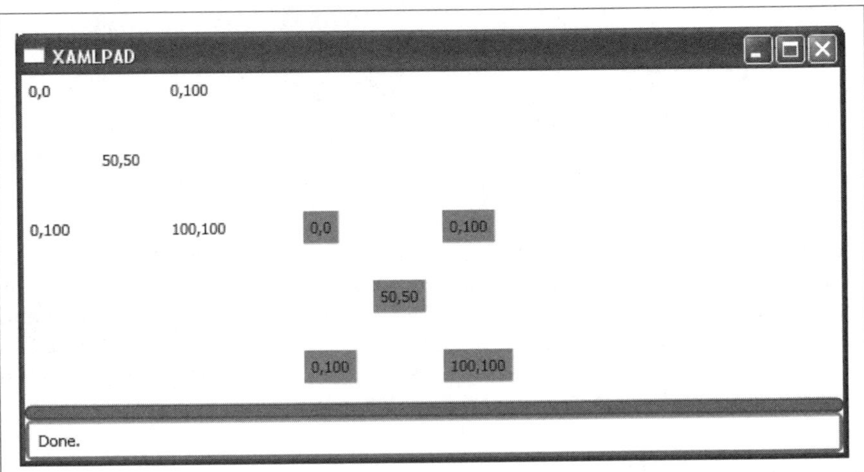

Figure 4-13. Canvas inside canvas, illustrating absolute positioning

Example 4-6. Canvas inside canvas, showing relative absolute positioning

```
<Page
    xmlns="http://schemas.microsoft.com/winfx/avalon/2005">
    <Canvas>
    <Canvas
        Canvas.Top="100"
        Canvas.Left="200">
        <Label Canvas.Top="0" Canvas.Left="0" Background="Red">0,0</Label>
        <Label Canvas.Top="0" Canvas.Left="100" Background="Red">0,100</Label>
        <Label Canvas.Left="50" Canvas.Top="50" Background="Red">50,50</Label>
        <Label Canvas.Left="100" Canvas.Top="100" Background="Red">100,100</Label>
        <Label Canvas.Left="0" Canvas.Top="100" Background="Red">0,100</Label>
```

Example 4-6. Canvas inside canvas, showing relative absolute positioning (continued)

```
    </Canvas>
        <Label Canvas.Top="0" Canvas.Left="0">0,0</Label>
        <Label Canvas.Top="0" Canvas.Left="100">0,100</Label>
        <Label Canvas.Left="50" Canvas.Top="50">50,50</Label>
        <Label Canvas.Left="100" Canvas.Top="100">100,100</Label>
        <Label Canvas.Left="0" Canvas.Top="100">0,100</Label>
    </Canvas>
</Page>
```

The rule is that even when using absolute coordinate values to specify the position of an element, the positioning is relative to its immediate parent element. An element considers its parent's layout area to be the whole world. Therefore, the positioning *is* absolute from the viewpoint of the element but could be relative from the view of the XAML developer. Didn't realize you were going to have to study philosophy to become a XAML developer, did you?

Example 4-7 shows how to use a `Canvas` element to position the elements required for the user-login interface. Each element must specify at least one of the attached attributes of `Canvas` in order to position itself correctly within the `Canvas` element. An element references an attached attribute by using the syntax `ElementName.AttachedAttribute`. In our example, `Canvas.Top` is declared for each element, assigning an appropriate value to position the elements on the canvas. The result, shown in Figure 4-14, is strikingly similar to the one defined using relative positioning with `StackPanel`.

Layout and Positioning

Example 4-7. Using a Canvas to absolutely position elements

```
<Page
    xmlns="http://schemas.microsoft.com/winfx/avalon/2005">
    <Canvas
        Margin="20"
        HorizontalAlignment="Left"
        VerticalAlignment="Top">
        <Label
            Canvas.Top="10"
            HorizontalAlignment="Left"
            Width="100">Username</Label>
        <TextBox
            Canvas.Top="30"
            Margin="0 0 0 10"
            Width="150">username@example.com</TextBox>
        <Label
            Canvas.Top="80"
            HorizontalAlignment="Left"
            Width="100">Password</Label>
        <PasswordBox
            Canvas.Top="100"
            Margin="0 0 0 10"
            Width="150"></PasswordBox>
        <Button
            Canvas.Top="150"
```

Example 4-7. Using a Canvas to absolutely position elements (continued)

```
            Margin="0 0 0 10"
            Content="Submit" />
    </Canvas>
</Page>
```

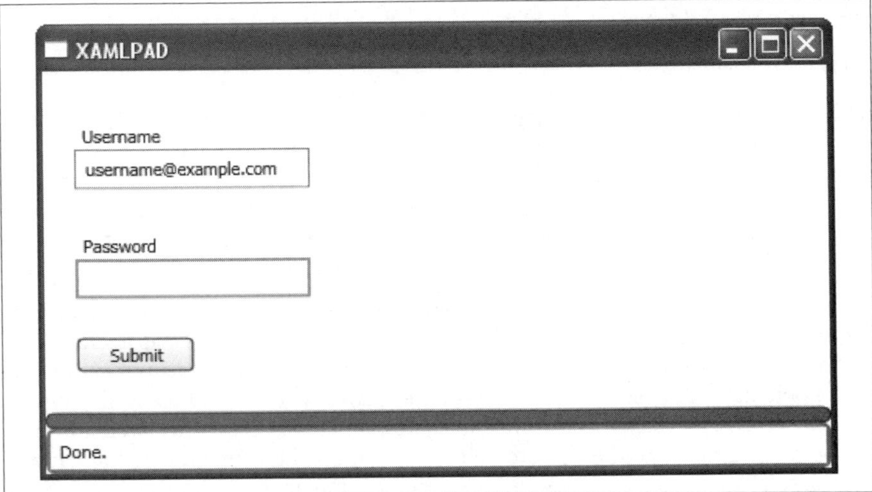

Figure 4-14. User-login interface created using Canvas and absolute positioning

You can mix and match the attached properties of `Canvas` to position elements exactly where you want them. By specifying `Canvas.Top` and `Canvas.Left` for the text field elements in the user interface (Example 4-8), the fields will line up, presenting a more typical user interface.

Example 4-8. Aligning elements using multiple attached properties of Canvas

```
<TextBox
            Canvas.Top="10"
            Canvas.Left="70"
            Margin="0 0 0 10"
            Width="150">username@example.com</TextBox>
<PasswordBox
            Canvas.Top="80"
            Cavas.Left="70"
            Margin="0 0 0 10"
            Width="150"></PasswordBox>
```

Setting `Canvas.Top` for each text field element to the same value as that specified for its `Label` lines up the elements vertically. Changing `Canvas.Left` modifies the anchor point of the left edge of the elements and lines the elements up with their respective labels (Figure 4-15).

Another way to accomplish this task is to group the label and field together in a `StackPanel` using a horizontal `Orientation` and then add the panel to the parent `Canvas`. This method has the benefit of aligning the elements in the `StackPanel`

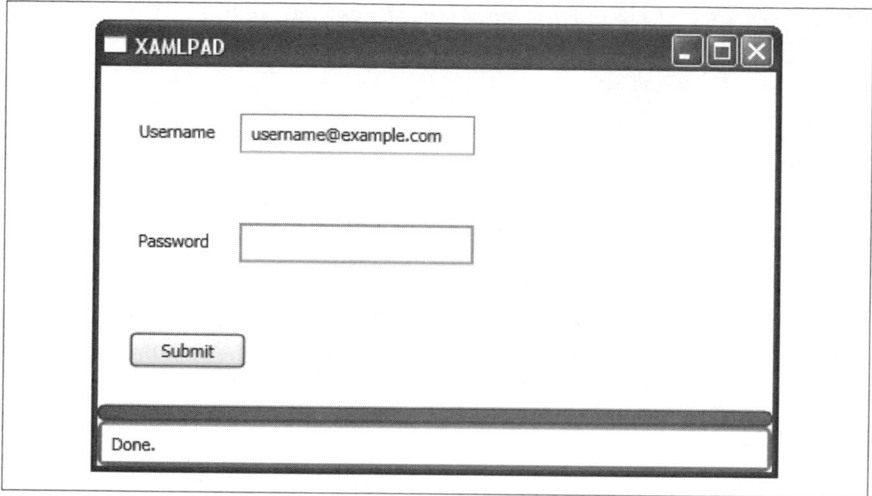

Figure 4-15. User interface with labels and elements aligned

Layout and Positioning

automatically and keeping them together as you move the panel around the Canvas. Don't forget that the stack panels must specify an absolute location on the Canvas or they'll stack on top of each other.

Example 4-9 shows possible XAML code for this technique. Notice that the absolute position is not specified for each element; only the StackPanel has a Canvas.Top declaration.

Example 4-9. Using StackPanel to group elements for absolute positioning

```
<Page
    xmlns="http://schemas.microsoft.com/winfx/avalon/2005">
    <Canvas
        Margin="20"
        HorizontalAlignment="Left"
        VerticalAlignment="Top">
        <StackPanel Orientation="Horizontal">
            <Label
                HorizontalAlignment="Left"
                Width="100">Username
            </Label>
            <TextBox
                Margin="0 0 0 10"
                Width="150">username@example.com
            </TextBox>
        </StackPanel>
        <StackPanel Orientation="Horizontal" Canvas.Top="50">
            <Label
                HorizontalAlignment="Left"
                Width="100">Password
            </Label>
            <PasswordBox
                Margin="0 0 0 10"
```

Example 4-9. Using StackPanel to group elements for absolute positioning (continued)

```
                Width="150">
            </PasswordBox>
        </StackPanel>
        <Button
            Canvas.Top="150"
            Margin="0 0 0 10"
            Content="Submit" />
    </Canvas>
</Page>
```

Unlike most fat-client programming models, individual elements cannot be absolutely positioned on their own. There are no Left or Right values for controls and elements such as Button, so the only way they can be positioned on the screen is by adding them to a container such as Canvas that offers a mechanism for absolute positioning.

Remember that although absolute positioning with elements such as Canvas can aid in designing your user interface, it can hamper localization efforts (as with hardcoding String values).

Next on the list of topics is styles and how to apply them globally, rather than locally, on each individual element. Chapter 5 will explore how to harness the power of XAML resources.

5
Resources

Every XAML element has a collection of resources. *Resources* provide a mechanism for defining common styles or elements that can be reused throughout the user interface. They also configure the actions that are carried out when a user interacts with a display element.

The benefit of using resources to define reusable, common styles is that modifications can be applied to one element, but they will take effect throughout the entire application. This reduces the chance of error and the possibility that an element might be missed when changes are applied. For example, you may want to define a specific `Point` from which all geometric shapes will originate. By defining the `Point` as a resource and referencing it as the appropriate attribute value of geometric elements, the origination point can easily be changed in one place—the resource declaration—without concern for mistakes made in multiple places throughout the user interface.

Local resources are defined on the element, while global resources are defined on the root element. Global resources can be used by all elements in the page while local resources are reserved for use by the element in which they are declared. Regardless of the type of resource (local or global), the syntax used to declare the resources is the same.

Although every element has a collection of resources, they are usually declared only on the root element.

Using Resources

When adding resources, you must add the appropriate namespace to the root element. You'll also need to give it a name to differentiate it from the default namespace. The default namespace, which references Avalon, contains the definitions of Avalon elements, such as Button, Page, and StackPanel. The namespace that must be added to define resources is the XAML namespace and describes the language itself.

Because resource definitions require the use of XAML-specific tags—which are not described by the default namespace—you must declare a reference to the XAML namespace and use it to prefix those attributes found only there, such as Key.

The key is a fully qualified attribute comprising the namespace, a colon, and the keyword Key. Elements defined as a resource must have a declared "key name" to be referenced by other elements. The value of the attribute is the name by which the resource will be referenced by other elements.

Resources are added by explicitly declaring elements as children of the Resources attribute of an element.

In Example 5-1, there are two instances of SolidColorBrush defined as resources: *RedBrush* and *BlueBrush*.

Example 5-1. Using resources to define global styles

```
<Page
    xmlns="http://schemas.microsoft.com/winfx/avalon/2005"
    xmlns:x="http://schemas.microsoft.com/winfx/xaml/2005"
    <Page.Resources>
        <SolidColorBrush
            x:Key="RedBrush"
            Color="red"/>
        <SolidColorBrush
            x:Key="BlueBrush"
            Color="blue"/>
    </Page.Resources>
    <StackPanel>
        <Button
            Background="{StaticResource RedBrush}" />
        <Ellipse
            Fill="{StaticResource BlueBrush}"
            Margin="40"
            Width="15"
            Height="25"/>
    </StackPanel>
</Page>
```

Resources must be declared in the file before they can be accessed. This is because the runtime engine interprets XAML as a stream of binary input and doesn't understand that a resource might be defined later in the stream. It can't render an element if a resource is required but hasn't yet been declared. In Example 5-2, the resource *RedBrush* is referenced *before* it is declared.

Example 5-2. Illegal use of a local resource

```
<Button
    Content="Click Me"
    Background="{StaticResource RedBrush}" >
```

Example 5-2. Illegal use of a local resource (continued)

```
    <Button.Resources>
        <SolidColorBrush
            x:Key="RedBrush"
            Color="Red" />
    </Button.Resources>
</Button>
```

This will result in an error in XamlPad and, although it will compile using MSBuild, it will raise a runtime exception. If you absolutely must declare a local resource, you'll have to declare it first, then explicitly declare the attribute that references the resource. Example 5-3 shows an example of declaring a local resource and then referencing it from within an explicitly declared attribute.

Example 5-3. Legal use of a resource

```
<Button Content="Click Me">
    <Button.Resources>
        <SolidColorBrush
                x:Key="RedBrush"
                Color="Red" />
    </Button.Resources>
    <Button.Background>
        {StaticResource RedBrush}
    </Button.Background>
</Button>
```

Resources

There are two ways to access a resource: statically and dynamically. An element references the resource by specifying either the keyword `StaticResource` or `DynamicResource`, followed by the key name of the resource. The two methods differ in how the resource in question behaves during the course of the application. If the resource can change through an outside source, it should be accessed dynamically because it will be reloaded and changes will be applied to it. Conversely, static resources assume that the resource in question will not change and therefore will not be reloaded during the application's execution.

In Example 5-1, the `Button` element declared its background color as the resource *RedBrush*. Similarly, the `Ellipse` element specified that its fill attribute should be defined by the resource *BlueBrush*.

Resources are hierarchical. Locally defined resources—those resources defined with the element—override resources defined for its parent, and so on. When the XAML processor encounters `{StaticResource RedBrush}` on the `Button`, it first checks the `Button` resources collection. Because `Button` does not have a definition of *RedBrush* (its resource collection is empty), it checks the parent of the `Button`, the `StackPanel`. When it does not find the definition in `StackPanel`, it checks its parent, `Page`, and finds the resource defined. The nature of resources allows you to apply a resource to all elements in the application simply by defining it on the root element.

The closest resource declaration of the same name for any given attribute will be the one applied. If *RedBrush* is declared as a global resource (in `Page.Resources`) as a red brush and then declared again locally on a button as a blue brush, the button will have a blue background. The rule is that local resources override global resources with the same key.

The most common use of resources is in defining styles and triggers to dynamically alter the appearance of user-interface elements.

Using Styles

A `Style` is a set of properties applied to an element that can be used to describe the appearance of an element. It is used in a similar manner as styles declared in CSS. A style can be applied locally to a single element, or it can be declared globally and referenced from the element. Styles can also be declared such that they affect all instances of a given type, such as `Button`.

A XAML `Style` is a collection of one or more `Setter` elements that act upon a specified dependency property, such as `Background` or `Foreground`. Remember that a `Key` value is required if the style will be applied by reference to an element. In Example 5-4, the `Style` *MyStyle* is declared as the value of the `Style` element on the `Button`, which sets the background, foreground, and width attributes to the values specified by the `Style` declaration.

Example 5-4. Example style applied to a Button element

```
<Page
    xmlns="http://schemas.microsoft.com/winfx/avalon/2005"
    xmlns:x="http://schemas.microsoft.com/winfx/xaml/2005">
    <Page.Resources>
        <Style
            x:Key="MyStyle">
            <Setter
                Property="Control.Background"
                Value="Red" />
            <Setter
                Property="Control.Foreground"
                Value="White" />
            <Setter
                Property="Control.Width"
                Value="100" />
        </Style>
    </Page.Resources>
    <StackPanel>
        <Button
            Style="{StaticResource MyStyle}"
            Content="A Red Button"/>
    </StackPanel>
</Page>
```

Figure 5-1 shows the result of evaluating Example 5-4 in XamlPad.

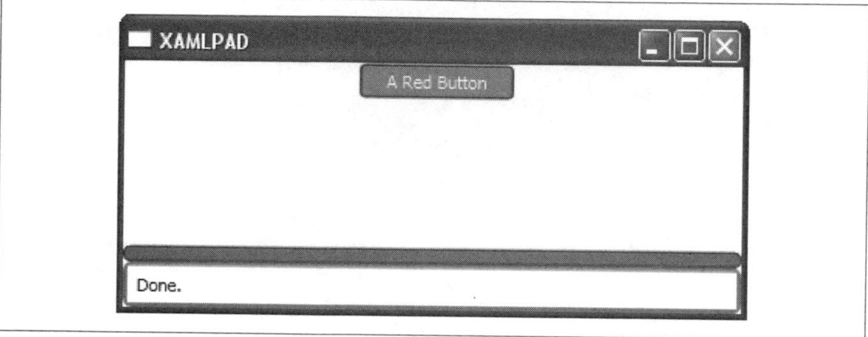

Figure 5-1. Application of a global style to a Button

Styles can also be applied to a class of elements by assigning the `TargetType` attribute of `Style` to the desired element type. Example 5-5 shows an example of applying a defined width and height to all elements of type `Button`.

Example 5-5. Example Style targeting a specific type of element

```
<Page
    xmlns="http://schemas.microsoft.com/winfx/avalon/2005"
    xmlns:x="http://schemas.microsoft.com/winfx/xaml/2005">
    <Page.Resources>
        <Style
            TargetType="{x:Type Button}">
            <Setter
                Property="Width"
                Value="200" />
            <Setter
                Property="Height"
                Value="50" />
        </Style>
    </Page.Resources>
    <StackPanel>
        <Button
            Content="A Button"/>
        <Button
            Content="Another Button"/>
    </StackPanel>
</Page>
```

In this example, we have omitted the `Control` prefix from the declared properties. This is because the style is targeting a specific type, namely `Button`, which inherits both properties used in the style (`Background` and `Foreground`) from `Control`. It is not necessary to prefix the property values when targeting a specific element type because of scoping rules, unless the property derives from a class outside the targeted element's hierarchy.

The result of evaluating Example 5-5 is shown in Figure 5-2.

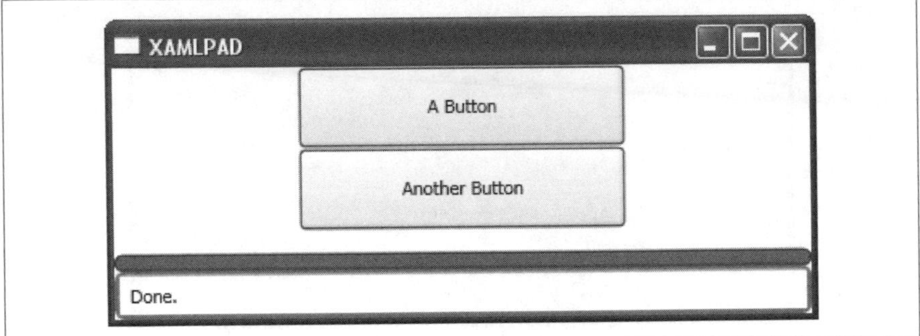

Figure 5-2. Result of evaluating Example 5-5 in XamlPad

In Example 5-5, neither `Button` element specifies its width or height. As discussed in Chapter 4, `StackPanel` defaults to a horizontal alignment value of `Stretch`. That means that elements added to the `StackPanel` with no specified width should fill the width of the panel. Yet when the XAML code in this example is interpreted, it will display both `Button` elements as though they have a specified height and width because the style is applied to all `Button` elements. Using the `Style` declared in Example 5-5 has the same effect as specifying the `Width` and `Height` attributes inline on both `Button` elements but saves space and makes changes to their appearance faster and with less margin for error.

`Style` is an extremely flexible element and, like all XAML elements, it can be extended to suit your needs. While other elements require code to be extended, `Style` can be extended purely within XAML by using the `BasedOn` attribute.

Extending `Style` using the `BasedOn` mechanism is like customizing a new car. You start with a "base" style and then specify changes such as color, heated seats, power windows, etc., that change the appearance of the final product. The plant that customizes your car applies all the base attributes to it but also makes the changes you specified, essentially assigning a new "style" to your car.

This technique is useful when you're given a standard corporate style to work with but are allowed to modify certain aspects of the style or to define previously undefined attributes. `BasedOn` allows you to essentially subclass a `Style`, much like using the `Inherits` VB.NET keyword to define a subclass. Example 5-6 demonstrates the use of `BasedOn` to extend a `Style`.

Example 5-6. Extending a Style using the BasedOn attribute

```
<Page
    xmlns="http://schemas.microsoft.com/winfx/avalon/2005"
    xmlns:x="http://schemas.microsoft.com/winfx/xaml/2005">
    <Page.Resources>
        <Style
            x:Key="MyStyle">
            <Setter
                Property="Control.Width"
                Value="200" />
            <Setter
                Property="Control.Height"
```

Example 5-6. Extending a Style using the BasedOn attribute (continued)

```
                Value="50" />
        </Style>
        <Style
            x:Key="MyStyle2"
            BasedOn="{StaticResource MyStyle}">
                <Setter
                    Property="Control.Width"
                    Value="300"/>
                <Setter
                    Property="Control.FontWeight"
                    Value="Bold" />
        </Style>
    </Page.Resources>
    <StackPanel>
        <Button
            Style="{StaticResource MyStyle}"
            Content="I use MyStyle"/>
        <Button
            Style="{StaticResource MyStyle2}"
            Content="I use MyStyle2"/>
    </StackPanel>
</Page>
```

As with polymorphism in object-oriented languages, overriding a `Property` value in a new `Style` that has been defined in its `BasedOn` style applies the new `Style`'s property whenever it is used. If the base style has not defined the property, then the new property is automatically used when it is referenced.

In Example 5-6, the width of the `Button` that references *`MyStyle2`* is 300, while the background of the `Button` referencing the style *`MyStyle`* has a width of 200. However, only the text on the `Button` that references *`MyStyle2`* will be bold, because the property `Control.FontWeight` has not been declared as part of *`MyStyle`*. Figure 5-3 shows the result of evaluating Example 5-6 with XamlPad.

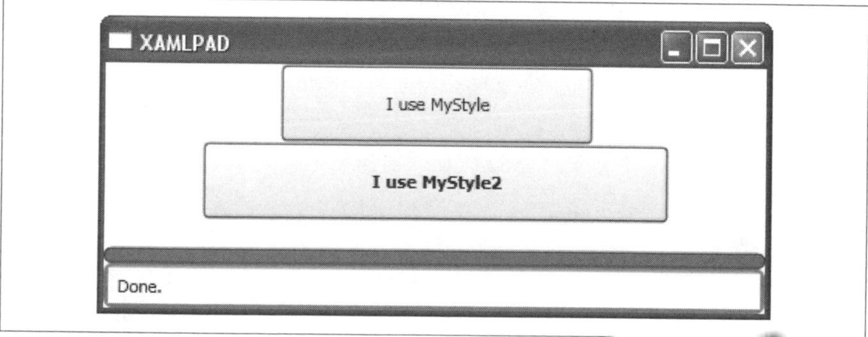

Figure 5-3. Using the BasedOn attribute to extend a style

Triggers

Triggers allow you to change attributes of an element when a specific action occurs. For example, you can change the font color of text when the mouse hovers over it, or change the width of a button once it has been clicked. Triggers can act on single instances of an element, or affect an entire class of elements.

Triggers are conditional. They are essentially a way to implement standard `if...then` logic without writing external code. In other words, a trigger evaluates an attribute and *if* the current value of that attribute matches the value specified by the trigger, *then* the style is applied. *If* the cursor moves over a `Button`, *then* change the background to green.

Example 5-7 defines a style that targets all elements of type `Button`. The code adds a `Trigger` that will fire when the property `Button.IsMouseOver` is `true`. Two `Setter` elements define the attributes we wish to change when the condition of the `Trigger` is met. In this case, it changes the foreground of the `Button` to green and the background to red.

Example 5-7. Using a Trigger to modify the appearance of Button elements

```
<Page
    xmlns="http://schemas.microsoft.com/winfx/avalon/2005"
    xmlns:x="http://schemas.microsoft.com/winfx/xaml/2005">
    <Page.Resources>
        <Style
            TargetType="{x:Type Button}">
            <Style.Triggers>
                <Trigger
                    Property="Button.IsMouseOver"
                    Value="true">
                    <Setter
                        Property = "Foreground"
                        Value="Green"/>
                    <Setter
                        Property = "Background"
                        Value="Red"/>
                </Trigger>
            </Style.Triggers>
        </Style>
    </Page.Resources>
    <StackPanel>
        <Button
            Content="My Button" />
    </StackPanel>
</Page>
```

Example 5-7 will modify the appearance of *all* `Button` elements declared in the page. To target only a specific `Button`, you must reference the style from the `Button` element. To do this, you must add a key name to the trigger and declare it as the `Style` attribute of the `Button`. The resulting code is shown in Example 5-8.

Example 5-8. Using a Trigger to modify the appearance of a single Button

```
<Page
    xmlns="http://schemas.microsoft.com/winfx/avalon/2005"
    xmlns:x="http://schemas.microsoft.com/winfx/xaml/2005">
    <Page.Resources>
        <Style
            x:Key="ButtonTriggers"
            TargetType="{x:Type Button}">
            <Style.Triggers>
                <Trigger
                    Property="Button.IsMouseOver"
                    Value="true">
                    <Setter
                        Property = "Control.Foreground"
                        Value="Green"/>
                    <Setter
                        Property = "Control.Background"
                        Value="Red"/>
                </Trigger>
            </Style.Triggers>
        </Style>
    </Page.Resources>
    <StackPanel>
        <Button
            Style="{StaticResource ButtonTriggers}"
            Content="My Button" />
    </StackPanel>
</Page>
```

Example 5-9 demonstrates how to declare Triggers local to an element by defining the Triggers within the local element's Resources attribute. As mentioned previously, local resources override global resources, so these resources will be applied to the element in which they are defined, but not to any others.

Example 5-9. Declaring a local Trigger

```
<Page
    xmlns="http://schemas.microsoft.com/winfx/avalon/2005"
    xmlns:x="http://schemas.microsoft.com/winfx/xaml/2005">
    <Page.Resources>
        <Style
            TargetType="{x:Type Button}">
            <Style.Triggers>
                <Trigger
                    Property="Button.IsPressed"
                    Value="true">
                    <Setter
                        Property = "Width"
                        Value="300"/>
                </Trigger>
            </Style.Triggers>
        </Style>
    </Page.Resources>
```

Example 5-9. Declaring a local Trigger (continued)

```
    <StackPanel>
        <Button
            Content="Button with global style" >
            <Button.Resources>
                <Style
                    TargetType="{x:Type Button}">
                    <Style.Triggers>
                    <Trigger
                        Property="IsMouseOver"
                        Value="true">
                        <Setter
                            Property="Background"
                            Value="Green" />
                    </Trigger>
                    </Style.Triggers>
                </Style>
            </Button.Resources>
        </Button>
        <Button
            Content="Button with no local style" />
    </StackPanel>
</Page>
```

Triggers can be used to modify the styles of specific elements, or they can be more generalized. By defining the Trigger's Property attribute as Control.IsMouseOver, the trigger can target any element that derives from Control. Assigning the Style attribute of controls as ButtonTriggers will then apply the conditional styling to any control. Example 5-10 shows how this use of Trigger can be applied to multiple control elements. All three elements (Button, ComboBox, and TextBox) assign the value of their Style attribute to the global Style *Triggers*. As these elements are ultimately derived from Control, the style is appropriately applied to all of them.

Example 5-10. Using a Trigger to modify the appearance of any Control

```
<Page
    xmlns="http://schemas.microsoft.com/winfx/avalon/2005"
    xmlns:x="http://schemas.microsoft.com/winfx/xaml/2005">
    <Page.Resources>
    <Style
        x:Key="Triggers">
        <Style.Triggers>
            <Trigger
                Property="Control.IsMouseOver"
                Value="true">
                <Setter
                    Property = "Control.Foreground"
                    Value="Green"/>
                <Setter
                    Property = "Control.Background"
                    Value="Red"/>
            </Trigger>
```

Example 5-10. Using a Trigger to modify the appearance of any Control (continued)

```
        </Style.Triggers>
    </Style>
    </Page.Resources>
    <StackPanel>
        <Button
            Style="{StaticResource Triggers}"
            Content="My Button" />
        <ComboBox
            Style="{StaticResource Triggers}">
            <ComboBoxItem>Item One</ComboBoxItem>
            <ComboBoxItem>Item Two</ComboBoxItem>
            <ComboBoxItem>Item Three</ComboBoxItem>
        </ComboBox>
        <TextBox
            Style="{StaticResource Triggers}">My Text
        </TextBox>
    </StackPanel>
</Page>
```

Thus far, the examples have concentrated on modifying color attributes for elements, but you can change other attributes as well, such as `Width`, `Height`, or even `Content`. Changing the content of an element might be useful if it is image-based, or if you want to provide more detailed information to the user when the mouse hovers over the element.

Example 5-11 modifies the background color, width, and content of a `Button` when the mouse hovers over the element. When the mouse is not over the element, a `Trigger` again modifies the content of the `Button`.

Example 5-11. Using a Trigger to modify multiple attributes of a Button

```
<Page
    xmlns="http://schemas.microsoft.com/winfx/avalon/2005"
    xmlns:x="http://schemas.microsoft.com/winfx/xaml/2005">
    <Page.Resources>
        <Style
            x:Key="Triggers" >
            <Style.Triggers>
                <Trigger
                    Property="Button.IsMouseOver"
                    Value="true">
                    <Setter
                        Property = "Control.Width"
                        Value="150"/>
                    <Setter
                        Property = "Control.Background"
                        Value="Red"/>
                    <Setter
                        Property = "Button.Content"
                        Value="Mouse Over" />
                </Trigger>
                <Trigger
```

Example 5-11. Using a Trigger to modify multiple attributes of a Button (continued)

```
                    Property="Button.IsMouseOver"
                    Value="false">
                    <Setter
                        Property = "Button.Content"
                        Value="Mouse Out" />
                </Trigger>
            </Style.Triggers>
        </Style>
    </Page.Resources>
    <StackPanel>
        <Button
            Style="{StaticResource Triggers}" />
    </StackPanel>
</Page>
```

This example includes a direct reference to the Content attribute as *Button.Content*, not one through Control as is done with Width and Background. This is because the base class Control does not have a Content attribute. As discussed in Chapter 3, only specific types of controls have a Content attribute. We could have made this example even more generic by specifying the property of the Setter as ContentControl.Content instead, because Button derives from ContentControl. This would allow this style to be applied to other classes derived from ContentControl (such as Label) as well as to all controls derived from HeaderedContentControl, which is a subclass of ContentControl. We would also need to change the Trigger property to ContentControl.IsMouseOver in order to apply the trigger style to elements other than Button.

This flexibility allows you to define conditional styling in a variety of ways, either by targeting a specific class of elements or individual elements. When used in conjunction with templated styles, triggers provide a powerful mechanism for designing rich, interactive user interfaces.

6 Storyboards and Animations

In the past, animations in user interfaces have been left to specialized developers and graphic designers. Most animations used in web applications require expertise in technologies such as Flash or GIF (Graphics Interchange Format). While these technologies vastly differ in how animations are created, they both utilize the basic building block of animation—frames.

The new presentation subsystem in Windows Vista (provided through the WinFX runtimes for Windows 2003 and XP) also supports the concept of animation using frames. In frame-based animation, each frame contains an object to be animated. That animation might be a change of color over time or movement from one point to another. Each frame specifies the state of the object at a given point in time. In frame 1, the circle is blue; in frame 2, it is blue-green; in frame 3, it is green, etc.

Flash developers have long been able to apply common animations to objects such as color changes, fades, and movement. Windows developers, however, had no such mechanism, so the task of coding such animations was time-consuming and difficult. XAML offers the ability to animate elements with the same ease as other technologies, making standard animations a breeze to create while providing the framework for more complex animations.

XAML uses storyboards to create animations. Standard animations, including fades, color changes, transforms, and even position changes, are easily accomplished through XAML—without any code—by using storyboards.

One of the hardest pieces of animations to nail down is timing. Timing involves determining how long an animation will last and how long each frame within it should take. If an object is being changed from green to blue, how long should each stage of the color change take? At what point does the object start looking more blue than green? And even more difficult, how many color changes (frames) will it take to go from blue to green in the time allotted for the total animation?

Thankfully, Avalon provides an efficient timing system that no longer requires a developer to manage timers himself. Instead, timing and redrawing the screen is handled by Avalon and defined in XAML. Like all XAML elements, `Animation` elements can be extended to create custom animations.

Animations in XAML are primarily created through the declaration of storyboards. A `Storyboard` is a collection of animations, each of which animates a specific property of an element (such as `Opacity`), which can be manipulated to make an element appear to fade in or out of view. So, you aren't really animating an element per se; you're animating an attribute of the target element.

A `Storyboard` accomplishes this by specifying one or more `SetterTimeline` elements. A `SetterTimeline` describes the target of the animation (a XAML element) and the attribute being animated. The attribute might be the `Background` color of an element, its position on a `Canvas`, its `Width`, or its `Height`.

The `SetterTimeline` element also declares one or more animation types to be applied to the element's attribute. As you might expect, common animations are already defined and ready for use, such as `ColorAnimation` and `DoubleAnimation`. The animation element really does all the work in the animation. It tells WPF everything it needs to know to perform the animation—the initial value of the attribute, the ending value of the attribute, and the length of the animation. From the animation declaration, WPF can determine how long each frame must be to accommodate the animation.

Storyboards

Storyboards can only be defined on root elements or as part of a style, even though every framework element has a `Storyboard` collection. The difference between setting the `Storyboard` attribute of the root element and setting the `Storyboard` attribute of a style can be summed up as follows:

- A style-based `Storyboard` can be applied to any element, not just the root element.
- The target of each `SetterTimeline` is assumed to be the element for which the style is defined, so you do not specify the `SetterTimeline` object's `TargetName`.

Every `Storyboard` must have at least one `SetterTimeline`. A `SetterTimeline` describes the target of the animation and the attribute being animated. In order to animate an attribute, it must be a dependency property. Animation in XAML is accomplished by modifying the value of an attribute over time. A `Path` indicates the element and the attribute to modify. The `Path` is another name for the target of an animation. An example of this is `(Button.Width)` or `(Button.Height)`.

The target is declared using the following syntax:

```
(ElementName.AttributeName)
```

Example 6-1 shows the XAML for targeting the width of a button with an animation.

Example 6-1. Targeting an element in a SetterTimeline

```
<SetterTimeline
            TargetName="myButton"
            Path="Button.Width" />
```

Only framework elements can be targeted. *Freezables*—elements deriving from the System.Windows.Freezable class—can only be targeted if they are used as an attribute value for another element. Brush is a freezable and is used to describe how to paint many attributes of elements, such as the Foreground and Background. Because Brush is used as the value of an attribute on an element, it can be targeted *through* the element, using syntax as follows:

```
(ElementName.AttributeName).(FreezableElementName.AttributeName)
```

An example of this is (Button.Background).(SolidColorBrush.*Red*), shown in Example 6-2.

Example 6-2. Targeting a Freezable in a SetterTimeline

```
<SetterTimeline
            TargetName="myButton"
            Path="(Button.Background).(SolidColorBrush.Red)" />
```

If you are trying to target the attribute of an element that is part of a collection, you'll need to push the path even deeper:

```
(ElementName.AttributeName).(CollectionTypeName.Children)[CollectionIndex].
(FreezableElementName.AttributeName)
```

An example of this is targeting a single Transform inside the RenderTransform collection of a Rectangle. (Rectangle.RenderTransform).(TransformGroup.Children)[0].(ScaleTransform.ScaleX) (Example 6-3).

Example 6-3. Targeting an element in a collection in a SetterTimeline

```
<SetterTimeline
    TargetName="myRectangle"
    Path="Rectangle.(Rectangle.RenderTransform).(TransformGroup.Children)[0].
(ScaleTransform.ScaleX)  />
```

XAML collections are zero-based, so the first element in the collection is referenced by the index 0.

The type of the animation you add to the SetterTimeline must match the type of the attribute you are targeting. If you target a Color, then you must use a ColorAnimation. If the attribute is a Double, you must use a DoubleAnimation, and so on. If the attribute on the target is not declared, the animation has no effect. If you do not specify the Background color for Button, the animation does not appear to work.

In Example 6-4, a SetterTimeline that targets the Button *myButton* is declared. The Path of the SetterTimeline is set to the SolidColorBrush used to paint the Background of the Button. A ColorAnimation that changes the background color from blue to yellow is then added to the SetterTimeline. The Color begins as blue and, as specified by the Duration attribute of the ColorAnimation, will change to yellow within five seconds of the animation starting. The RepeatBehavior of the animation is declared as Forever, which means that once the animation ends, it will begin again, resetting the color to blue and continuing to iterate until the application closes.

Example 6-4. Animating the Background Color of a Button

```
<Page
     xmlns="http://schemas.microsoft.com/winfx/avalon/2005"
     xmlns:x="http://schemas.microsoft.com/winfx/xaml/2005">
     <Page.Storyboards>
         <SetterTimeline
             TargetName="myButton"
             Path="(Button.Background).(SolidColorBrush.Color)">
             <ColorAnimation
                 From="Blue"
                 To="Yellow"
                 Duration="0:0:5"
                 RepeatBehavior="Forever" />
         </SetterTimeline>
    </Page.Storyboards>
    <StackPanel >
        <Button
            Name="myButton"
            Width="120"
            Background="White">A Button
        </Button>
    </StackPanel>
</Page>
```

All elements of *Type*Animation have a From, To, By, Duration, and RepeatBehavior attribute. The value of From, To, and By varies according to the type. A DoubleAnimation, for example, requires Double values for these attributes. A RectAnimation requires a Rect, and so on. The animation starts at the value From and changes according to the To or By values. Setting the To attribute means that the animation value will move from the From value to the To value in the time period specified by Duration. Setting the By attribute means that the value will change by the By value during the time period specified by Duration. You are not allowed to set both the To and By attributes at the same time.

You determine the type of animation to use based on the attribute you are trying to animate. If you're animating the width of an element, use a DoubleAnimation because the data type of the Width attribute is a Double.

Example 6-5 shows the code used to animate the width of a Button using a DoubleAnimation. Over the course of five seconds, the Button will change width from 100 pixels to 200 pixels. Figures 6-1 through 6-4 illustrate the animation in effect at different times.

Example 6-5. Animating the width of a Button using DoubleAnimation

```
<Page
     xmlns="http://schemas.microsoft.com/winfx/avalon/2005"
     xmlns:x="http://schemas.microsoft.com/winfx/xaml/2005">
     <Page.Storyboards>
         <SetterTimeline
             TargetName="myButton"
             Path="(Button.Width)">
             <DoubleAnimation
                 From="100"
                 To="200"
                 Duration="0:0:5"
                 RepeatBehavior="Forever" />
         </SetterTimeline>
    </Page.Storyboards>
    <StackPanel >
        <Button
            Name="myButton">A Button
        </Button>
    </StackPanel>
</Page>
```

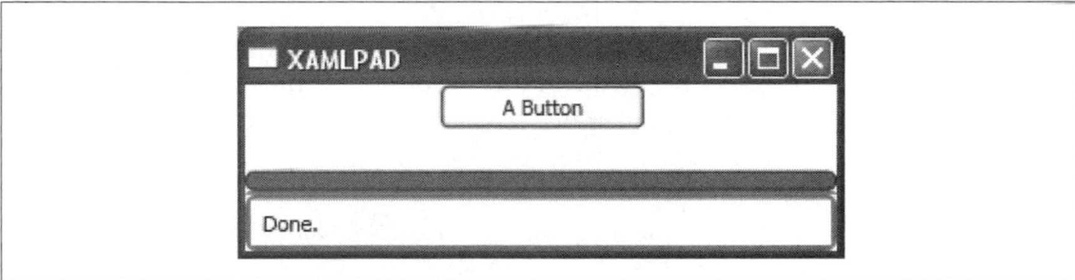

Figure 6-1. Animation of Button width at time 0:0:0

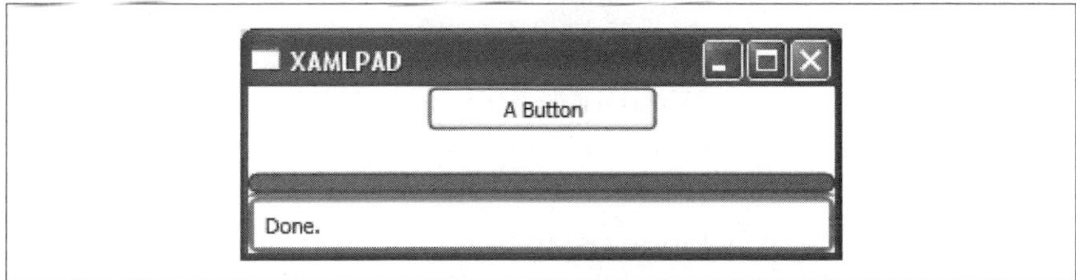

Figure 6-2. Animation of Button width at time 0:0:1

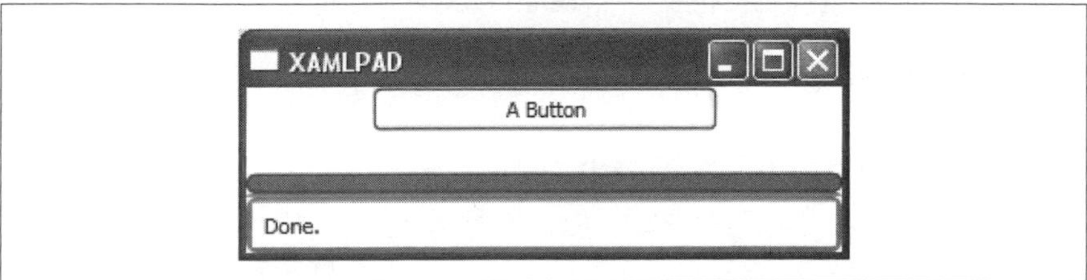

Figure 6-3. Animation of Button width at time 0:0:3

Figure 6-4. Animation of Button width at time 0:0:5

Once the animation completes (Figure 6-4), it returns to the beginning (Figure 6-1) and starts again, its width suddenly dropping from 200 to 100 in the process. There are mechanisms that allow you to change this behavior. Using attributes of the animation, you can expand the button's width and then reverse the animation so that it decreases its width gradually instead of returning to its original size. The next section discusses how to control different aspects of animations, such as speed and behavior.

Controlling Animations

Animation elements inherit several attributes from `Timeline` that control the speed and behavior of the animation. One of the more useful attributes is `SpeedRatio`, which controls the speed at which the animation moves. The attribute `AutoReverse` is also noteworthy. `AutoReverse` controls the behavior of the `Timeline` when it reaches the end of its `Duration`. Setting this value to `true` will cause the animation to reverse itself when it reaches the end of its iteration. Setting it to `false` will cause the animation to begin again—if `RepeatBehavior` indicates that it should continue—either for a specified number of iterations through the animation, for a specified period of time, or forever.

Example 6-6 shows the same animation from Example 6-4, but `RepeatBehavior` is now declared as `2x` and `AutoReverse` has been added and set to `true`. This animation will repeat twice, reversing itself each time. Although the animation declaration makes it appear that the `Button` will have a yellow background at the end of the animation, the background will actually be blue because we have set `AutoReverse` to `true`.

Example 6-6. Modifying the behavior of an Animation using AutoReverse and RepeatDuration

```
<Page
    xmlns="http://schemas.microsoft.com/winfx/avalon/2005"
    xmlns:x="http://schemas.microsoft.com/winfx/xaml/2005">
    <Page.Storyboards>
        <SetterTimeline
            TargetName="myButton"
            Path="(Button.Background).(SolidColorBrush.Color)">
            <ColorAnimation
                From="Blue"
                To="Yellow"
                Duration="0:0:5"
```

Example 6-6. Modifying the behavior of an Animation using AutoReverse and RepeatDuration (continued)

```
                AutoReverse="true"
                RepeatBehavior="2x" />
        </SetterTimeline>
    </Page.Storyboards>
    <StackPanel >
        <Button
            Name="myButton"
            Width="120"
            Background="White">A Button
        </Button>
    </StackPanel>
</Page>
```

You can mix and match animations within a SetterTimeline to create more interesting effects. For example, to yield the code in Example 6-7, modify Example 6-4 by adding a second animation that animates the width of the Button using a DoubleAnimation. Then, coordinate the Duration of the DoubleAnimation with the Duration of the ColorAnimation and, for both animations, set the AutoReverse to true and the RepeatBehavior to Forever. This creates a Button that begins with a width of 100 and a background color of blue and then slowly expands to a width of 200 and changes its background color to yellow. Both animations then reverse themselves and repeat.

Example 6-7. Coordinating multiple animations for a Button

```
<Page
    xmlns="http://schemas.microsoft.com/winfx/avalon/2005"
    xmlns:x="http://schemas.microsoft.com/winfx/xaml/2005">
        <Page.Storyboards>
        <SetterTimeline
            TargetName="myButton"
            Path="(Button.Background).(SolidColorBrush.Color)">
            <ColorAnimation
                From="Blue"
                To="Yellow"
                Duration="0:0:5"
                RepeatBehavior="Forever"
                AutoReverse="true"/>
        </SetterTimeline>
        <SetterTimeline
            TargetName="myButton"
            Path="(Button.Width)">
            <DoubleAnimation
                From="100"
                To="200"
                Duration="0:0:5"
                RepeatBehavior="Forever"
                AutoReverse="true"/>
        </SetterTimeline>
    </Page.Storyboards>
    <StackPanel >
```

Example 6-7. Coordinating multiple animations for a Button (continued)

```
        <Button
            Name="myButton"
            Width="120"
            Background="White">A Button</Button>
    </StackPanel>
</Page>
```

XAML also includes elements that can transform the position of other elements. `RotateTransform`, `SkewTransform`, `TranslateTransform`, and `ScaleTransform` provide basic 2-D transformation capabilities that can easily be used within animations to change the position and size of other elements.

Example 6-8 shows the code to rotate a rectangle in a circle around a specified point. The unnamed `Rectangle` is placed in the background with an `Opacity` of 0.25 to illustrate its starting position. The `RotateTransform` does not actually rotate the rectangle, because the `Angle` of the rotation is set to 0 degrees. It exists only to provide a way for the `SetterTimeline` to direct the `DoubleAnimation` to animate its `Angle` attribute from 0 degrees to 360 degrees over the course of four seconds (as indicated by the `Duration` attribute on the `DoubleAnimation`). Figures 6-5 through 6-7 show a few of the frames from this animation.

Example 6-8. Animating the RotateTransform of a Rectangle

```
<Page xmlns="http://schemas.microsoft.com/winfx/avalon/2005"
   xmlns:x="http://schemas.microsoft.com/winfx/xaml/2005" >
   <Page.Storyboards>
         <SetterTimeline
             TargetName="MyRectangle"
             Path="(Rectangle.RenderTransform).(RotateTransform.Angle)">
             <DoubleAnimation
                 From="0"
                 To="360"
                 RepeatBehavior="Forever"
                 Duration="0:0:4" />
         </SetterTimeline>
   </Page.Storyboards>
   <StackPanel>
       <Canvas
           Width="400"
           Height="550">
           <Rectangle
               Canvas.Top="100"
               Canvas.Left="100"
               Fill="Blue"
               Width="100"
               Height="100"
               Stroke="black"
               StrokeThickness="5"
               Opacity="0.25" />
          <Rectangle
              Name="MyRectangle"
              Canvas.Top="100"
```

Example 6-8. Animating the RotateTransform of a Rectangle (continued)

```
            Canvas.Left="100"
            Fill="blue"
            Width="100"
            Height="100"
            Stroke="black"
            StrokeThickness="5">
            <Rectangle.RenderTransform>
                <RotateTransform
                    Angle="0"
                    Center="50,50" />
            </Rectangle.RenderTransform>
        </Rectangle>
      </Canvas>
    </StackPanel>
</Page>
```

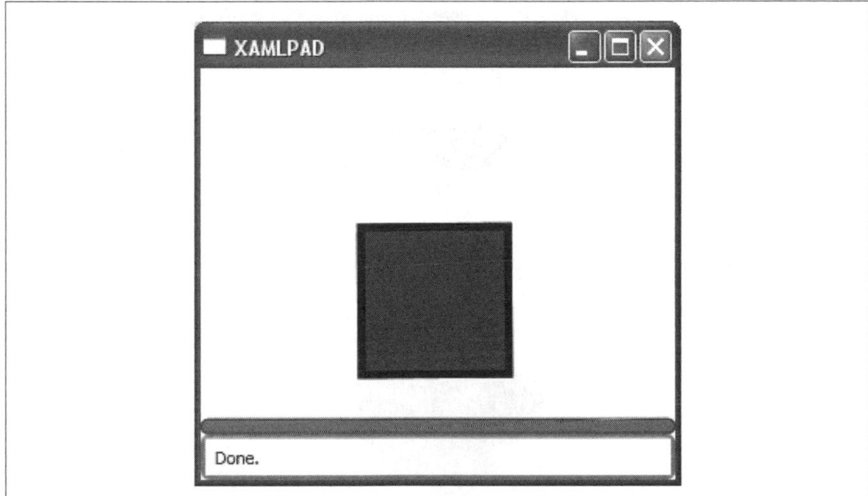

Figure 6-5. Animated Rectangle transform

As with animations involving attributes of elements, you can mix and match the animations to create interesting effects. Using a `ParallelTimeline` to manage multiple `SetterTimeline` elements allows different aspects of the `Rectangle` to be animated. A `ParallelTimeline` allows child timelines to overlap and use their `Begin` attribute, if specified, to determine when they begin animating. Without using `ParallelTimeline`, each animation would become active in the order it was added, and the `Begin` attribute would be evaluated relative to the end time of the previous animation. (This is useful for performing animations in a specific sequence rather than as a combination of effects.) A `ColorAnimation` has been added to change the color from blue to yellow with the same `Duration` as the `DoubleAnimation`. Evaluating Example 6-9 in XamlPad will produce a rotating rectangle with a changing fill color. It may not be very useful, but it sure is fun to watch.

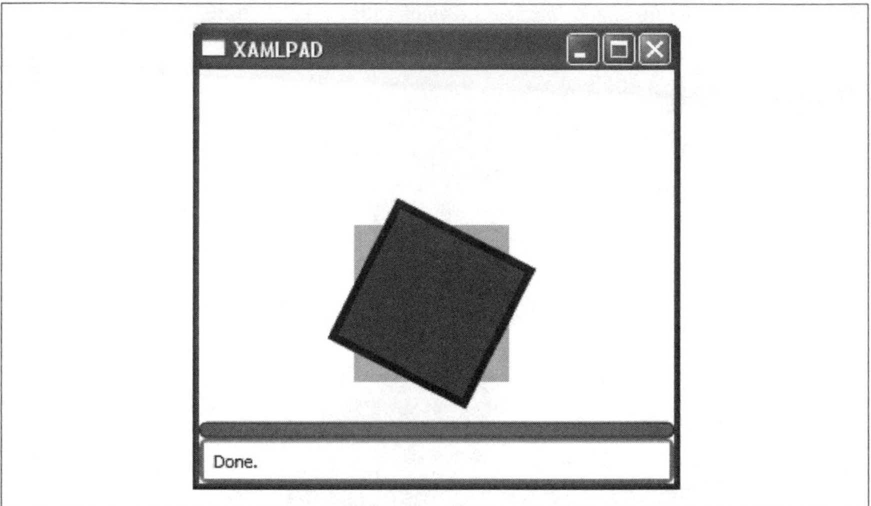

Figure 6-6. Animated rectangle at 40 degrees

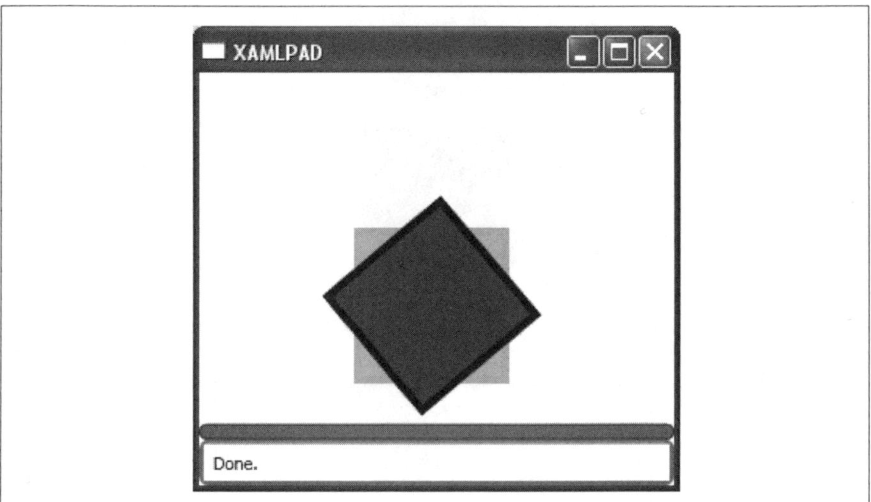

Figure 6-7. Animated rectangle at 60 degrees

Example 6-9. Animating multiple attributes of an element with ParallelTimeline

```
<Page xmlns="http://schemas.microsoft.com/winfx/avalon/2005"
   xmlns:x="http://schemas.microsoft.com/winfx/xaml/2005">
   <Page.Storyboards>
      <ParallelTimeline>
         <SetterTimeline
             TargetName="MyRectangle"
             Path="(Rectangle.Fill).(SolidColorBrush.Color)">
             <ColorAnimation
                From="Blue"
```

Example 6-9. Animating multiple attributes of an element with ParallelTimeline (continued)

```
                To="Yellow"
                Duration="0:0:4"
                RepeatBehavior="Forever"
                AutoReverse="true" />
        </SetterTimeline>
        <SetterTimeline
            TargetName="MyRectangle"
            Path="(Rectangle.RenderTransform).(RotateTransform.Angle)">
            <DoubleAnimation
                From="0"
                To="360"
                RepeatBehavior="Forever"
                Duration="0:0:4" />
        </SetterTimeline>
      </ParallelTimeline>
   </Page.Storyboards>
   <StackPanel>
      <Canvas
         Width="400"
         Height="550">
         <Rectangle
             Canvas.Top="100"
             Canvas.Left="100"
             Fill="Blue"
             Width="100"
             Height="100"
             Stroke="black"
             StrokeThickness="5"
             Opacity="0.25" />
        <Rectangle
            Name="MyRectangle"
            Canvas.Top="100"
            Canvas.Left="100"
            Fill="blue"
            Width="100"
            Height="100"
            Stroke="black"
            StrokeThickness="5">
            <Rectangle.RenderTransform>
                <RotateTransform
                    Angle="0"
                    Center="50,50" />
            </Rectangle.RenderTransform>
        </Rectangle>
      </Canvas>
   </StackPanel>
</Page>
```

Adding DoubleAnimation elements that target the Height and Width of the rectangle can make it seem to disappear and reappear as the animation progresses. The flexibility of Avalon's animation system means that you are generally limited only by your imagination.

Animation Using Key Frames

KeyFrame animations are another method for animating elements in XAML. They differ from non-key animations in that they use a number of key frames (values) as the destination rather than allowing the system to iterate through the values. KeyFrame animations allow you to control the specific values—and the interpolation methods used to arrive at them—across a number of key frames that make up the animation.

KeyFrame animations use different classes than non-key frame animations, but they are easily recognizable because each one uses the term "KeyFrame" in its name. As with non-key animations, there are KeyFrame animations for almost every primitive data type and some XAML elements.

Creating a KeyFrame animation requires the following steps:

1. Set a Duration for the animation.
2. For each key frame, select its appropriate type, set its value and key time, and add it to the animation's KeyFrame collection.
3. Associate the animation with an element's attribute, just as you would for a non-key animation.

Recreating the animation from Example 6-8 using KeyFrame animations instead of a non-key animation is a good way to illustrate the concept of a KeyFrame. The first step is to understand KeyTime, which is required for each key frame added to the animation's KeyFrames collection.

A KeyTime specifies when the key frame will end, as illustrated in the following example. It is tempting to view KeyTime as the amount of time the key frame will play, but this is incorrect. That value is determined by when the key frame ends, when the previous key frame ended, and the animation's duration.

```
<DoubleAnimationUsingKeyFrames Duration="0:0:10">
    <LinearDoubleKeyFrame Value="0" KeyTime="0:0:3" />
    <LinearDoubleKeyFrame Value="100" KeyTime="0:0:10" />
```

In this XAML fragment, the animation has a Duration of 10 seconds. The first key frame's KeyTime is set to 0:0:3, which means it will end three seconds into the animation. The second key frame's KeyTime is set to 0:0:10, which means it will end when the animation ends. Because the previous key frame ends at 3 seconds, and the second key frame is set to end at 10 seconds, the second key frame will play for a total of 7 seconds.

The KeyTime attribute can be specified using other values. It is most commonly specified as a duration, but you can also express the key time as a percentage of the total duration, or you can allow the interpreter to allocate time based on a distribution pattern that either spreads the duration equally over all frames or distributes it across key frames such that the animation will progress at a steady pace.

The possible values for KeyTime are:

KeyTime
: This value can be specified as a duration (hours:minutes:seconds) or as a percentage of the total duration, e.g., 20%.

Uniform
: This value automatically distributes the duration across all key frames based on how many there are. If the Duration is set to 10 seconds and there are five key frames, each key frame will play for 2 seconds (10/5 = 2). This can result in non-uniform speed because it is based on the number of key frames, not the change in values!

Paced
: This value automatically distributes the duration based on the number of key frames and value changes to ensure a smooth, even speed.

Example 6-10 uses key frame animation to construct the same animation created in Example 6-8 using non-key animation. The only real difference between the two examples is the declaration of the animation type. Using LinearDoubleKeyFrame elements produces a similar result to the one produced by using DoubleAnimation to animate the rotation angle value linearly from the previous value to the destination value.

Example 6-10. Animating a Rectangle using key frame animation

```
<Page xmlns="http://schemas.microsoft.com/winfx/avalon/2005"
   xmlns:x="http://schemas.microsoft.com/winfx/xaml/2005"
   <Page.Storyboards>
         <SetterTimeline
             TargetName="MyRectangle"
             Path="(Rectangle.RenderTransform).(RotateTransform.Angle)">
             <DoubleAnimationUsingKeyFrames Duration="0:0:20" >
                <LinearDoubleKeyFrame Value="90" KeyTime="0:0:5" />
                <LinearDoubleKeyFrame Value="180" KeyTime="0:0:10" />
                <LinearDoubleKeyFrame Value="270" KeyTime="0:0:15" />
                <LinearDoubleKeyFrame Value="360" KeyTime="0:0:20" />
             </DoubleAnimationUsingKeyFrames>
         </SetterTimeline>
   </Page.Storyboards>
   <StackPanel>
       <Canvas
           Width="400"
           Height="550">
           <Rectangle
               Canvas.Top="100"
               Canvas.Left="100"
               Fill="Blue"
               Width="100"
               Height="100"
               Stroke="black"
               StrokeThickness="5"
               Opacity="0.25" />
         <Rectangle
```

Example 6-10. Animating a Rectangle using key frame animation (continued)

```
                Name="MyRectangle"
                Canvas.Top="100"
                Canvas.Left="100"
                Fill="blue"
                Width="100"
                Height="100"
                Stroke="black"
                StrokeThickness="5">
                <Rectangle.RenderTransform>
                    <RotateTransform
                        Angle="0"
                        Center="50,50" />
                </Rectangle.RenderTransform>
            </Rectangle>
        </Canvas>
    </StackPanel>
</Page>
```

Most KeyFrame elements have three distinct types: linear, discrete, and spline. Each uses a different interpolation technique to move from the previous value to the destination value. The interpolation technique used can be determined from the name of the KeyFrame, e.g., SplineDoubleKeyFrame uses a spline interpolation technique, while LinearDoubleKeyFrame uses a linear interpolation technique.

Core XAML Reference

7

Elements

XAML elements are components whose primary purpose is to display information either graphically or textually. They are used to create and display text and graphics either as standalone elements or as ones nested within controls. Users do not generally interact with elements unless they are nested within a control, such as using an `Image` to paint the foreground of a `Button` or defining a `Hyperlink` within a `TextBlock`.

Many of the elements in XAML, particularly those such as `Brush` and `Color`, are used as attributes for other elements and derive from `System.Windows.DependencyObject`. `DependencyObject` is a standard .NET object and can be used by developers to create their own custom attributes.

Bold

Hierarchy: DependencyObject → ContentElement → FrameworkContentElement → TextElement → Inline

```
<Bold>Text to be bold</Bold>
```

`<Bold .../>` is an `Inline`-derived class that is applied to text-based elements. `Bold` makes the font appear darker, increasing its weight. Its only properties are those inherited from `Inline`. (See Figure 7-1.)

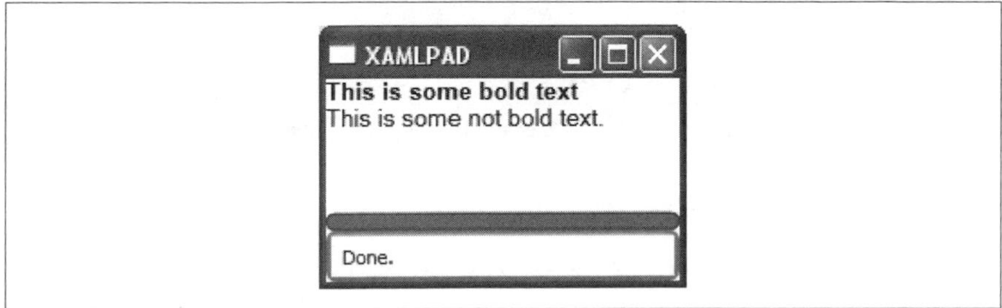

Figure 7-1. Bold text

Brush

Hierarchy: DependencyObject → Freezable → Animatable

`<Brush .../>` is an abstract component that defines how an area is painted. `SolidColorBrush` is most commonly referenced by other components through the use of the predefined colors in the `Colors` class (see Appendix G).

When a `Brush` is referenced as one of the colors from `Colors`, no explicit declaration is required and the element may be referenced simply by its predefined color name. (See Example 7-1.)

Example 7-1. Implicit declaration of a Brush using a predefined color

```
<Rectangle Fill="Blue" Width="100" Height="100" />
```

Color

Color is a structure and has no class hierarchy.

```
<Color
    ScA="1.0"
    ScR="0.0"
    ScG="0.0"
    ScB="1.0" />
```

`<Color .../>` defines a color.

Attributes

`ScA` *(required)*
: Defines the alpha channel of this `Color`. The alpha channel of a `Color` structure determines the amount of transparency the color has. An alpha value of 1 indicates the color is completely opaque, and a value of 0 indicates that it is completely transparent.

`ScB` *(required)*
: The blue component of this `Color`. The value is a single precision floating-point number. The range of this value is 0–1, inclusive.

`ScG` *(required)*
: The green component of this `Color`. The value is a single precision floating-point number. The range of this value is 0–1, inclusive.

`ScR` *(required)*
: The red component of this `Color`. The value is a single precision floating-point number. The range of this value is 0–1, inclusive.

Figure

DependencyObject → ContentElement → FrameworkContentElement → TextElement → Block

```
<Figure
    CanDelayPlacement="true|false"
    Height="200"
    HorizontalAnchor="ContentCenter|ContentLeft|ContentRight|
                      PageCenter|PageLeft|PageRight|ParagraphCenter|
                      ParagraphLeft|ParagraphRight"
    HorizontalOffset="10"
```

```
    VerticalAnchor="ContentBottom|ContentTop|ContentCenter|PageBottom|PageTop|
                    PageCenter|ParagraphTop"
       VerticalOffset="10"
       Width="200"
       WrapDirection="Both|Left|None|Right" />
```

`<Figure .../>` is used to display inline content within a `FlowDocument` with special placement properties. Figure 7-2 shows a `Figure` that displays both an image and text and is placed in the paragraph according to its declared anchor attributes.

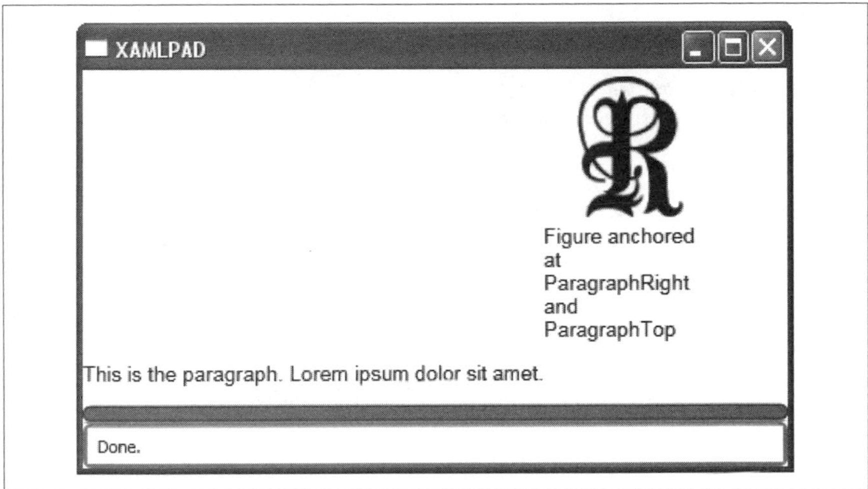

Figure 7-2. Using Figure to display an image and text within a FlowDocument

Attributes

`CanDelayPlacement` *(optional)*
: Specifies whether the `Figure` can wait to place itself into the layout until after other elements have been rendered in the `FlowDocument`.

  `true`
  : Placement can be delayed.

  `false`
  : Placement cannot be delayed.

`Height` *(optional)*
: A `Double` value specifying the height of the element.

`HorizontalAnchor` *(optional)*
: Specifies the position that content is anchored horizontally.

  `ContentCenter`
  : The figure is anchored to the center of the page content area.

  `ContentLeft`
  : The figure is anchored to the left of the page content area.

  `ContentRight`
  : The figure is anchored to the right of the page content area.

  `PageCenter`
  : The figure is anchored to the center of the page area.

`PageLeft`
: The figure is anchored to the left of the page area.

`PageRight`
: The figure is anchored to the right of the page area.

`ParagraphCenter`
: The figure is anchored to the center of the current paragraph.

`ParagraphLeft`
: The figure is anchored to the left of the current paragraph.

`ParagraphRight`
: The figure is anchored to the right of the current paragraph.

`HorizontalOffset` *(optional)*
: A `Double` value representing the distance this `Figure` is offset from its horizontal baseline.

`VerticalAnchor` *(optional)*
: Specifies the position that content is anchored vertically.

`ContentBottom`
: The figure is anchored to the bottom of the page content area.

`ContentCenter`
: The figure is anchored to the center of the page content area.

`ContentTop`
: The figure is anchored to the top of the page content area.

`PageBottom`
: The figure is anchored to the bottom of the page area.

`PageCenter`
: The figure is anchored to the center of the page area.

`PageTop`
: The figure is anchored to the top of the page area.

`ParagraphTop`
: The figure is anchored to the top of the current paragraph.

`VerticalOffset` *(optional)*
: A `Double` value representing the distance this `Figure` is offset from its vertical baseline.

`Width` *(optional)*
: A `Double` value specifying the width of the element.

`WrapDirection` *(optional)*
: Specifies the allowable directions in which content can wrap about the `Figure`.

`Both`
: Content may flow around both sides of the element.

`None`
: Content may not flow around this element.

`Left`
: Content only flows around the left side of the element.

`Right`
: Content only flows around the right side of the element.

Floater

Hierarchy: DependencyObject → ContentElement → FrameworkContentElement → TextElement → Block

```
<Floater
    HorizontalAlignment="Center|Right|Left|Stretch"
    Width="100" />
```

`<Floater .../>` displays images and other content parallel to the main content flow within a container. Floaters are always positioned parallel to the main flow of content. Unlike `Figure`, `Floater` may not span multiple columns. (See Figure 7-3.)

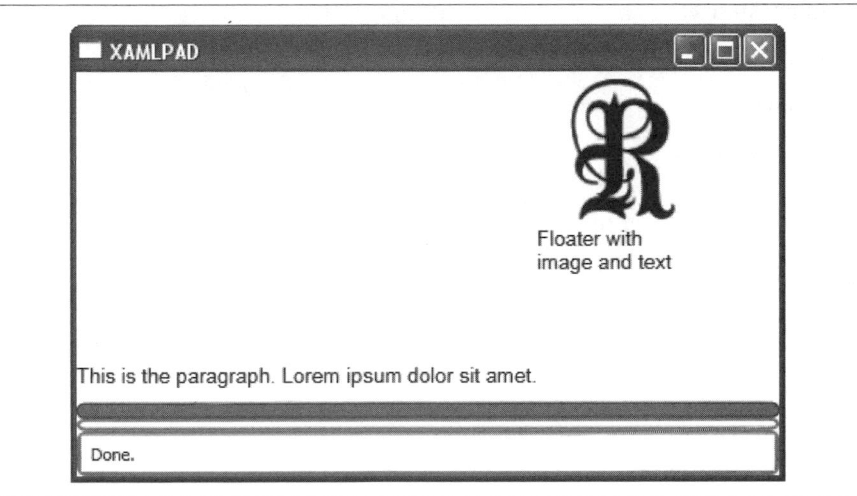

Figure 7-3. Floater with image and text positioned in a paragraph

Attributes

`HorizontalAlignment` *(optional)*

Indicates where the `Floater` should be aligned relative to its parent's layout slot.

`Center`
: Align the element at the center of its parent's layout slot.

`Left`
: Align the element to the left of its parent's layout slot.

`Right`
: Align the element to the right of its parent's layout slot.

`Stretch`
: Stretch the element to fit to the width of its parent's layout slot.

`Width` *(optional)*

A `Double` value indicating the width of the element.

Frame

Hierarchy: UIElement → FrameworkElement → ContentControl

```
<Frame
    Source="Page1.xaml" />
```

`<Frame .../>` implements an area that can load the contents of another markup tree. It is similar to the `<Frame>` tag in HTML. `Frame` uses the application navigation model; therefore, its content model is determined by the navigation service pointing to the URI to be loaded.

Attributes

`Source` *(optional)*
: The URI of the document containing the XAML markup to be displayed. The default value is `null`.

GradientStop

Hierarchy: DependencyObject → Freezable → Animatable

```
<GradientStop
    Color="Yellow"
    Offset="0.5" />
```

`<GradientStop .../>` describes the location and `Color` of the transitional point in a gradient. It is used by `RadialGradientBrush` and `LinearGradientBrush`.

Attributes

`Color` *(optional)*
: Describes the color of the transitional point in a gradient. The `Color` may be predefined in the `Color` class (see Appendix G) or described as a `Color` element. The default value is `Transparent`.

`Offset` *(optional)*
: This `Double` value represents the stop location in a gradient vector.

Image

Hierarchy: DependencyObject → Freezable → Animatable → Brush

```
<Image
    Source="filename"
    Stretch="None|Uniform|UniformFill|Fill"
/>
```

`<Image .../>` provides a means for displaying an image in a document or application. `Image` supports bitmaps of the following types: BMP, GIF, JPG, ICO, PNG, and TIFF.

Attributes

`Source` *(required)*
: The source URI for the image. It may be relative to the XAML application (e.g., `/images/`*`myimage`*`.png`), or it may be a remote image (e.g., `http://www.`*`example`*`.com/`*`myimage`*`.png`).

`Stretch` *(optional)*
: Defines how the image should be stretched to fill the destination rectangle. If defined, this attribute must be one of the following:

  `Fill`
  : Resizes the content to fit the destination. The aspect ratio is not preserved.

  `None`
  : The original size is preserved; the image is not stretched.

`Uniform`
: Resizes the original content to fit the destination and preserves the native aspect ratio.

`UniformToFill`
: Resizes the original content to fit the destination and preserves the native aspect ratio. If the aspect ratio of the destination is different than the original image, the image will be clipped to fit into the destination.

ImageBrush

Hierarchy: DependencyObject → ContentElement → FrameworkContentElement → Brush

```
<ImageBrush
    Viewport="0,0,0.5,0.5"
    ViewportUnits="Absolute|RelativeToBoundingBox"
    Viewbox="0,0 10 10"
    ViewboxUnits="Absolute|RelativeToBoundingBox"
    TileMode="FlipX|FlipXY|FlipY|None|Tile"
    AlignmentX="Center|Left|Right"
    AlignmentY="Center|Top|Bottom"
    ImageSource="sampleImages\cherries_larger.jpg"
    Stretch="Fill|None|Uniform|UniformFill"

/>
```

`<ImageBrush .../>` allows you to paint an area using an image. Using the attributes, you can modify how the image is used to paint the area. For example, the `TileMode` attribute allows you to modify the view of the image itself, flipping it horizontally or vertically if desired. Figure 7-4 shows the result of evaluating Example 7-2, which uses an `ImageBrush` to paint the rectangle indicated by the outlined area.

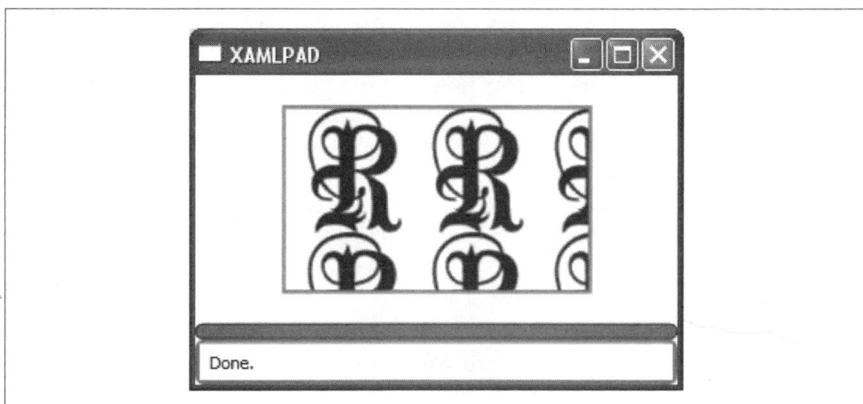

Figure 7-4. Using ImageBrush to paint a Rectangle

Example 7-2. Using an ImageBrush to paint a Rectangle

```
<Page
    xmlns="http://schemas.microsoft.com/winfx/avalon/2005"
    xmlns:x="http://schemas.microsoft.com/winfx/xaml/2005">
    <Rectangle
```

Example 7-2. Using an ImageBrush to paint a Rectangle (continued)

```
        Width="200"
        Height="120"
        StrokeThickness="2"
        Stroke="Red" >
        <Rectangle.Fill>
            <ImageBrush
                TileMode="Tile"
                AlignmentX="Left"
                AlignmentY="Top"
                ImageSource="c:\r.gif"
                Stretch="None" />
        </Rectangle.Fill>
    </Rectangle>
</Page>
```

Attributes

`AlignmentX` *(optional)*
: Describes how the image is aligned horizontally.

`AlignmentY` *(optional)*
: Describes how the image is aligned vertically.

`ImageSource` *(required)*
: Defines the source of the image used to paint the area.

`Stretch` *(optional)*
: Specifies how the brush's selected content is displayed in the brush's tiles.

  `Fill`
  : Resizes the content to fit the destination. The aspect ratio is not preserved.

  `None`
  : The original size is preserved; the image is not stretched.

  `Uniform`
  : Resizes the original content to fit the destination and preserves the native aspect ratio.

  `UniformToFill`
  : Resizes the original content to fit the destination and preserves the native aspect ratio. If the aspect ratio of the destination is different than the original image, the image will be clipped to fit into the destination.

`TileMode` *(optional)*
: Specifies how the tile fills out the object.

  `FlipX`
  : The same as `Tile`, but alternate columns of tiles are flipped horizontally. The base tile is drawn untransformed.

  `FlipXY`
  : The combination of `FlipX` and `FlipY`. The base tile is drawn untransformed.

  `FlipY`
  : The same as `Tile`, but alternate rows of tiles are flipped vertically. The base tile is drawn untransformed.

None
: Do not tile. Only the base tile is drawn; the remaining area is left transparent.

Tile
: The basic tile mode. The base tile is drawn, and the remaining area is filled by repeating the base tile such that the right edge of one tile abuts the left edge of the next, and likewise for bottom and top.

Viewbox *(optional)*
: Sets the position and dimensions of the Brush content in terms of the top-left corner, width, and height. The default is (0,0) with a width and height of 1, and it is defined as a Rect.

ViewboxUnits *(optional)*
: Sets the units for the Viewbox.

  Absolute
  : The coordinate system is not relative to the Brush output area. Values are interpreted directly in local space.

Viewport *(optional)*
: Sets the position and dimensions of the brush's tiles in terms of the top-left corner, width, and height. The default is (0,0) with a width and height of 1, and it is defined as a Rect.

ViewportUnits *(optional)*
: Sets the units for the ViewPort.

  Absolute
  : The coordinate system is not relative to the Brush output area. Values are interpreted directly in local space.

  RelativeToBoundingBox
  : The coordinate system is relative to the Brush output area, with 0 indicating 0 percent of the output area and 1 indicating 100 percent of the output area.

  RelativeToBoundingBox
  : The coordinate system is relative to the Brush output area, with 0 indicating 0 percent of the output area and 1 indicating 100 percent of the output area.

Inline

Hierarchy: DependencyObject → ContentElement → FrameworkContentElement → TextElement

```
<Inline
    BaselineAlignment="Baseline|Bottom|Center|Superscript|
                       Subscript|TextTop|Top|TextBottom"
    TextDecorations="Collection of TextDecoration" />
```

<Inline .../> defines an inline element with no inherent rendering properties. Inline is the base class for several inline elements designed to apply formatting to text and text-based elements. Derived classes are:

- AccessKey
- Bold
- Italic
- Underline

Elements

Attributes

`BaselineAlignment` *(optional)*

: `Baseline`
  : Aligns the text at the baseline

  `Bottom`
  : Aligns the bottom toward the bottom of the container

  `Center`
  : Centers the text vertically

  `Subscript`
  : Aligns the baseline to the subscript position of the container

  `Superscript`
  : Aligns the baseline to the superscript position of the container

  `TextBottom`
  : Aligns toward text's bottom of container

  `TextTop`
  : Aligns toward text's top of container

  `Top`
  : Aligns toward the top of the container

`TextDecorations` *(optional)*

: Specifies a collection of `TextDecoration` elements that will be applied to the content of `Inline`.

Italic

Hierarchy: DependencyObject → ContentElement → FrameworkContentElement → TextElement → Inline

```
<Italic>Text to be italicized</Italic>
```

`<Italic .../>` is an inline element that is applied to italicize text-based elements. Its only properties are those inherited from `Inline`. (See Figure 7-5.)

Figure 7-5. Italicized text using the Italic element

Label

Hierarchy: UIElement → FrameworkControl → Control → ContentControl

```
<Label
    Content="Text"
    Target="{Binding ElementName=UIElement}" />
```

or:

```
<Label
    Target="UIElement">
    Label Text
</Label>
```

<Label .../> defines a component that can be a text label for a control as well as providing mnemonic support.

Attributes

`Content` *(optional)*
: The text that will be displayed by the label. This attribute can be omitted if the second declaration syntax is used.

`Target` *(optional)*
: Defines the target element of the `Label`. The target element must be of type `UIElement` and must exist in the XAML document. Assigning a `Target` to the `Label` keeps the label grouped with the element during the rendering process.

LinearGradientBrush

Hierarchy: DependencyObject → Freezable → Animatable → Brush → GradientBrush

```
<LinearGradientBrush
    StartPoint="0,0"
    EndPoint="5,5"
    <LinearGradientBrush.GradientStops>
        <GradientStop Color="Yellow" Offset="0" />
        <GradientStop Color="Green" Offset="0.5" />
    </LinearGradientBrush.GradientStops>
</LinearGradientBrush>
```

or:

```
<LinearGradientBrush>
    <LinearGradientBrush.StartPoint>
        <Point X="0" Y="0" />
    </LinearGradientBrush.StartPoint>
    <LinearGradientBrush.EndPoint>
        <Point X="5" Y="5" />
    </LinearGradientBrush.EndPoint>
    <LinearGradientBrush.GradientStops>
        <GradientStop Color="Yellow" Offset="0" />
        <GradientStop Color="Green" Offset="0.5" />
    </LinearGradientBrush.GradientStops>
</LinearGradientBrush>
```

<LinearGradientBrush .../> paints an area with a linear gradient. Colors in the gradient are interpolated along a diagonal path. `LinearGradientBrush` can be specified as an attribute on XAML elements using abbreviated markup syntax (Example 7-3). Figure 7-6 shows an example of using a `LinearGradientBrush` to paint a Rectangle element.

Example 7-3. Abbreviated markup syntax for a LinearGradientBrush

```
<element attribute="LinearGradientBrush StartPoint EndPoint StartColor
StopColor"/>
```

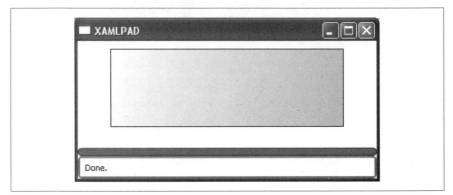

Figure 7-6. Painting a Rectangle with a LinearGradientBrush

Attributes

`EndPoint` *(optional)*
: The ending `Point` of the linear gradient. Specified either as a `Point` through abbreviated markup or explicitly declared as a `Point`. The default is the lower-right corner (1,1).

`GradientStops` *(optional)*
: A collection of `GradientStop` elements specifying the location and color of each change in the gradient.

: To simplify the creation of linear gradients, two gradient types can be quickly created through abbreviated markup syntax: `HorizontalGradient` and `VerticalGradient`:

```
<element attribute="HorizontalGradient StartColor EndColor" />
<element attribute="VerticalGradient UpperColor LowerColor" />
```

: These gradients are assumed to encompass the entire layout region of the element to which they are attached. `HorizontalGradient` paints the region with a gradient from left (`StartColor`) to right (`EndColor`), while `VerticalGradient` paints the region with a gradient from top (`UpperColor`) to bottom (`LowerColor`). An example of each is shown in Figure 7-7.

`StartPoint` *(optional)*
: The starting `Point` of the linear gradient. Specified either as a `Point` through abbreviated markup or explicitly declared as a `Point`. The default is the upper-left corner (0,0).

LineBreak

Hierarchy: DependencyObject → ContentElement → FrameworkContentElement

```
<Paragraph>
    Lorem ipsum dolor sit amet, consecteteur adipscing elit.
    <LineBreak/>
</Paragraph>
```

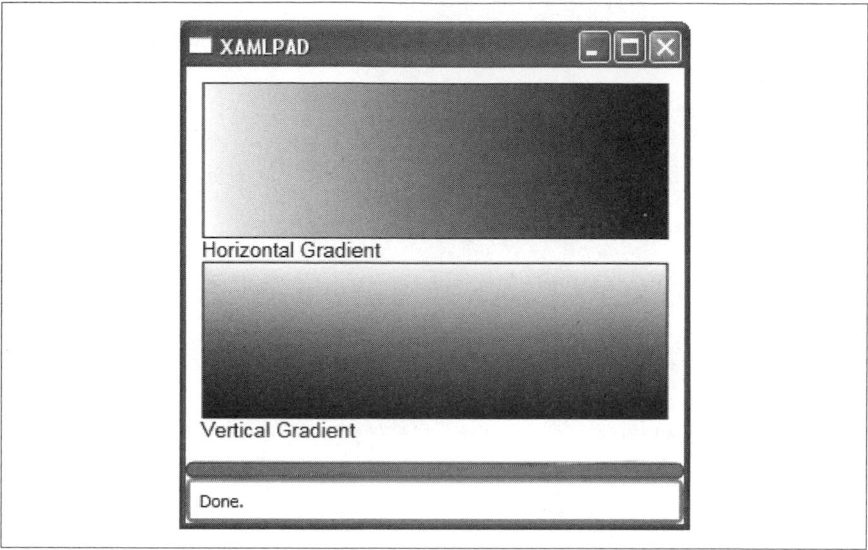

Figure 7-7. Example of Horizontal and Vertical linear gradient brushes

`<LineBreak .../>` forces a line break. This element cannot be a root-level element.

List

Hierarchy: DependencyObject → FrameworkContentElement → TextElement → Block

```
<List
    MarkerOffset="2"
    MarkerStyle="Box|Circle|Decimal|Disc|LowerLatin|LowerRoman|None|
                 Square|UpperLatin|UpperRoman"
    StartIndex="1" />
```

`<List .../>` implements an element that presents child content in the form of an ordered or unordered list. `List` may contain only `ListItem` elements as children.

Attributes

`MarkerOffset` *(optional)*
: The desired distance, as a `Double`, between the `ListElement` and the edge of the marker.

`MarkerStyle` *(optional)*
: The desired style of marker for the list.

`Box`
: A solid square box

`Circle`
: A hollow disc circle

`Decimal`
: A numeric value, starting at 1

`Disc`
: A solid disc circle

Elements

`LowerLatin`
: Lowercase ASCII characters in alphabetic sequence, i.e., a, b, c, d, etc.

`LowerRoman`
: Lowercase Roman numerals, i.e., i, ii, iii, iv, etc.

`None`
: No marker

`Square`
: A hollow square shape

`UpperLatin`
: Uppercase ASCII characters in alphabetic sequence, i.e., A, B, C, D, etc.

`UpperRoman`
: Uppercase Roman numerals, i.e., I, II, III, IV, etc.

`StartIndex` *(optional)*
: The index, as an `Integer`, of the first `ListItem` child for this `List`.

ListItem

Hierarchy: DependencyObject → FrameworkContentElement → TextElement → Block

```
<ListItem />
```

`<ListItem .../>` is similar to `Section` but has features to support bullets and numbering. `ListItem` cannot directly contain text, so it must contain other elements that can. It is used with `List` to format information into ordered or unordered lists. (See Example 7-4.)

Example 7-4. List element with multiple items

```
<List MarkerStyle="Square" MarkerOffset="2">
    <ListItem><Paragraph>Item One</Paragraph></ListItem>
    <ListItem><Paragraph>Item Two</Paragraph></ListItem>
    <ListItem><Paragraph>Item Three</Paragraph></ListItem>
    <ListItem><Paragraph>Item Four</Paragraph></ListItem>
</List>
```

Paragraph

Hierarchy: DependencyObject → FrameworkContentElement → TextElement → Block

```
<Paragraph
    MinOrphanLines="1"
    MinWidowLines="1"
    TextIndent="1.0"
    TextTrimming="WordEllipsis|CharacterEllipsis|None"
    TextDecorations="Collection"
    KeepTogether="true|false"
    KeepWithNext="true|false"
    />
```

`<Paragraph .../>` implements a block-level element that is analogous to an HTML paragraph, except that `Paragraph` can contain only inline elements. Unlike HTML, you cannot nest `Paragraph` elements within other `Paragraph` elements. This element cannot be a root-level element.

Attributes

`KeepTogether` *(optional)*

This attribute determines how text should be handled in the case of page breaks.

`true`

Text in this paragraph should be kept together, even if it means moving the entire paragraph to the next logical section.

`false`

Text can be separated.

`KeepWithNext` *(optional)*

This attribute determines how text should be handled in the case of page breaks.

`true`

Indicates that this block should be kept with the next block in the track. (This also implies that the paragraph itself will not be broken.)

`false`

Text can be separated.

`MinOrphanLines` *(optional)*

Designates the minimum number of lines that can be left behind when a paragraph is broken on a page or column break.

`MinWidowLines` *(optional)*

Specifies the minimum number of lines after a break that can be put on the next page or column.

`TextDecorations` *(optional)*

Specifies a collection of `TextDecoration` elements that are applied to the `Paragraph`.

`TextIndent` *(optional)*

Specifies the indentation of the first line of a paragraph.

`TextTrimming` *(optional)*

Determines how text that flows past the end of the element is treated. Must be one of:

`CharacterEllipsis`

Text is trimmed at a character boundary. Remaining text is replaced with an ellipsis (...).

`None`

Text is not trimmed.

`WordEllipsis`

Text is trimmed at a word boundary. Remaining text is replaced with an ellipsis (...).

Pen

Hierarchy: DependencyObject → Freezable → Animatable

```
<Pen
    Brush="Blue"
    Thickness="1"
    DashCap="Flat|Round|Square|Triangle"
    EndLineCap="Flat|Round|Square|Triangle"
    LineJoin="Bevel|Miter|Round"
```

```
        MiterLimit="1"
        StartLineCap="Flat|Round|Square|Triangle" />
```

<Pen .../> describes how an element is outlined. Figure 7-8 shows two drawings, each drawn with a different Pen. The first Pen is black with a thickness of 2 and uses Triangle and Round as start and end line caps. The second Pen is blue with a thickness of 1 and uses Square and Flat as start and end line caps. The code to produce this figure is shown in Example 7-5.

Figure 7-8. Different styles of Pen

Example 7-5. Declaring different styles of Pen

```
<Page
    xmlns="http://schemas.microsoft.com/winfx/avalon/2005"
    xmlns:x="http://schemas.microsoft.com/winfx/xaml/2005">
    <DockPanel>
        <StackPanel Margin="10" Width="50">
            <StackPanel.Background>
                <DrawingBrush>
                    <DrawingBrush.Drawing>
                        <GeometryDrawing
                            Brush="MediumBlue">
                            <GeometryDrawing.Geometry>
                                <GeometryGroup>
                                    <LineGeometry
                                        StartPoint="10,10"
                                        EndPoint="20,10" />
                                    <LineGeometry
                                        StartPoint="20,10"
                                        EndPoint="20,20" />
                                </GeometryGroup>
                            </GeometryDrawing.Geometry>
                            <GeometryDrawing.Pen>
                                <Pen
                                    Thickness="2"
                                    Brush="Black"
                                    StartLineCap="Triangle"
                                    EndLineCap="Round" />
                            </GeometryDrawing.Pen>
                        </GeometryDrawing>
                    </DrawingBrush.Drawing>
                </DrawingBrush>
```

Example 7-5. Declaring different styles of Pen (continued)

```
            </StackPanel.Background>
        </StackPanel>
        <StackPanel Margin="10" Width="50">
            <StackPanel.Background>
                <DrawingBrush>
                    <DrawingBrush.Drawing>
                        <GeometryDrawing
                            Brush="MediumBlue">
                            <GeometryDrawing.Geometry>
                                <GeometryGroup>
                                    <LineGeometry
                                        StartPoint="10,10"
                                        EndPoint="20,10" />
                                    <LineGeometry
                                        StartPoint="20,10"
                                        EndPoint="20,20" />
                                </GeometryGroup>
                            </GeometryDrawing.Geometry>
                            <GeometryDrawing.Pen>
                                <Pen
                                    Thickness="1"
                                    Brush="MediumBlue"
                                    StartLineCap="Square"
                                    EndLineCap="Flat" />
                            </GeometryDrawing.Pen>
                        </GeometryDrawing>
                    </DrawingBrush.Drawing>
                </DrawingBrush>
            </StackPanel.Background>
        </StackPanel>
    </DockPanel>
</Page>
```

Attributes

`Brush` *(optional)*

Describes how the object is filled. The value of this attribute may be a reference to a predefined `Color` (see Appendix G) or it may be a defined `Brush`. Although the `Brush` attribute is optional, no outline will be shown if it is not set to something other than the default, `Transparent`.

`DashCap` *(optional)*

Describes how the ends of a dash are drawn.

`Flat`
: No line cap. This is the default.

`Round`
: The line is capped with a semicircle equal in diameter to the line thickness.

`Square`
: The line is capped with a square whose sides are equal in length to the line thickness.

`Triangle`
: The line is capped with a triangle equal in height to the line thickness.

Elements

`EndLineCap` *(optional)*
: Sets the shape used to end a stroke.

  `Flat`
  : No line cap. This is the default.

  `Round`
  : The line is capped with a semicircle equal in diameter to the line thickness.

  `Square`
  : The line is capped with a square whose sides are equal in length to the line thickness.

  `Triangle`
  : The line is capped with a triangle equal in height to the line thickness.

`LineJoin` *(optional)*
: Sets the type of joint used at the vertices of a shape's outline.

  `Bevel`
  : Beveled vertices

  `Miter`
  : Regular angular vertices

  `Round`
  : Rounded vertices

`MiterLimit` *(optional)*
: A miter is created when the ends of two surfaces with angles other than 90 degrees are joined to form a corner. This attribute sets the limit on the ratio of the miter length to the thickness of the `Pen`. This value must be a positive number greater than or equal to 1.0 and is expressed as a `Double`.

`StartLineCap` *(optional)*
: Sets the type of shape to be used at the beginning of a line.

  `Flat`
  : No line cap. This is the default.

  `Round`
  : The line is capped with a semicircle equal in diameter to the line thickness.

  `Square`
  : The line is capped with a square whose sides are equal in length to the line thickness.

  `Triangle`
  : The line is capped with a triangle equal in height to the line thickness.

`Thickness` *(optional)*
: The width of the stroke. The default is 1.0. This attribute is expressed as a `Double`.

RadialGradientBrush

Hierarchy: DependencyObject → Freezable → Animatable → Brush → GradientBrush

```
<RadialGradientBrush
    RadiusX="20"
    RadiusY="20"
    Center="0,0"
    GradientOrigin="0,0" >
    RadialGradientBrush.GradientStops>
```

```
            <GradientStop Color="Red" Offset="5" />
            <GradientStop Color="Orange" Offset="10" />
        </RadialGradientBrush.GradientStops>
    </RadialGradientBrush>
```

or:

```
    <RadialGradientBrush
        RadiusX="20"
        RadiusY="20" >
        <RadialGradientBrush.Center>
            <Point X="0" Y="0" />
        </RadialGradientBrush.Center>
        <RadialGradientBrush.GradientOrigin>
            <Point X="0" Y="0" />
        </RadialGradientBrush.GradientOrigin>
        RadialGradientBrush.GradientStops>
            <GradientStop Color="Red" Offset="5" />
            <GradientStop Color="Orange" Offset="10" />
        </RadialGradientBrush.GradientStops>
    </RadialGradientBrush>
```

`<RadialGradientBrush .../>` paints an area with a radial gradient. The focal point is the beginning of the gradient, and a circle defines the outer boundary. `RadialGradientBrush` can be declared using abbreviated markup syntax as an attribute of an element:

```
    <element attribute="RadialGradientBrush InnerColor OuterColor" />
```

Figure 7-9 shows the result of evaluating Example 7-6, which uses a `RadialGradientBrush`.

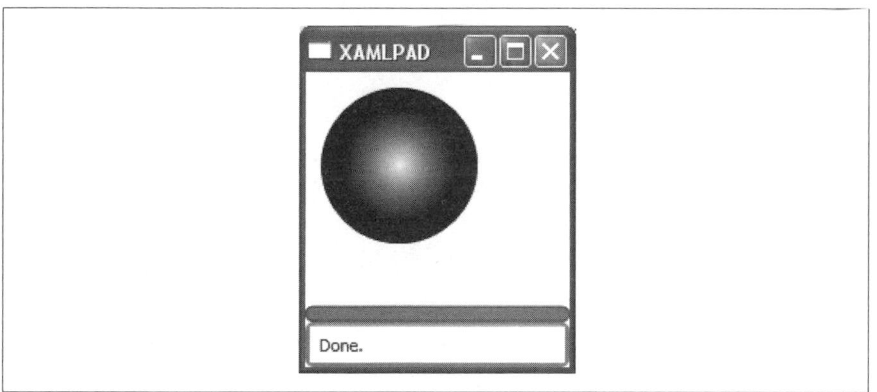

Figure 7-9. A RadialGradientBrush filling an Ellipse

Example 7-6. Filling an Ellipse with a RadialGradientBrush

```
<Page
    xmlns="http://schemas.microsoft.com/winfx/avalon/2005"
    xmlns:x="http://schemas.microsoft.com/winfx/xaml/2005">
    <StackPanel Margin="10" >
        <Ellipse CenterX="50" CenterY="50">
            <Ellipse.Fill>
                <RadialGradientBrush
                    RadiusX=".5"
                    RadiusY=".5"
```

Example 7-6. Filling an Ellipse with a RadialGradientBrush (continued)

```
                    Center=".5,.5"
                    GradientOrigin=".5,.5" >
                    <RadialGradientBrush.GradientStops>
                        <GradientStop Color="White" Offset="0" />
                        <GradientStop Color="Black" Offset=".75" />
                    </RadialGradientBrush.GradientStops>
                </RadialGradientBrush>
            </Ellipse.Fill>
        </Ellipse>
    </StackPanel>
</Page>
```

Attributes

`Center` *(optional)*
: A `Point` describing the location of the center of the radial gradient. The default is (0.5,0.5). `Center` may be described using abbreviated markup syntax or explicitly declared as a `Point`.

`GradientOrigin` *(optional)*
: A `Point` describing the focal point of the gradient. The default is (0.5,0.5). `GradientOrigin` may be described using abbreviated markup syntax or explicitly declared as a `Point`. This value is between 0 and 1.0, inclusive.

`RadialGradientStops` *(optional)*
: A collection of `GradientStop` elements specifying the location and color of each change in the gradient. This value is between 0 and 1.0, inclusive.

`RadiusX` *(optional)*
: A `Double` value describing the horizontal outermost radius of the gradient. The default value is 0.5. This value is between 0 and 1.0, inclusive.

`RadiusY` *(optional)*
: A `Double` value describing the vertical outermost radius of the gradient. The default value is 0.5. This value is between 0 and 1.0, inclusive.

Section

Hierarchy: DependencyObject → FrameworkContentElement → TextElement → Block

```
<Section> Lorem ipsum dolar sit amet, consecteteur adipscing elit.</Section>
```

`<Section ...>` is intended to group block elements. It does not generate any specific rendering other than grouping elements together. `Section` must have at least one child element.

SolidColorBrush

Hierarchy: DependencyObject → Freezable → Animatable → Brush

```
<SolidColorBrush>
    <SolidColorBrush.Color>
        <Color
            ScA="1.0"
            ScR="0.0"
```

```
            ScG="0.0"
            ScB="1.0" />
    </SolidColorBrush.Color>
</SolidColorBrush>
```

`<SolidColorBrush .../>` defines a `Brush` that paints an object or region in a solid color.

Attributes

`Color` *(required)*
: Defines the color of the `Brush` either using one of the predefined colors or one described by using `ScRGB` values.

TextBlock

Hierarchy: UIElement → FrameworkElement

```
<TextBlock
    TextAlignment="Center|End|Justify|Left|Right|Start"
    TextWrap="Wrap|NoWrap|Emergency"
    TextTrimming="CharacterEllipsis|WordEllipsis|None"
    TextEffects="Collection"
    TextContent="Lorem ipsum dolar sit amet, consecteteur adipscing elit."
    BaselineOffset="10" />
```

or:

```
<TextBlock
    TextAlignment="Center|End|Justify|Left|Right|Start"
    TextWrap="Wrap|NoWrap|Emergency"
    TextTrimming="CharacterEllipsis|WordEllipsis|None"
    TextEffects="Collection"
    BaselineOffset="10">
    Lorem ipsum dolar sit amet, consecteteur adipscing elit.
</TextBlock>
```

`<TextBlock .../>` displays a block of text. `TextBlock` is similar to `Paragraph` in terms of formatting and display, but `TextBlock` is a `UIElement`, which means that it can be used outside the context of documents. This element is optimized for UI display.

Attributes

`BaselineOffset` *(optional)*
: The amount to adjust the baseline offset position. Essentially, this drops the text down the specified distance. This attribute is attached to inline children of `TextBlock`. The following code fragment raises the baseline of the inline `TextBlock` so that the text appears above the surrounding text:

```
<TextBlock>
    This text is normal.
    <TextBlock BaselineOffset="20">This text is raised</TextBlock>
    This text is normal again.
</TextBlock>
```

`TextAlignment` *(optional)*
: Describes how text is aligned horizontally.

Elements

`Center`
: Text is center-aligned.

`End`
: Text is aligned on the end of the inline progression, as determined by the current text advance direction.

`Justify`
: Text is justified. This will increase spacing between words if necessary to keep text justified across the width of the `TextBox`.

`Left`
: In horizontal inline progression, the text is aligned on the left.

`Right`
: In horizontal inline progression, the text is aligned on the right.

`Start`
: The text is aligned on the start of the inline progression, as determined by the current text advance direction.

`TextContent` *(optional)*
: This attribute contains the text being displayed.

`TextEffects` *(optional)*
: A collection of `TextEffect` elements.

`TextTrimming` *(optional)*
: Determines how to treat text that flows past the end of the element.

`CharacterEllipsis`
: Text is trimmed at a character boundary. Remaining text is replaced with an ellipsis (…).

`None`
: Text is not trimmed.

`WordEllipsis`
: Text is trimmed at a word boundary. Remaining text is replaced with an ellipsis (…).

`TextWrap` *(optional)*
: Determines the behavior of text when it reaches the boundary of its containing box.

`Emergency`
: Text is wrapped even if the line-breaking algorithm cannot determine an optimal wrapping opportunity. This is the default behavior.

`NoWrap`
: Text is not wrapped.

`Wrap`
: Text is wrapped.

TextDecoration

Hierarchy: DependencyObject → Freezable → Animatable

```
<TextDecoration
    Location="Baseline|Overline|Underline|Strikethrough"
    PenThicknessUnit="FontRecommended|FontRenderingEmSize|Pixel"
```

```
        PenOffset="1.0"
        PenOffsetUnit="FontRecommended|FontRenderingEmSize|Pixel">
        <TextDecoration.Pen>
            <Pen .../>
        </TextDecoration.Pen>
    </TextDecoration>
```

`<TextDecoration .../>` specifies a decoration to be applied to text, such as underlining or strikethrough.

Attributes

`Location` *(optional)*
: Specifies the vertical location at which the decoration will appear. Must be one of the following:

  `Baseline`
  : Decoration appears at the vertical position of baseline.

  `Overline`
  : Decoration appears at the vertical position of overline.

  `Strikethrough`
  : Decoration appears at the vertical position of strikethrough.

  `Underline`
  : Decoration appears at the vertical position of underline.

`PenOffset` *(optional)*
: Specifies the decoration's offset from its `Location`, expressed as a `Double` and interpreted based on the `PenOffsetUnit`.

`PenOffsetUnit` *(optional)*
: Defines the thickness unit of the `PenOffset`.

  `FontRecommended`
  : The value is relative to the Avalon-calculated recommended value. This is the default value.

  `FontRenderingEmSize`
  : The value is relative to the font em size. The effective value is the thickness or offset multiplied by the font em size.

  `Pixel`
  : The value is expressed in pixels.

`PenThicknessUnit` *(optional)*
: Defines the thickness unit of the `Pen`.

  `FontRecommended`
  : The value is relative to the Avalon-calculated recommended value. This is the default value.

  `FontRenderingEmSize`
  : The value is relative to the font em size. The effective value is the thickness or offset multiplied by the font em size.

  `Pixel`
  : The value is expressed in pixels.

`TextDecoration.Pen` *(optional)*
: Specifies the `Pen` to be used to draw the `TextDecoration`.

TextDecorationCollection

Hierarchy: DependencyObject → Freezable → Animatable

```
<TextDecorationCollection>
    <TextDecoration .../>
     ...
    <TextDecoration .../>
</TextDecorationCollection>
```

<TextDecorationCollection .../> specifies a collection of TextDecoration elements. Multiple TextDecoration elements are used to specify formatting for text-based elements. If you want text to have an overline and underline, use a collection of TextDecoration elements (Example 7-7).

Example 7-7. Using TextDecorations to modify the appearance of text

```
<TextBlock>This is underlined and overlined text
    <TextBlock.TextDecorations>
         <TextDecoration Location="Underline"
            PenThicknessUnit="FontRecommended">
            <TextDecoration.Pen>
               <Pen Brush="Red" Thickness="1" />
            </TextDecoration.Pen>
         </TextDecoration>
         <TextDecoration Location="Overline">
            <TextDecoration.Pen>
               <Pen Brush="Blue" Thickness="1" />
            </TextDecoration.Pen>
        </TextDecoration>
    </TextBlock.TextDecorations>
</TextBlock>
```

TextEffect

Hierarchy: DependencyObject → Freezable → Animatable

```
<TextEffect
    Location="Baseline|Overline|Strikethrough|Underline"
    CharacterIndex="0"
    Count="999">
    <TextEffect.Transform>
        <TranslateTransform|ScaleTransform|SkewTransform|RotateTransform />
    </TextEffect.Transform>
</TextEffect>
```

<TextEffect .../> defines a text effect such as an animation. A TextEffect can be placed in the same location (underline, overline, etc.) as a TextDecoration. TextEffect performs a transformation (essentially animating the text effect), while a TextDecoration is a static entity.

Attributes

`CharacterIndex` *(optional)*

`Count` *(optional)*

`Location` *(optional)*

Specifies the vertical location at which the decoration will appear.

`Baseline`

Decoration appears at the vertical position of baseline.

`Overline`

Decoration appears at the vertical position of overline.

`Strikethrough`

Decoration appears at the vertical position of strikethrough.

`Underline`

Decoration appears at the vertical position of underline.

`Transform` *(optional)*

Specifies the type of `Transform` that will be applied. Must be the name of a class that inherits from the abstract class `Transform`. Transforms are discussed further in Chapter 11. Built-in transforms are:

- `RotateTransform`
- `ScaleTransform`
- `SkewTransform`
- `TranslateTransform`

Thickness

Thickness is a structure and has no class hierarchy.

```
<Object AttributeName="Left, Top, Right, Bottom" />
```

`<Thickness ... />` is used to describe the size of the outline of an element. It is also commonly used to describe the size of a `Pen` used to draw an element, as well as the border of an element such as `Rectangle` or `Ellipse`. Furthermore, it describes the `Margin` and `Padding` attributes of elements deriving from `UIElement` (see Chapter 8).

`Thickness` can be declared either explicitly or through the use of abbreviated markup syntax. Example 7-8 demonstrates the explicit declaration of a `Thickness`. The `Button` will have a uniform margin of 10. The same result can be achieved by using the abbreviated markup syntax shown in Example 7-9.

Example 7-8. Explicit declaration of a Thickness

```
<Button Content="Click Me">
    <Button.Margin>
        10,10,10,10
    </Button.Margin>
</Button>
```

Example 7-9. Abbreviated markup syntax declaration of a Thickness

```
<Button Margin="10,10,10,10" Content="Click Me" />
```

If you are declaring a uniform thickness (meaning all four sides are equal), you can shorten the syntax even further. Example 7-10 shows the declaration of a Thickness with only one value, 10. When declaring a Thickness using a single value, that value is applied to all four attributes (Left, Top, Right, and Bottom). All three examples will produce the same Margin.

Example 7-10. Abbreviated markup syntax declaring a uniform Thickness

```
<Button Margin="10" Content="Click Me" />
```

Attributes

Left
: This Double value describes the thickness of the left side of the element's associated rectangle.

Right
: This Double value describes the thickness of the right side of the element's associated rectangle.

Top
: This Double value describes the thickness of the top side of the element's associated rectangle.

Bottom
: This Double value describes the thickness of the bottom side of the element's associated rectangle.

Underline

Hierarchy: DependencyObject → FrameworkContentElement → TextElement → Inline

```
<Underline>Text to be underlined</Underline>
```

<Underline .../> is an inline element that formats text-based elements with an underline. Its only properties are those inherited from Inline.

8
Controls

With the exception of Hyperlink, which is included because it is unique among non-control elements in its support of the Click event, all controls in this chapter belong to the System.Windows.Controls namespace and are ultimately children of the same base class, Control. This gives them a common set of properties and events, but this chapter will detail those specific to each control. Two controls, Grid and StackPanel, are not detailed in this chapter because they provide layout control and are therefore documented in Chapter 10.

Because XAML controls represent .NET CLR controls, they share a common hierarchy (UIElement → FrameworkElement → Control). For the most part, these base classes are abstract and will never be explicitly declared as XAML elements. Their attributes are inherited by subclasses and have been included to avoid redundancy. Each element description contains a hierarchy so that you can easily reference the inherited attributes.

Attributes that have both a get and set method are generally accessible through XAML, and these values are set in exactly the same way as the properties detailed below. Although an attribute's data type may be type Boolean or Integer, XAML requires that the attribute value be specified as a String. Some elements have *attached attributes*. These are specifically designated as such, and the concept behind them is discussed in depth in Chapter 3.

There are several structures and elements, detailed in other chapters, that are commonly used to declare attributes. For example, Thickness, detailed in Chapter 7, is the data type for several common Control attributes, such as Margin and Padding. Similarly, Brush is used to describe how to fill the Background attribute of elements. Brush is most often described as a simple, predefined Color (see Appendix G). Table 8-1 lists these common structures/elements, as well as where they are detailed.

Table 8-1. Structures and elements commonly used as attribute types

Structure/element	Description	Where detailed
`Brush`	Used to fill a region, such as the background area of an element	Chapter 7
`Pen`	Used to render text or draw outlines	Chapter 7
`Thickness`	The size of a specific edge of an element	Chapter 7
`Color`	Describes a color using ScA values or by referencing a predefined `Color`	Chapter 7 and Appendix G
`Style`	Describes a specific set of attributes such as `Color`, `Thickness`, `Pen`, etc., to be applied to one or more elements	Chapter 10

This chapter also includes a brief reference to common events. A detailed explanation of all events can be found in Chapter 12.

Base Control Reference

This section details the attributes associated with the hierarchy common to controls. It includes the attributes for `UIElement`, `FrameworkElement`, and the `Control` classes (`ContentControl`, `ItemsControl`, `HeaderedItemsControl`, and `HeaderedContentControl`).

UIElement

`UIElement` is the base class for most XAML controls. It provides attributes that determine how elements are displayed.

Attributes

`AllowDrop`
: This `Boolean` value determines whether the element can be the target of a drag-and-drop operation.

  `true`
  : The element may be targeted.

  `false`
  : The element may not be targeted. This is the default.

`Opacity`
: This `Double` value describes the opacity factor applied to the element when it is rendered. The range for this value is 0.0–1.0. The default value is 1.0.

`OpacityMask`
: This `Brush` is applied to any alpha-channel masking for the rendered control.

`RenderTransform`
: This property specifies a `Transform` (detailed in Chapter 11) to apply to the element.

`Visibility`
: This attribute determines the visibility of the control.

Collapsed
: The element is not displayed and does not occupy layout space.

Hidden
: The element is not displayed but does occupy layout space.

Visible
: The element is displayed.

FrameworkElement

`FrameworkElement` is the base class for elements in the core presentation set. It also implements many of the virtual methods defined in its parent class, `UIElement`.

Attributes

`Focusable`

This `Boolean` value determines whether the element is focusable.

`true`
: The element is focusable. The default for controls is `true`.

`false`
: The element is not focusable.

`Height`

This attribute determines the height of the control.

`Margin`

This `Thickness` (detailed in Chapter 7) describes the margin of an element.

`Name`

This attribute sets the name of the object and must be used if `codebehind` routines will reference the object.

`Style`

This attribute allows a `Style` (detailed in Chapter 10) to be applied through a `StaticResource` or `DynamicResource` or to be described inline.

`ToolTip`

This attribute describes the prompt displayed when the mouse hovers over the element. If the `ToolTip` is a `String`, then it can be declared inline; otherwise, it must be declared explicitly.

`Width`

This attribute determines the width of the control.

Control

Hierarchy: UIElement → FrameworkElement

`Control` is the base class for all interactive XAML elements.

Attributes

`Background`

This attribute sets the `Brush` used to paint the control's background. This can be one of the colors from the `Color` class (see Appendix G). This attribute defaults to `Transparent`.

Controls

`BorderBrush`
: This attribute sets the `Brush` used to paint the control's border. This attribute defaults to `Transparent`.

`BorderThickness`
: This `Thickness` determines the thickness of the control's border. The default is 0. This attribute is not applicable to `RadioButton` controls.

`FontFamily`
: This `String` describes the font used in this control. Examples are Arial and Times New Roman.

`FontSize`
: This `Double` value describes the size of the font. The default is the system dialog font size.

`FontStyle`
: This attribute describes the style of the font. Options are italic, normal, and oblique.

`FontWeight`
: This attribute describes the weight of the font. Options are bold and normal.

`Foreground`
: This `Brush` describes the foreground color.

`HorizontalContentAlignment`
: This enumeration determines how the control's content should be aligned horizontally.

  `Center`
  : The content is aligned to the center of the control's layout slot.

  `Left`
  : The content is aligned to the left of the control's layout slot.

  `Right`
  : The content is aligned to the right of the control's layout slot.

  `Stretch`
  : The content is stretched to fill the entirety of the control's layout slot.

`Padding`
: This `Thickness` describes the amount of padding around a control.

`TabIndex`
: This `Integer` determines the order in which a control will receive focus. Lower index controls receive focus before higher index controls. The default value is 1.

`TextDecorations`
: This `TextDecorationCollection` describes any `TextDecoration` elements (detailed in Chapter 7) to be added to the control's text. `TextDecoration` elements specify formatting, such as underlines and overlines, and provide details of the color and placement of such decorations.

`TextTrimming`
: This enumeration determines how text will be treated if it runs off the edge of the control.

`CharacterEllipsis`
: Text is trimmed at a character boundary. Remaining text is replaced with an ellipsis (...).

`None`
: Text is not trimmed.

`WordEllipsis`
: Text is trimmed at a word boundary. Remaining text is replaced with an ellipsis (...).

`VerticalContentAlignment`
: This enumeration determines how the control's content should be aligned vertically.

`Bottom`
: The content is aligned at the bottom of the control's layout slot.

`Center`
: The content is aligned at the center of the control's layout slot.

`Stretch`
: The content is stretched to fill the entirety of the control's layout slot.

`Top`
: The content is aligned at the top of the control's layout slot.

ContentControl

Hierarchy: UIElement → FrameworkElement → Control

`ContentControl` is the base class for all elements that display a single piece of content, such as `ListBoxItem` and `Label`.

Attributes

`Content`
: `Content` may be an element of any type. When used to describe the text displayed in or on a control, it is declared inline. When used to hold other types of elements, `Content` is assumed to comprise those elements declared between the element's beginning and ending tags.

`<Button Content="This is content" />` is equivalent to declaring `<Button>This is content</Button>`. Complex attribute types must be declared explicitly between the beginning and end tags of the `ContentControl`-derived element. Example 8-1 demonstrates the explicit declaration of a non-text element as the single piece of content for a `Button`.

Example 8-1. Explicit declaration of an element within a ContentControl

```
<Button Height="100" Width="100">
    <Ellipse CenterX="25" CenterY="25" Fill="Blue" />
</Button>
```

Controls

HeaderedItemsControl

Hierarchy: UIElement → FrameworkElement → ItemsControl

`HeaderedItemsControl` is the base class for all elements that have multiple items as well as a Header. Examples of a `HeaderedItemsControl` are `MenuItem` and `ToolBar`.

`Header`
: The `Header` attribute acts as a label for all `HeaderedItemsControl`-derived classes, such as `MenuItem` and `ToolBar`.

HeaderedContentControl

Hierarchy: UIElement → FrameworkElement → Control → ContentControl

`HeaderedContentControl` is the base class for all elements that have a single content element and a header. Examples of `HeaderedContentControl` classes are `Expander` and `TabItem`.

Attributes

`Header`
: The `Header` attribute acts as a label for all `HeaderedContentControl`-derived classes, such as `Expander` and `TabItem`.

ItemsControl

Hierarchy: UIElement → FrameworkElement → Control

`ItemsControl` is the base class for all elements that hold multiple elements. Examples of `ItemsControl` classes are `ComboBox`, `ListBox`, and `RadioButtonList`.

Attributes

`Items`
: This implicitly declared attribute is common to all child elements of `ItemsControl`, which include `HeaderedItemsControl`, `Selector`, `MenuBase`, and `StatusBar`.

Common Event Reference

Elements deriving from `UIElement` inherit a set of common events. Events are used in XAML to specify the `codebehind` handler that will be executed when the specified event is raised. All events can be assigned a `codebehind` handler using the following syntax:

```
<Element Name="ElementName" EventName="CodeBehindHandler" />
```

Elements specifying a `codebehind` handler must declare the `Name` attribute in order to be referenced in the `codebehind` class. Examples 8-2 and 8-3 demonstrate the event-handling code in C# and VisualBasic, respectively, which is executed when the mouse cursor enters or leaves the `Button` declared in Example 8-4.

Example 8-2. C# implementation of event handlers

```
public partial class MouseEnterMouseLeave
{
    void MouseEnterHandler(object sender, MouseEventArgs e)
    {
        MyButton.Background=Brushes.Red;
        MyButton.Content="Mouse is over me";
    }
    void MouseLeaveHandler(object sender, MouseEventArgs e)
    {
        MyButton.Background=Brushes.White;
        MyButton.Content="Mouse is not over me";
    }
}
```

Example 8-3. VisualBasic implementation of event handlers

```
Partial Public Class MouseEnterMouseLeave
    Sub MouseEnterHandler(ByVal sender as Object, ByVal e As MouseEventArgs
        MyButton.Background = Brushes.Red
        MyButton.Content = "Mouse is over me"
    End Sub
    Sub MouseLeaveHandler(ByVal sender As Object, ByVal e as MouseEventArgs
        MyButton.Background = Brushes.White
        MyButton.Content = "Mouse is not over me"
    End Sub
End Class
```

Example 8-4. XAML declaration of event handlers for Button

```
<StackPanel
    xmlns="http://schemas.microsoft.com/winfx/avalon/2005"
    xmlns:x="http://schemas.microsoft.com/winfx/xaml/2005"
    x:Class="ButtonExample.MouseEnterMouseLeave"
    <Button
        Content="Mouse is not over me"
        MouseEnter="MouseEnterHandler"
        MouseLeave="MouseLeaveHandler"
        Name="MyButton" />
</StackPanel>
```

The following events are common to all `UIElement`-derived elements. Events specific to the element are listed with the element description. Events are fully detailed in Chapter 12, along with a more thorough exploration of the event subsystem.

- `DragEnter`
- `DragLeave`
- `DragOver`
- `Drop`
- `GotFocus`

- IsVisibleChanged
- IsEnableChanged
- IsFocusChanged
- KeyUp
- KeyDown
- LayoutUpdated
- LostFocus
- MouseEnter
- MouseLeave
- MouseMove
- MouseLeftButtonDown
- MouseLeftButtonUp
- MouseRightButtonDown
- MouseRightButtonUp
- PreviewDragOver
- PreviewDragEnter
- PreviewDragLeave
- PreviewDrop
- PreviewKeyUp
- PreviewKeyDown
- PreviewMouseLeftButtonDown
- PreviewMouseLeftButtonUp
- PreviewMouseRightButtonDown
- PreviewMouseRightButtonUp
- PreviewMouseMove

Core Control Reference

Button

Hierarchy: UIElement → FrameworkElement → Control → ContentControl → ButtonBase

```
<Button
    Click="OnSubmitButtonClicked">
    Button Label
</Button>
```

or:

```
<Button
    Click="OnSubmitButtonClicked"
    Content="Button Label" />
```

<Button .../> displays a push button.

Attributes

Click *(optional)*
: This attribute sets the name of the codebehind handler that executes when the button is clicked.

Content *(optional)*
: This attribute sets the value that is displayed on the button.

Events

Click

CheckBox

Hierarchy: UIElement → FrameworkElement → Control → ContentControl → ButtonBase → ToggleButton

```
<CheckBox
    IsChecked="true|false"
    Content="This box is checked"
    IsCheckedChanged="OnCheckedChangedEvent" />
```

or:

```
<CheckBox
    IsChecked="true|false"
    IsCheckedChanged="OnCheckedChangedEvent">
        This is a checkbox label
</CheckBox>
```

<CheckBox .../> displays a checkbox.

Attributes

Click *(optional)*
: This attribute sets the name of the codebehind handler that executes when the button is clicked.

Content *(optional)*
: This attribute describes the element that is displayed next to the CheckBox. This is usually a text-based value, but can be any single UIElement.

IsChecked *(optional)*
: This attribute sets the initial state of the checkbox.

  true
  : The CheckBox is checked.

  false
  : The CheckBox is not checked. This is the default.

IsCheckedChanged *(optional)*
: This attribute sets the name of the codebehind handler that executes when the checkbox changes state.

Events

Click
IsCheckedChanged

ComboBox

Hierarchy: UIElement → FrameworkElement → Control → ItemsControl → Selector

```
<ComboBox
    IsEditable="true|false"
    IsSelectionRequired="true|false"
    SelectionChanged="SelectionChangedHandler">
</ComboBox>
```

`<ComboBox .../>` displays a selection control in a drop-down list form. A `ComboBox` is a container for `ComboBoxItems`.

Attributes

`IsEditable` *(optional)*

This attribute determines whether users can edit the `ComboBoxItems`. If it is `true`, the user can type in the `ComboBox` as though it were a text field.

`true`

The items are editable by the user.

`false`

The items are not editable.

`IsSelectedRequired` *(optional)*

This attribute determines whether the first `ComboBoxItem` will be selected when the control is initially drawn.

`true`

The `ComboBox` will be displayed with an empty selection.

`false`

The first `ComboBoxItem` will be initially selected.

`SelectionChanged` *(optional)*

This attribute sets the name of the `codebehind` handler that executes when the selection changes.

Events

`SelectionChanged`

ContextMenu

Hierarchy: UIElement → FrameworkElement → Control → ItemsControl → MenuBase

```
<ContextMenu
    Opened="OpenedHandler"
    Closed="ClosedHandler"
/>
```

`<ContextMenu .../>` represents a menu control containing a contextually accurate pop-up menu for the control to which it is attached. `ContextMenu` is a container for a collection of `MenuItem` elements and must be nested within another control. `ContextMenu` is automatically placed inside a `Popup` element.

Example of a fully defined `ContextMenu`:

```
ContextMenu Opened="OpenedHandler Closed="ClosedHandler">
    <MenuItem Header="File"/>
```

```
        <MenuItem Header="Save"/>
        <MenuItem Header="SaveAs"/>
        <MenuItem Header="Recent Files">
            <MenuItem Header="Readme.txt"/>
            <MenuItem Header="Schedule.xls"/>
        </MenuItem>
    </ContextMenu>
```

Attributes

`Closed` *(optional)*
: This attribute sets the name of the codebehind handler that executes when the `ContextMenu` closes.

`Opened` *(optional)*
: This attribute sets the name of the codebehind handler that executes when the `ContextMenu` opens.

Events

`Closed`
`Opened`

DocumentViewer

Hierarchy: UIElement → FrameworkElement → Control

```
<DocumentViewer
    FirstVisiblePage="0" // 0 based integer
    GridColumnCount="1" // sets the number of columns in the viewer
    HorizontalOffset="0.5" // Double, ele scrolls to value
    HorizontalPageSpacing="2" // Double, space between pages
    IsToolBarMaximized="true|false"
    ShowPageBorders="true|false"
    VerticalOffset="2" // double, sets vert scroll
    VerticalPageSpacing="10" // vert page spacing
    ZoomPercentage="5.0 ... 5000.0" //default 100.0
/>
```

`<DocumentViewer .../>` implements a control that allows users to view paginated documents in a fixed or flow format. It may contain only child elements of either `FlowDocument` or `FixedDocument`.

Attributes

`FirstVisiblePage` *(optional)*
: This attribute is a zero-based `Integer` indicating the first visible page of content. This value must be non-negative. Setting this value causes the `DocumentViewer` to load the specified page and scroll to the top if necessary.

`GridColumnCount` *(optional)*
: This `Integer` value represents the number of grid columns in the `DocumentViewer`. The value must be non-negative and cannot be greater than the total page count.

`HorizontalOffset` *(optional)*
: This `Double` value represents the horizontal scroll position in 1/96". It must be non-negative.

Controls

`HorizontalPageSpacing` *(optional)*
: This `Double` value specifies the amount of horizontal space between pages. It must be non-negative. The default value is 10.0.

`IsToolBarMaximized` *(optional)*
: This attribute determines whether the `DocumentViewer` toolbar is visible or hidden.

  `true`
  : The toolbar is visible. This is the default.

  `false`
  : The toolbar is hidden.

`ShowPageBorders` *(optional)*

`VerticalOffset` *(optional)*
: This `Double` value represents the vertical scroll position in 1/96". It must be non-negative.

`VerticalPageSpacing` *(optional)*
: This `Double` value specifies the amount of vertical space between pages. It must be non-negative. The default value is 10.0.

`ZoomPercentage` *(optional)*
: This attribute is a `Double` value between 5.0 and 5000.0 that represents the zoom percentage. The default value is 100.0.

Attached Attributes

`ContentHost`
: The `ContentHost` for a `DocumentViewer` must be a `ScrollViewer`. The attribute is a `Boolean` that marks the `ScrollViewer` as the `ContentHost`:

```
<ScrollViewer DocumentViewer.ContentHost="true|false" />
```

Expander

Hierarchy: UIElement → FrameworkElement → Control → ContentControl → HeaderedContentControl

```
<Expander
    IsExpanded="true|false"
    Header="this is an Expander"      Content="content"/>
```

or:

```
<Expander
    IsExpanded="true|false"
    Header="this is an Expander">
      Content string
</Expander>
```

`<Expander .../>` allows a user to collapse an element to show only the header, or to expand it to show more content. An `Expander` object may contain only one child element, but there are no limitations on how many children that element may have. Figure 8-1 shows the result of evaluating Example 8-5 in XamlPad and shows the `Expander` both closed (on the left) and open (on the right).

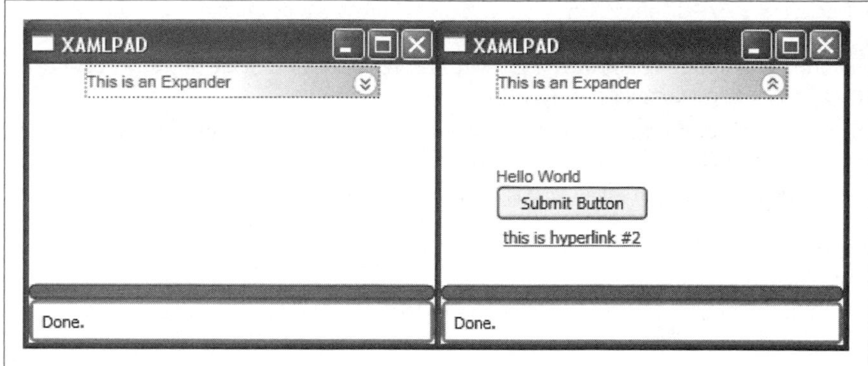

Figure 8-1. An Expander in collapsed state and fully expanded

Example 8-5. Expander with a StackPanel as Content to accommodate multiple objects

```
<Expander
    Width="200"
    IsExpanded="true"
    Header="This is an Expander" >
    <StackPanel>
        <TextBlock>Hello World</TextBlock>
        <Button Background="Yellow">Submit Button</Button>
        <Label>
            <Hyperlink NavigateUri="#Paragraph2">this is hyperlink #2</Hyperlink>
        </Label>
    </StackPanel>
</Expander>
```

Attributes

`Content` *(optional)*
: The value of this attribute will be displayed when the `Expander` state is expanded and hidden when the `Expander` state is collapsed.

`IsExpanded` *(optional)*
: This attribute sets the initial state of the `Expander`.

  `true`
  : The initial state is open.

  `false`
  : The initial state is closed.

`Header` *(optional)*
: The value of this attribute will be displayed in the header area.

Hyperlink

Hierarchy: DependencyObject → FrameworkContentElement → TextElement → Inline

```
<Hyperlink
    NavigateUri="Page2.xaml">Next Page
</Hyperlink>
```

<Hyperlink .../> displays a hyperlink. A Hyperlink is a mechanism used to load a new page or to navigate to an inline section of a document. This element can only be included where text is allowed, e.g., within a TextBlock or Label object. It cannot be defined as a standalone or root element.

Navigating to an inline section of a document uses the same syntax as linking to an anchor in an HTML document:

```
<Hyperlink NavigateUri="#paragraph3">Paragraph 3</Hyperlink>
```

Attributes

Click *(optional)*
: This attribute sets the name of the codebehind handler that executes when the element is clicked.

NavigateUri *(required)*
: This attribute loads the page designated by the hyperlink or navigates to the appropriate place within a document.

Events

Click

ListBox

Hierarchy: UIElement → FrameworkElement → Control → ItemsControl → Selector

```
<ListBox
    SelectionChanged="SelectionChangedHandler"
    SelectionMode="Single|Multiple|Extended" />
```

<ListBox .../> is a control that implements a list of selectable items. Like ComboBox, ListBox is a container for other elements, namely ListBoxItem. (See Example 8-6.)

Example 8-6. An example of a complete ListBox

```
<ListBox
    SelectionChanged="SelectionChangedHandler"
    SelectionMode="Single|Multiple|Extended" >
        <ListBoxItem>Item 1</ListBoxItem>
        <ListBoxItem>Item 2</ListBoxItem>
        <ListBoxItem>Item 3</ListBoxItem>
</ListBox>
```

Attributes

SelectionChanged *(optional)*
: This attribute sets the name of the codebehind handler that executes when the selection changes.

SelectionMode *(optional)*
: This attribute determines how items are selected.

`Extended`
: Multiple items may be selected in groups by using the Shift key with either the mouse or the arrow keys.

`Multiple`
: Multiple items may be selected.

`Single`
: A single item may be selected.

Events

`SelectionChanged`

MediaElement

Hierarchy: UIElement → FrameworkElement

```
<MediaElement
    Source="c:\\media\\mymedia.wmv"
    Stretch="Fill|None|Uniform|UniformFill"
    StretchDirection="Both|DownOnly|UpOnly"/>
```

`<MediaElement .../>` provides a mechanism for including media resources, such as video, in a XAML interface.

Attributes

`Source` *(optional)*
: A `MediaTimeline` (detailed in Chapter 11) describing the source video.

`MediaTimeline` requires an absolute path to the media source.

`Stretch` *(optional)*
: Determines how the `MediaElement` will be drawn.

  `Fill`
  : The content is stretched to fill the destination. Aspect ratio is not preserved.

  `None`
  : The content's original size is preserved.

  `Uniform`
  : Content is resized to fit the destination. Aspect ratio is preserved.

  `UniformFill`
  : Content is resized to fit the destination. Aspect ratio is preserved. If the resized content overflows the destination, it is clipped.

`StretchDirection` *(optional)*
: Determines how content is stretched to fit the `Viewbox`.

`Both`
: Content is stretched to fit the `Viewbox` according to the `Stretch` attribute.

`DownOnly`
: Content is scaled downward if it is larger than the parent `Viewbox`.

`UpOnly`
: Content is scaled upward if it is smaller than the parent `Viewbox`.

Menu

Hierarchy: UIElement → FrameworkElement → Control → ItemsControl → MenuBase

```
<Menu />
```

`<Menu .../>` defines a control that allows you to hierarchically represent commands. On its own, `Menu` has very little meaning and must contain child elements of type `MenuItem` to be useful.

MenuItem

Hierarchy: UIElement → FrameworkElement → Control → ItemsControl → HeaderedItemsControl

```
<MenuItem
    Header="File"
    IsCheckedChanged="CheckedChangedHandler"
    Click="ClickHandler"
    IsChecked="true|false"
    InputGestureText="Ctrl+X"
    Command="ApplicationCommand"
    Mode="Default|Separator|Checked" />
```

In the previous code block, `Header` is used to represent text. To use other elements for display, define the desired elements between the tags instead of using `Header`, e.g., `<MenuItem ...>` *`<element .../>`*`</MenuItem>`.

`<MenuItem .../>` is used by both `Menu` and `ContextMenu` as a child element that represents menu options. `MenuItem` headers may be defined inline using the `Header` attribute or in context. `MenuItem` can be:

- Checked or unchecked
- Selected to invoke commands
- Used as a header for submenus
- Used as a separator

Attributes

`Click` *(optional)*
: This attribute sets the name of the `codebehind` handler that executes when the `MenuItem` is clicked.

`Command` *(optional)*
: This attribute is used to assign an application command to the menu item, which automatically assigns the command's associated input gesture to the object. This

attribute must be one of the commands defined by the `System.Windows.Input.ApplicationCommands` class. For a full listing of these commands, see Appendix F.

`Header` *(optional)*
: This attribute defines the visible text of the menu item that is displayed.

`InputGestureText` *(optional)*
: This attribute describes the sequence of keystrokes that accesses this menu item. An example is Ctrl-X or Ctrl-Z. This text is displayed on the right side of the menu item as a user prompt. Figure 8-2 shows an example of declaring `InputGestureText="Ctrl+N"` and `InputGestureText="Ctrl+X"` for two separate instances of `MenuItem`.

`IsChecked` *(optional)*
: This attribute sets the initial state of the `MenuItem`.

  `true`
  : The `MenuItem` is checked.

  `false`
  : The `MenuItem` is not checked.

  Figure 8-2 shows the result of declaring `<MenuItem Header= "Open" IsChecked= "true" />`.

`IsCheckedChanged` *(optional)*
: This attribute sets the name of the `codebehind` handler that executes when the `MenuItem` state changes from checked to unchecked, or vice versa.

`Mode` *(optional)*
: This attribute defines the operational mode of the menu item.

  `Checkable`
  : The menu item can be clicked, which toggles its checked state.

  `Default`
  : The menu item can be clicked. This is the default mode and is assigned if a mode is not explicitly declared.

  `Separator`
  : The menu item is a separator and cannot be clicked.

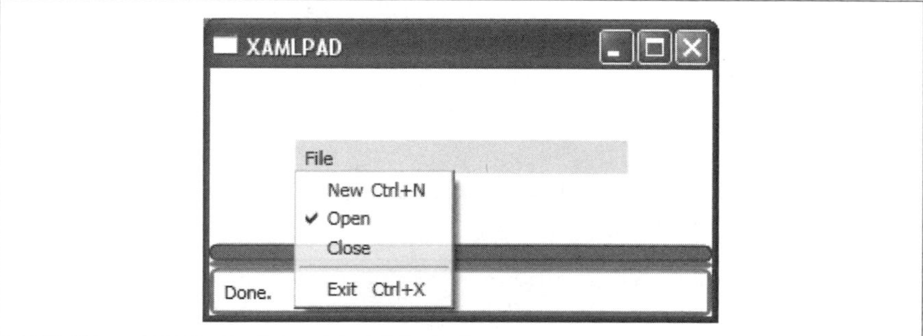

Figure 8-2. A Menu with InputGestureText and IsChecked declared

Events

`Click`
`IsCheckedChanged`

NavigationWindow

Hierarchy: UIElement → FrameworkElement → Control → ContentControl → Window

```
<NavigationWindow
    StartupUri="StartPage.xaml" />
```

`<NavigationWindow .../>` extends `Window` and adds standard back and forward web navigation capabilities. `NavigationWindow` is always created with a navigation "chrome," which contains the controls that allow a user to move forward and backward through the navigation stack. The navigation chrome is indicated in Figure 8-3 by the space containing the back and forward navigation arrows.

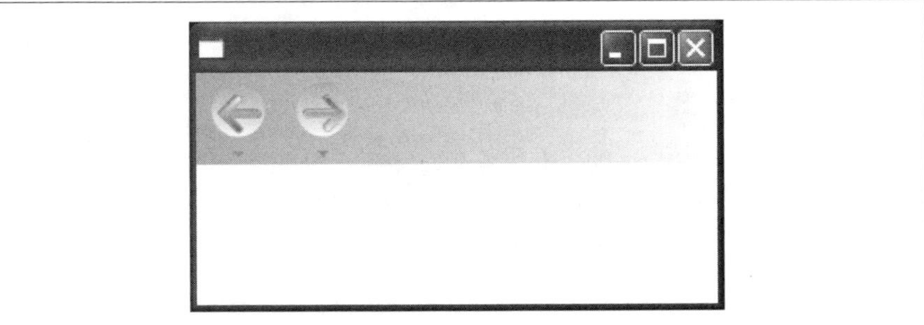

Figure 8-3. Navigation chrome

Attributes

`StartUri` *(required)*
: Specifies the URI of the starting page

Page

Hierarchy: UIElement → FrameworkElement

```
<Page
    xmlns="http://schemas.microsoft.com/winfx/avalon/2005"
    xmlns:x="http://schemas.microsoft.com/winfx/xaml/2005"
    x:Class="Page_API.Page1"
    Name="myWindow"
    WindowHeight="400"
    WindowWidth="400"
    Text="Title of the Page"
    WindowState="Maximized|Minimized|Normal"
    <Page.Resources>
     ...
    </Page.Resources>
</Page>
```

Note that *x* is replaceable both for `Class` and the namespace declaration. It refers to the XAML namespace (`http://schemas.microsoft.com/winfx/xaml/2005`), which must be included when using this method of reference .

<Page .../> is a root-level element that can be used to set window properties and event handlers.

Attributes

`Name` *(optional)*
: This attribute determines the name of the `Page`. `Name` must be set in order to access the element instance from `codebehind` functions.

`Resources` *(optional)*
: This attribute determines a collection of `Style`, `Trigger`, and `Storyboard`.

`Text` *(optional)*
: Sets the title of the `Page`. The default value is `null`; no title is displayed.

`WindowHeight` *(optional)*
: This `Double` value specifies the height of the `Page`.

`WindowState` *(optional)*
: This attribute determines the initial state of the window.

  `Maximized`
  : The `Page` starts maximized.

  `Minimized`
  : The `Page` starts minimized.

  `Normal`
  : The `Page` starts at its specified dimensions.

`WindowWidth` *(optional)*
: This `Double` value specifies the width of the `Page`.

`x:Class` *(optional)*
: This attribute defines the name of the `codebehind` class responsible for implementing event handlers. The namespace for this class is determined by the declaration of the WinFX XAML namespace. `x` may be replaced with any namespace reference you desire, as long as it matches the declaration of the `codebehind` class in which event handlers and other application logic will be implemented. If the declaration in XAML for the `Page` `codebehind` class is `x:Class="Page_API.Page1"`, then the associated C# `codebehind` file would appear as shown in Example 8-7.

Example 8-7. Declaring a codebehind class for Page

```
namespace XAML_Space
{
    public partial class Page1 : Page
    {
     // code goes here for page level event handlers
    }
}
```

PasswordBox

Hierarchy: UIElement → FrameworkElement → Control

```
<PasswordBox
    MaxLength="0"
    PasswordTextChanged="PasswordChangedHandler"
```


Controls

```
        PasswordChar="*"
        Password="MyPassword" />
```

<PasswordBox .../> implements a TextBox with special provisions for handling passwords.

Attributes

MaxLength *(optional)*
: This attribute is an Integer value specifying the maximum length of the password. A 0 indicates there is no maximum. The default value is 0.

Password *(optional)*
: This attribute is a SecureString representing the password to be displayed.

PasswordChar *(optional)*
: This attribute is the Char displayed in place of typed characters in the password box. The default value is *.

PasswordTextChanged *(optional)*
: This attribute describes the codebehind handler that executes when the PasswordTextChanged event is raised.

Events

PasswordTextChanged

Popup

Hierarchy: UIElement → FrameworkElement

```
<Popup
    Child="MyChild"
    HasDropShadow="true|false"
    HorizontalOffset="3"
    IsOpen="true|false"
    Placement="Absolute|AbsolutePoint|Top|Bottom|Right|Center|Left|Relative|
               RelativePoint|Mouse|MousePoint"
    PlacementRectangle="0,0 5 10"
    PlacementTarget="Target"
    PopupAnimation="None|Fade|Scroll|Slide"
    StaysOpen="true|false"
    VerticalOffset="5"
    CustomPopupPlacementCallback="CustomCallback"
    Opened="OpenedHandler"
    Closed="ClosedHandler"
/>
```

<Popup .../> creates a top-level window that displays content. It is not affected by styles or properties in the existing tree unless it is specifically bound to them.

Attributes

Child *(optional)*
: This attribute sets the child element. Child elements can also be defined between the tags.

Closed *(optional)*
: This attribute sets the name of the codebehind handler that executes when the Popup is closed.

`CustomPopupPlacementCallback` *(optional)*

This attribute identifies a `codebehind` callback function, which returns the placement for this element.

`HasDropShadow` *(optional)*

This attribute determines whether the `Popup` has a drop shadow.

`true`

The element has a drop shadow.

`false`

The element does not have a drop shadow. This is the default.

`HorizontalOffset` *(optional)*

This attribute determines the offset of the `Popup` from the left. It is of type `Double`.

`IsOpen` *(optional)*

This attribute determines whether the `Popup` is visible.

`true`

The element is visible.

`false`

The element is not visible.

`Opened` *(optional)*

This attribute sets the name of the `codebehind` handler that executes when the `Popup` is opened.

`Placement` *(optional)*

This attribute determines where the `PopUp` appears.

`Absolute`

Uses `HorizontalOffset` and `VerticalOffset` to position the `Popup` relative to the upper-left corner of the screen.

`AbsolutePoint`

Uses `HorizontalOffset` and `VerticalOffset` to position the `Popup` relative to the upper-left corner of the screen. If the `Popup` extends beyond the edges of the screen, it flips to the other side of the point.

`Bottom`

Positions the `Popup` on the bottom edge of its parent, aligning left edges.

`Center`

Centers the `Popup` over the parent.

`Left`

Positions the `Popup` on the left side of the parent, aligning upper edges.

`Mouse`

Behaves the same way as `Bottom` but uses the bounding box of the mouse cursor.

`MousePoint`

Behaves the same way as `RelativePoint`, but its reference point is the tip of the mouse cursor.

`Relative`

Uses `HorizontalOffset` and `VerticalOffset` to position the `Popup` relative to the upper-left corner of the parent element.

`RelativePoint`
: Uses `HorizontalOffset` and `VerticalOffset` to position the `Popup` relative to the upper-left corner of the parent element. If the popup extends beyond the edges of the screen, it flips to the other side of the point.

`Right`
: Positions the `Popup` on the right side of the parent, aligning upper edges.

`Top`
: Positions the `Popup` on the top edge of the parent, aligning left edges.

`PlacementRectangle` *(optional)*
: If this attribute is `null`, then the `Popup` will be placed relative to its visual parent. If this attribute is set, then the `Popup` will be placed relative to the rectangle it describes. `PlacementRectangle` is of type `Rect` and can be expressed through markup as the top-left coordinate pair, height, and width, e.g., `5,5 10 10`.

`PlacementTarget` *(optional)*
: This attribute specifies the element used to calculate the position of the `Popup` as though it were the parent element.

`PopupAnimation` *(optional)*
: This attribute specifies the animation used when the element opens.

`Fade`
: Animates the opacity. The element appears to fade in.

`None`
: No animation is used.

`Scroll`
: Animates the height of the element.

`Slide`
: Animates the width and height at the same time.

`StaysOpen` *(optional)*
: This attribute determines the automatic closure behavior of the `Popup`.

`true`
: The element stays open and must be closed programmatically.

`false`
: The element automatically closes.

`VerticalOffset` *(optional)*
: This attribute determines the offset of the `Popup` from the bottom. It is of type `Double`.

Events

`Opened`
`Closed`

RadioButton

Hierarchy: UIElement → FrameworkElement → Control → ContentControl → ButtonBase → ToggleButton

```
<RadioButton
    IsChecked="true|false"
    Content="Checked Radio Button"
```

```
        IsCheckedChanged="CheckedChangedHandler"
        Click="ClickHandler"/>
```

or:

```
    <RadioButton
        IsChecked="true|false"
        IsCheckedChanged="CheckedChangedHandler"
        Click="ClickHandler">
        Checked Radio Button
    </RadioButton>
```

`<RadioButton .../>` displays a single button that can be selected but not deselected. To display a group of `RadioButton` elements, use `RadioButtonList`.

Although the content of a `RadioButton` is usually text, any `UIElement` can be used, as demonstrated in Example 8-8. Figure 8-4 shows an example of several `RadioButton` elements using text, `Button`, and `Ellipse` as content.

Example 8-8. Using elements as RadioButton content instead of text

```
<StackPanel
    xmlns="http://schemas.microsoft.com/winfx/avalon/2005"
    Margin="20">
    <RadioButtonList >
        <RadioButton
            Name="rb1">Radio Button 1
        </RadioButton>
        <RadioButton
            Name="rb2">
            <Ellipse
                CenterX="15"
                CenterY="5"
                Fill="Blue" />
        </RadioButton>
        <RadioButton
            Name="rb3">
            <Button Content="Button" />
        </RadioButton>
    </RadioButtonList>
</StackPanel>
```

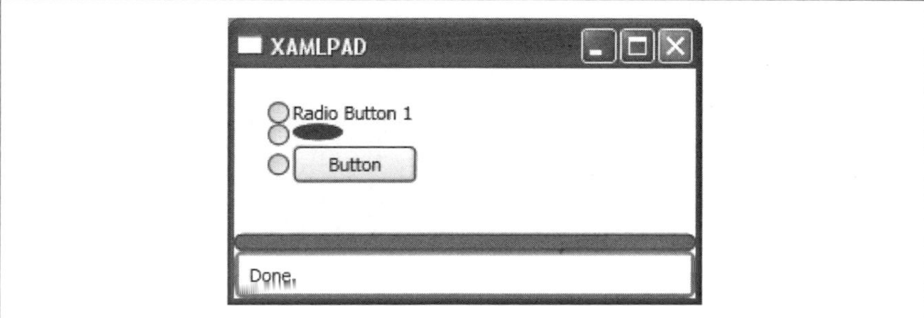

Figure 8-4. RadioButton using non-text content

Attributes

`Click` *(optional)*

This attribute sets the name of the codebehind handler that executes when the RadioButton is clicked.

`Content` *(optional)*

This attribute's value will be displayed as the RadioButton label.

`IsChecked` *(optional)*

This attribute sets the initial state of the RadioButton.

`true`

Sets the initial state to selected

`false`

Sets the initial state to unselected

`IsCheckedChanged` *(optional)*

This attribute sets the name of the codebehind handler that executes when the RadioButton changes state.

Events

`Click`
`IsCheckedChanged`

RadioButtonList

Hierarchy: UIElement → FrameworkElement → Control → ItemsControl → Selector

```
<RadioButtonList
    SelectionChanged="RadioButtonSelectionChangedHandler">
        <RadioButton Name="rb1">Radio Button 1</RadioButton>
        <RadioButton Name="rb2">Radio Button 2</RadioButton>
        <RadioButton Name="rb3">Radio Button 3</RadioButton>
</RadioButtonList>
```

`<RadioButtonList .../>` is a selector containing a group of RadioButton elements and is limited to a single selection mode. RadioButtonList can contain any type of element, but all elements declared within its beginning and ending tags will be interpreted as a RadioButton and displayed as the RadioButton's label. If you declare a Button in the middle of the list, the user interface will display a typical RadioButton with a Button next to it instead of a text-based prompt.

Attributes

`SelectionChanged` *(optional)*

This attribute sets the name of the codebehind handler that executes when the selection changes.

Events

`SelectionChanged`

RepeatButton

Hierarchy: UIElement → FrameworkElement → Control → ContentControl → ButtonBase

```
<RepeatButton
    Delay="500"
    Interval="100"
    Click="ClickHandler"
    Content="Increment Counter" />
```

`<RepeatButton .../>` is a button that continually raises its `Click` event until it is released. The interval between `Click` events is controlled through the event's properties. `RepeatButton` is used to implement the composite components `HorizontalSlider` and `VerticalSlider`.

Attributes

`Click` *(optional)*
: This attribute sets the name of the `codebehind` handler that executes when the `RepeatButton` is clicked.

`Content` *(optional)*
: This attribute's value will be displayed as the `RepeatButton` label.

`Delay` *(optional)*
: This attribute sets the amount of time, in milliseconds, that the `RepeatButton` waits before it starts repeating. This value must be a non-negative `Integer`.

`Interval` *(optional)*
: This attribute sets the amount of time, in milliseconds, between repeats. This value must be a non-negative `Integer`.

Events

`Click`

ScrollViewer

Hierarchy: UIElement → FrameworkElement → Control → ContentControl

```
ScrollViewer
    HorizontalScrollBarVisibility="Auto|Visible|Hidden|Disabled"
    VerticalScrollBarVisibility=" Auto|Visible|Hidden|Disabled"
    ScrollChanged="ScrollChangedHandler"
    CanContentScroll="true|false" >
    ...
</ScrollViewer>
```

`<ScrollViewer .../>` represents a scrollable area that contains other visible elements. The visible area of the content is called the viewport. The viewport for the `ScrollViewer` is defined by the `Height` and `Width` properties.

Attributes

`CanContentScroll` *(optional)*

Determines whether content is scrollable

`true`

The content is scrollable.

`false`

The content is not scrollable.

`HorizontalScrollBarVisibility` *(optional)*

Determines the properties of the horizontal scrollbar

`Auto`

The scrollbar will be visible only if there is more content than can fit in the viewport.

`Disabled`

No scrolling is allowed.

`Hidden`

The scrollbar should never be visible or have space reserved for it.

`Visible`

The scrollbar should always be visible and have space reserved for it.

`ScrollChanged` *(optional)*

Sets the name of the `codebehind` handler that executes when a scrollbar changes position

`VerticalScrollBarVisibility` *(optional)*

Determines the properties of the vertical scrollbar

`Auto`

The scrollbar will be visible only if there is more content than can fit in the viewport.

`Disabled`

No scrolling is allowed.

`Hidden`

The scrollbar should never be visible or have space reserved for it.

`Visible`

The scrollbar should always be visible and have space reserved for it.

Events

`ScrollChanged`

Slider

Hierarchy: UIElement → FrameworkElement → Control → RangeBase

`Slider` controls provide a thumb that slides from side to side to change a value, usually a number with a large range or a percentage. `Slider` is the parent of two objects: `HorizontalSlider` and `VerticalSlider`. These elements are controlled in a like fashion and have the same attributes. Attributes are applied based on whether the slider is displayed vertically or horizontally, but the two components are identical in all other respects.

HorizontalSlider

Hierarchy: UIElement → FrameworkElement → Control → RangeBase → Slider

```
<HorizontalSlider
    IsSnapToTickEnabled="true|false"
    Minimum="0"
    Maximum="3"
    Delay="100"
    Interval="100"
    TickPlacement=" Both|BottomRight|TopLeft|None"
    AutoToolTipPlacement="BottomRight|TopLeft|None"
    AutoToolTipPrecision="2"
    SmallChange="0.5"
    LargeChange="1"
    Ticks="0, 1, 2, 3"
    TickFrequency="1"
    Value="2" />
```

`<HorizontalSlider .../>` is a composite component that allows the user to select a range of values using a sliding control displayed horizontally.

VerticalSlider

Hierarchy: UIElement → FrameworkElement → Control → RangeBase → Slider

```
<VerticalSlider
    IsSnapToTickEnabled="true|false"
    Minimum="0"
    Maximum="3"
    Delay="100"
    Interval="100"
    TickPlacement="Both|BottomRight|TopLeft|None"
    AutoToolTipPlacement="BottomRight|TopLeft|None"
    AutoToolTipPrecision="2"
    SmallChange="0.5"
    LargeChange="1"
    Ticks-"0, 1, 2, 3"
    TickFrequency="1"
    Value="2" />
```

`<VerticalSlider .../>` is a composite component that allows the user to select a range of values using a sliding control displayed vertically.

Attributes

`AutoToolTipPlacement` *(optional)*

Determines whether an auto-generated `ToolTip` will be shown and where it will appear.

`BottomRight`

Shows the auto `ToolTip` at the bottom edge of the `Thumb` in a `HorizontalSlider` and at the right edge in a `VerticalSlider`.

`None`

Auto `ToolTips` will not be shown.

`TopLeft`

Shows the auto `ToolTip` at the top edge of the `Thumb` in a `HorizontalSlider` and at the left edge in a `VerticalSlider`.

`AutoToolTipPrecision` *(optional)*
: Determines the number of decimal places shown in the auto-generated `ToolTip`.

`Delay` *(optional)*
: The amount of time, in milliseconds, that the object's `RepeatButton` waits before processing an increase or decrease command.

`Interval` *(optional)*
: Sets the amount of time, in milliseconds, between repeats. This value must be non-negative.

`IsSnapToTickEnabled` *(optional)*
: Determines whether the `Thumb` will snap to tick marks. *Snap* describes the behavior of a thumb control when the mouse is clicked either to its left or right.

    `true`
    : `Thumb` will snap.

    `false`
    : `Thumb` will not snap.

`LargeChange` *(optional)*
: The amount added or subtracted from the `Value` when the scrollbar is clicked. The default is 1.

`Maximum` *(optional)*
: Determines the maximum value for this object. The `Value` attribute will not be allowed to increase beyond this value.

`Minimum` *(optional)*
: Determines the minimum value for this object. The `Value` attribute will not be allowed to decrease beyond this value.

`SmallChange` *(optional)*
: The amount added or subtracted from the `Value` when the `Thumb` is moved. The default is 0.1.

`TickFrequency` *(optional)*
: Sets the distance between `Ticks`. The default value for this attribute is 1.0. Ticks start at `Minimum` and end at `Maximum`.

`TickPlacement` *(optional)*
: Determines where `Ticks` should be displayed relative to the slidebar.

    `Both`
    : Displays tick marks on both sides of the slidebar.

    `BottomRight`
    : Displays tick marks below the track in a `HorizontalSlider` and to the right in a `VerticalSlider`.

    `None`
    : No tick marks are shown.

    `TopLeft`
    : Displays tick marks above the track in a `HorizontalSlider` and to the left in a `VerticalSlider`.

`Ticks` *(required)*
: A collection of `Double` values that indicates the values of displayed tick marks.

`Value` *(optional)*
: The initial value of the control.

TabControl

Hierarchy: UIElement → FrameworkElement → Control → ItemsControl → Selector

```
<TabControl
      TabStripPlacement="Bottom|Top|Right|Left"
      SelectionChanged="SelectionChangedHandler" />
```

`<TabControl .../>` allows content to be organized in tabbed panes. It must contain at least one `TabItem` to be useful.

Attributes

`SelectionChanged` *(optional)*
: Sets the name of the `codebehind` handler that executes when the selected `TabItem` changes

`TabStripPlacement` *(optional)*
: Determines where individual `TabItem` objects will be placed

  `Bottom`
  : Tabs are placed at the bottom of content.

  `Left`
  : Tabs are placed to the left of content.

  `Right`
  : Tabs are placed to the right of content.

  `Top`
  : Tabs are placed at the top of content.

Events

`SelectionChanged`

TabItem

Hierarchy: UIElement → FrameworkElement → Control → ContentControl → HeaderedItemsControl

```
<TabItem
    Header="Tab 1"
    IsSelected="true|false"
    Content="Content" />
```

`<TabItem .../>` is a child of `TabControl` and defines individual tabs. `Content` may be omitted if elements other than text will be included.

Figure 8-5 shows a `TabControl` with three `TabItem` declarations.

Attributes

`Content` *(optional)*
: This attribute determines the text-based content of the `TabItem`.

`Header` *(optional)*
: This attribute sets the title of the `TabItem`.

Figure 8-5. A TabControl with three elements

`IsSelected` *(optional)*
: This `Boolean` determines whether a `TabItem` is initially selected.

  `true`
  : The `TabItem` is initially selected.

  `false`
  : The `TabItem` is not selected.

TextBox

Hierarchy: UIElement → FrameworkElement → Control → TextBoxBase

```
<TextBox
    MaxLength="10"
    AcceptsDigitsOnly="true|false"
    TextChanged="TextChangedHandler"
    CaretIndex="3"
    CharacterCasing="Upper|Normal|Lower"
    AcceptsReturn="true|false"
    AcceptsTab="true|false"
    TextTrimming="CharacterEllipsis|WordEllipsis|None"
    Text="123" />
```

`<TextBox .../>` defines an editable region in which a user can enter text.

Attributes

`AcceptsDigitsOnly` *(optional)*
: Determines whether this element will accept alphanumeric characters or numeric only.

  `true`
  : This element accepts only numeric input.

  `false`
  : This element accepts alphanumeric input.

`AcceptsReturn` *(optional)*

Determines the element's behavior when the Enter key is pressed.

`true`
: The Enter key inserts a new line at the current cursor position. This is the default behavior.

`false`
: Enter is ignored.

`AcceptsTab` *(optional)*

Determines the element's behavior when the Tab key is pressed.

`true`
: The Tab key inserts a tab character at the current cursor position. This is the default behavior.

`false`
: The Tab key moves to the next control in the tab order; no tab character is inserted.

`CaretIndex` *(optional)*

Determines the position of the caret. The value is of type `Integer` and is zero-based.

`CharacterCasing` *(optional)*

Determines the casing of characters during input. Typed characters are automatically converted according to this attribute.

`Lower`
: Converts typed characters to lowercase

`Normal`
: Does not convert typed characters

`Upper`
: Converts typed characters to uppercase

`MaxLength` *(optional)*

Determines the maximum length of the string that this element will accept. The default is 0 and is of type `Integer`. The string can be set to a longer value programmatically.

`Text` *(optional)*

Sets the initial content of the `TextBox`.

`TextChanged` *(optional)*

Sets the name of the `codebehind` handler that executes when the text changes.

`TextTrimming` *(optional)*

Determines how text that flows past the end of the element is treated.

`CharacterEllipsis`
: Text is trimmed at a character boundary. Remaining text is replaced with an ellipsis (...).

`None`
: Text is not trimmed.

`WordEllipsis`
: Text is trimmed at a word boundary. Remaining text is replaced with an ellipsis (...).

Events

TextChanged

ToolBar

Hierarchy: UIElement → FrameworkElement → Control → ItemsControl → HeaderedItemsControl

```
<ToolBar
    BandIndex="0"
    Band="0"
    OverflowMode="Always|Never|AsNeeded|Never" />
```

`<ToolBar .../>` represents a standard UI toolbar with facilities to handle the overflow of items. ToolBar holds objects of type UIElement. Figure 8-6 shows the result of evaluating Example 8-9, which builds a ToolBar out of Button elements. Each Button contains an Image element—a common mechanism for building toolbars.

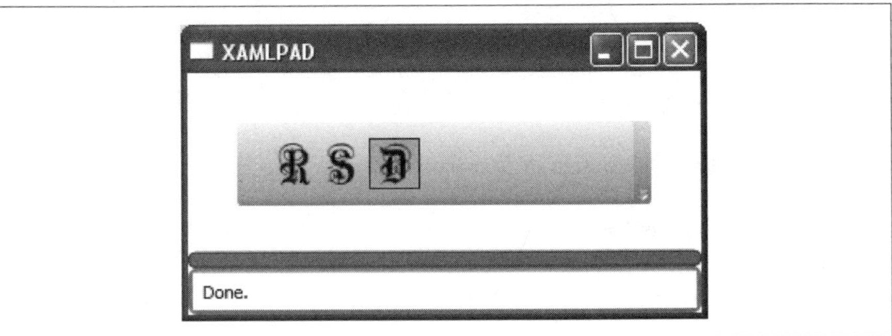

Figure 8-6. ToolBar containing Buttons with images

Example 8-9. ToolBar containing elements

```
<StackPanel
    xmlns="http://schemas.microsoft.com/winfx/avalon/2005"
    Margin="20">
    <ToolBar
        BandIndex="0"
        Band="0"
        Margin="10"
        Padding="10">
        <Button Width="32" Height="32"><Image Source="c:\r.gif"/></Button>
        <Button Width="32" Height="32"><Image Source="c:\s.gif"/></Button>
        <Button Width="32" Height="32"><Image Source="c:\d.gif"/></Button>
    </ToolBar>
</StackPanel>
```

The Band and BandIndex attributes are useful only when more than one ToolBarPanel is contained within a ToolBar. Example 8-9 contains example code and figures that demonstrate the usefulness of these two attributes.

Attributes

`Band` *(optional)*

This `Integer` value determines which band, or row, in the `ToolBarTray` this `ToolBar` should occupy.

`BandIndex` *(optional)*

This `Integer` value determines which band, or row, in the `ToolBarTray` this `ToolBar` should occupy.

`IsOverFlowOpen` *(optional)*

This `Boolean` determines the initial state of the `ToolBarOverflowPanel`.

`true`

The overflow panel is open.

`false`

The overflow panel is closed.

Attached Attributes

`ToolBar.OverflowMode`

Determines how an element should be added to the overflow panel, if ever

`Always`

This element should always be added to the overflow panel.

`AsNeeded`

This element should be added to the overflow panel if necessary.

`Never`

This element should never be added to the overflow panel.

ToolBarOverflowPanel

Hierarchy: UIElement → FrameworkElement → Panel

```
<ToolBarOverflowPanel
    WrapWidth="100" />
```

`<ToolBarOverflowPanel .../>` describes the overflow panel for a `ToolBar`. It is used in conjunction with a `ToolBarPanel` to determine which elements are automatically placed into the overflow panel when there is not enough room in the `ToolBar` to display all of them. If there is not enough room for even one element in the `ToolBar`, then all elements declared in the `ToolBarOverflowPanel` will appear there. If there is enough room for all the elements declared in the `ToolbarOverflowPanel` to be displayed on the `ToolBarPanel`, then they will appear there.

Attributes

`WrapWidth` *(optional)*

This `Integer` value sets the width at which items will begin to flow into the overflow panel.

ToolBarPanel

Hierarchy: UIElement → FrameworkElement → Panel → StackPanel

```
<ToolBarPanel />
```

<ToolBarPanel .../> is responsible for arranging items in a ToolBar and determining which elements will fit there and which will be placed into the ToolBarOverflowPanel. Example 8-10 describes a ToolBarPanel with two ToolBar elements, one of which is always an overflow item and one that is not. The result is shown in Figure 8-7.

Example 8-10. ToolBarPanel with overflow panel

```
<StackPanel
    xmlns="http://schemas.microsoft.com/winfx/avalon/2005"
    Margin="20">
    <ToolBar
        BandIndex="0"
        Band="0" Margin="10" Padding="10">
        <ToolBarPanel Orientation="Horizontal">
            <Button Width="32" Height="32"><Image Source="c:\r.gif"/></Button>
            <Button Width="32" Height="32"><Image Source="c:\s.gif"/></Button>
            <Button Width="32" Height="32"><Image Source="c:\d.gif"/></Button>
        </ToolBarPanel>
        <ToolBarPanel ToolBar.OverflowMode="Always">
            <Button Width="32" Height="32"><Image Source="c:\m.gif"/></Button>
            <Button Width="32" Height="32"><Image Source="c:\s.gif"/></Button>
            <Button Width="32" Height="32"><Image Source="c:\d.gif"/></Button>
        </ToolBarPanel>
    </ToolBar>
</StackPanel>
```

Figure 8-7. A ToolBarPanel with overflow

ToolBarTray

Hierarchy: UIElement → FrameworkElement → Panel → Canvas

```
<ToolBarTray
    IsLocked="true|false"
    Orientation="Vertical|Horizontal" >
```

<ToolBarTray .../> defines a toolbar tray that holds a group of ToolBar elements. The BandIndex and Band attributes indicate the order of these elements in the ToolBarTray.

Figure 8-8 shows the result of specifying Band="0" for both ToolBar elements. Specifying the same Band for both ToolBar elements lines them up horizontally. Changing the first value to Band="1" results in Figure 8-9, in which the ToolBar elements line up vertically. Example 8-11 demonstrates the code for a ToolBarTray with multiple ToolBars.

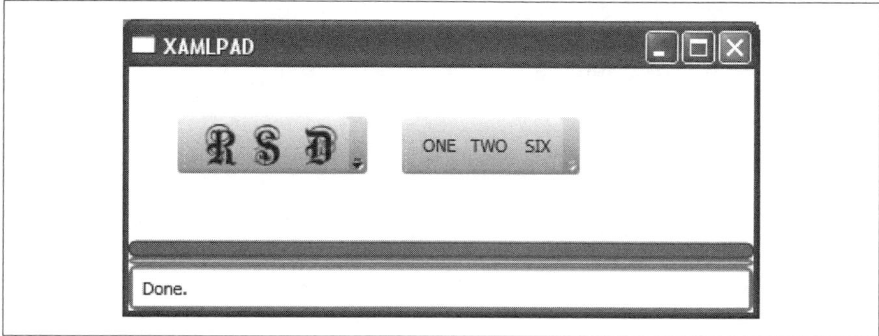

Figure 8-8. Specifying the same value for Band in a ToolBarTray

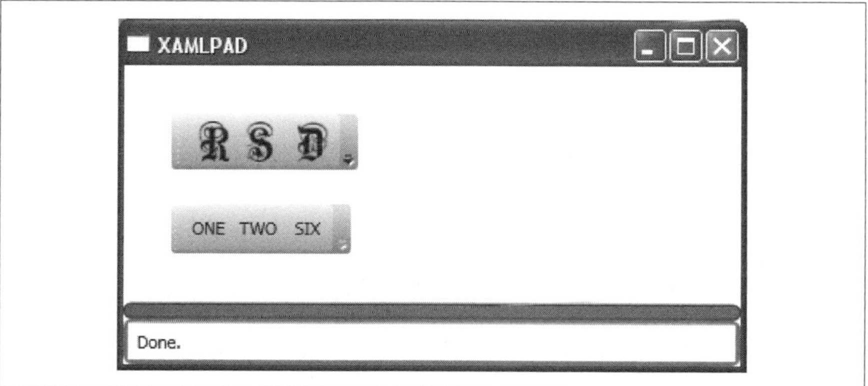

Figure 8-9. Specifying two different values for Band in a ToolBarTray

Example 8-11. ToolBarTray with multiple ToolBars

```
<StackPanel
    xmlns="http://schemas.microsoft.com/winfx/avalon/2005"
    Margin="20">
    <ToolBarTray>
        <ToolBar BandIndex="1" Band="0" Margin="10">
            <Button Width="32" Height="32" Content="ONE" />
            <Button Width="32" Height="32" Content="TWO" />
            <Button Width="32" Height="32" Content="SIX" />
        </ToolBar>
        <ToolBar
            BandIndex="0"
            Band="0" Margin="10" Padding="2">
            <ToolBarPanel Orientation="Horizontal">
```

Example 8-11. ToolBarTray with multiple ToolBars (continued)

```
                <Button Width="32" Height="32"><Image Source="c:\r.gif"/>
</Button>
                <Button Width="32" Height="32"><Image Source="c:\s.gif"/>
</Button>
                <Button Width="32" Height="32"><Image Source="c:\d.gif"/>
</Button>
            </ToolBarPanel>
            <ToolBarPanel ToolBar.OverflowMode="Always">
                <Button Width="32" Height="32"><Image Source="c:\m.gif"/>
</Button>
                <Button Width="32" Height="32"><Image Source="c:\s.gif"/>
</Button>
                <Button Width="32" Height="32"><Image Source="c:\d.gif"/>
</Button>
            </ToolBarPanel>
        </ToolBar>
    </ToolBarTray>
</StackPanel>
```

Attributes

`IsLocked` *(optional)*

Specifies whether child instances of `ToolBar` can be moved within the `ToolBarTray`

`true`
: `ToolBar` elements may not be moved.

`false`
: `ToolBar` elements may be moved. This is the default behavior.

`Orientation` *(optional)*

Determines the orientation of the `ToolBarTray`

`Horizontal`
: The element is oriented horizontally.

`Vertical`
: The element is oriented vertically.

ToolTip

Hierarchy: UIElement → FrameworkElement → Control → ContentControl

```
<ToolTip

Placement="Absolute|AbsolutePoint|Top|Bottom|Right|Center|Left|Relative|
                RelativePoint|Mouse|MousePoint"
    HorizontalOffset="50"
    VerticalOffset="20"
    StaysOpen="true|false"
    Opened="OpenedHandler"
    Closed="ClosedHandler"
    PlacementTarget="Target"
    HasDropShadow="true|false" />
```

`<ToolTip .../>` displays a small pop-up window after particular events are raised or when the mouse hovers over a control. Assigning a `ToolTip` to a control requires the explicit declaration of the ToolTip attribute, which is inherited from FrameworkElement. ToolTip can be declared inline as a String, in which case the system automatically displays the tool tip with its default style. ToolTip can also be explicitly declared, as shown in Example 8-12, as any derivative of UIElement.

Example 8-12. Assigning an Image as a ToolTip for a control

```
<StackPanel
    xmlns="http://schemas.microsoft.com/winfx/avalon/2005"
    Margin="20">
    <Button
        Content="Button with ToolTip">
        <Button.ToolTip>
            <ToolTip
                Placement="Mouse">
                <Image Source="c:\tooltipimage.gif" />
            </ToolTip>
        </Button.ToolTip>
    </Button>
</StackPanel>
```

Attributes

Closed *(optional)*
: Sets the name of the codebehind handler that executes when the ToolTip closes.

HasDropShadow *(optional)*
: Determines whether the ToolTip has a drop shadow.

    true
    : ToolTip has a drop shadow.

    false
    : ToolTip does not have a drop shadow. This is the default value.

HorizontalOffset *(optional)*
: Determines the offset of the pop up from the left. It is of type Double.

Opened *(optional)*
: Sets the name of the codebehind handler that executes when the ToolTip opens.

Placement *(optional)*
: Determines where the ToolTip appears.

    Absolute
    : Uses HorizontalOffset and VerticalOffset to position the ToolTip relative to the upper-left corner of the screen.

    AbsolutePoint
    : Uses HorizontalOffset and VerticalOffset to position the ToolTip relative to the upper-left corner of the screen. If the pop up extends beyond the edges of the screen, it flips to the other side of the point.

    Bottom
    : Positions the pop up on the bottom edge of its parent, aligning left edges.

    Center
    : Centers the pop up over the parent.

    Left
    : Positions the pop up on the left side of the parent, aligning upper edges.

`Mouse`
: Behaves the same way as `Bottom` but uses the bounding box of the mouse cursor.

`MousePoint`
: Behaves the same way as `RelativePoint`, but its reference point is the tip of the mouse cursor.

`Relative`
: Uses `HorizontalOffset` and `VerticalOffset` to position the `ToolTip` relative to the upper-left corner of the parent element.

`RelativePoint`
: Uses `HorizontalOffset` and `VerticalOffset` to position the `ToolTip` relative to the upper-left corner of the parent element. If the pop up extends beyond the edges of the screen, it flips to the other side of the point.

`Right`
: Positions the pop up on the right side of the parent, aligning upper edges.

`Top`
: Positions the pop up on the top edge of the parent, aligning left edges.

`PlacementTarget` *(optional)*
: Determines the element relative to which the `ToolTip` is displayed. This element is used to calculate placement. If `null`, the parent element is used.

`StaysOpen` *(optional)*
: Determines the behavior of the `ToolTip` when opened.

`true`
: The `ToolTip` stays open.

`false`
: The `ToolTip` automatically closes after a specified period of time. This is the default behavior.

`VerticalOffset` *(optional)*
: Determines the offset of the pop up from the top. It is of type `Double`.

Events

`Closed`
`Opened`

Window

Hierarchy: UIElement → FrameworkElement → Control → ContentControl

```
<Window
    Left="10"
    ResizeMode="CanMinimize|CanResize|CanResizeWithGrip|NoResize"
    ShowInTaskbar="true|false"
    StatusBarContent="My Status Bar Content"
    Text="Window Title"
    Topmost="true|false"
    WindowState="Maximized|Minimized|Normal"
    WindowStyle="None|SingleBorderWindow|ThreeDBorderWindow|ToolWindow" />
```

Attributes

`HasStatusBar` *(optional)*

A `Boolean` value determining whether the `Window` has a status bar.

`true`

The `Window` has a status bar.

`false`

The `Window` has no status bar. This is the default.

`Left` *(optional)*

An `Integer` value that describes the location of the left edge of the window in logical units (1/96").

`ResizeMode` *(optional)*

Determines how, if at all, the user can resize the `Window`.

`CanMinimize`

The user can only minimize the window and restore it from the task bar. Only the minimize box is enabled, even though the maximize box is shown.

`CanResize`

The user can resize the window.

`CanResizeWithGrip`

The user can resize the window, and a resize grip is displayed in the window's lower-right corner.

`NoResize`

The user cannot resize the window. The maximize and minimize boxes are not displayed.

`ShowInTaskbar` *(optional)*

A `Boolean` value that determines whether the window shows up in the task bar.

`true`

The window shows up in the task bar and can be accessed through Alt-Tab.

`false`

The window does not show up in the task bar.

`StatusBarContent` *(optional)*

The content shown in the status bar. This attribute is meaningless if `HasStatusBar` is set to `false`.

`Text` *(optional)*

The title of the `Window`.

`Top` *(optional)*

An `Integer` value that describes the location of the top edge of the window in logical units (1/96").

`Topmost` *(optional)*

A `Boolean` value determining whether this window should be on top at all times.

`true`

The window always appears on top.

`false`

The window behaves normally.

`WindowState` *(optional)*
: Determines the initial state of the window.

  `Maximized`
  : The `Window` starts maximized.

  `Minimized`
  : The `Window` starts minimized.

  `Normal`
  : The `Window` starts at its specified dimensions.

`WindowStyle` *(optional)*
: Determines the core style for the `Window`.

  `None`
  : The `Window` has no border or caption.

  `SingleBorderWindow`
  : The `Window` will have a single border. This is the default.

  `ThreeDBorderWindow`
  : The `Window` will have a 3-D border.

  `ToolWindow`
  : The `Window` will appear as a fixed-tool window.

9
Shapes and Geometry

Shape and Geometry are both used to render 2-D objects. While the two have much in common, there are important differences between the two sets of drawing objects. The most important is that instances of Geometry cannot draw themselves; they must be drawn by another class. There are other differences, but the easiest way to differentiate the two is to remember that Geometry is used to describe a region and Shape determines how that region is drawn and filled. Because Shapes are UI elements, they can be used inside panels and most controls. Geometry elements cannot.

Geometry elements are also used to define clipping regions. A *clipping region* defines the visible area of another element, such as an Image. For example, if you have a large image but only want to display part of it, you could use a Geometry element to clip it. You could also use Geometry elements to clip the image to simulate a frame, as Example 9-1 and Figure 9-1 illustrate.

Example 9-1. Clipping an image with EllipseGeometry

```
<StackPanel
    xmlns="http://schemas.microsoft.com/winfx/avalon/2005"
    Margin="20">
    <Image
        Source="c:\image.jpg"
        HorizontalAlignment="Left">
        <Image.Clip>
            <EllipseGeometry
                RadiusX="100"
                RadiusY="75"
                Center="100,75"/>
        </Image.Clip>
    </Image>
</StackPanel>
```

Figure 9-1. Using EllipseGeometry to clip an image

Geometries are categorized as either simple or path. A *simple* geometry is used to describe basic geometric shapes, such as line, ellipse, and rectangle. *Path* geometry describes more complex geometric figures, such as ones created by tracing a path.

Although shapes are most commonly drawn on a `Canvas`, they may be used with any `Panel` or control that supports non-text elements. This chapter details the shapes and geometry available for use in XAML.

All shapes derive from the base class `Shape` and therefore share a common set of attributes, which is detailed in Table 9-1.

Table 9-1. Attributes common to all Shape elements

Property name	Data type	Purpose
`Fill`	`Brush`	Describes how the shape's interior is filled. The default is `null`. A list of pre-defined `Brush` colors is in Appendix G.
`StrokeDashArray`	`DoubleCollection`	Describes the series of dashes and gaps used to outline the shape. Each `Double` in the collection specifies the length of a dash or gap relative to the thickness of the pen. For example, a value of 1 creates a dash or gap with the same length as the thickness of the pen (a square). The first item in the collection, located at index 0, specifies the length of a dash; the second item, located at index 1, specifies the length of a gap; and so on. Objects with an even index value specify dashes, and objects with an odd index value specify gaps.

Table 9-1. Attributes common to all Shape elements (continued)

Property name	Data type	Purpose

StrokeDashCap	Enumeration	Describes how the ends of a dash are drawn. Must be one of the following:
		`Flat`
		No line cap.
		`Round`
		The line is capped with a semicircle equal in diameter to the line thickness.
		`Square`
		The line is capped with a square whose sides are equal in length to the line thickness.
		`Triangle`
		The line is capped with a triangle equal in height to the line thickness.
		The default is `Flat`.

StrokeDashOffset	Double	Describes the distance in the dash pattern at which the dash will start.

StrokeEndLineCap	Enumeration	Describes the shape used at the end of the element's stroke. Must be one of the following:
		`Flat`
		No line cap.
		`Round`
		The line is capped with a semicircle equal in diameter to the line thickness.
		`Square`
		The line is capped with a square whose sides are equal in length to the line thickness.
		`Triangle`
		The line is capped with a triangle equal in height to the line thickness.
		The default is `Flat`.

StrokeLineJoin	Enumeration	Sets the type of joint used at the vertices of a shape's outline. Must be one of the following:
		`Bevel`
		Beveled vertices
		`Miter`
		Regular angular vertices
		`Round`
		Rounded vertices

StrokeMiterLimit	Double	Specifies a limit on the ratio of the miter length to the `StrokeThickness` of a `Shape` element. The value is always greater than or equal to 1.
Stroke	Brush	Describes how the outline of the shape will be drawn. The default is `null`.

Table 9-1. Attributes common to all Shape elements (continued)

Property name	Data type	Purpose

`StrokeStartLineCap`	`Enumeration`	Describes the shape used to draw the start of a line. Must be one of:
		`Flat`
		No line cap.
		`Round`
		The line is capped with a semicircle equal in diameter to the line thickness.
		`Square`
		The line is capped with a square whose sides are equal in length to the line thickness.
		`Triangle`
		The line is capped with a triangle equal in height to the line thickness.
		The default is `Flat`.

`StrokeThickness`	`Double`	Sets the width of the shape's outline.
`Height`	`Double`	Describes the height of the element.
`Width`	`Double`	Describes the width of the element.

Most `Shape` and `Geometry` elements use instances of the structure `Point`, which is detailed in this chapter.

ArcSegment

Type: Geometry

Hierarchy: Freezable → Animatable → PathSegment

```
<ArcSegment
    LargeArc="true|false"
    Point="5,5"
    Size="10,10"
    SweepFlag="true|false"
    XRotation="45" />
```

or:

```
<ArcSegment
    LargeArc="true|false"
    Size="10,10"
    SweepFlag="true|false"
    XRotation="45">
    <ArcSegment.Point>
        <Point X="5" Y="5" />
    </ArcSegment.Point>
</ArcSegment>
```

`<ArcSegment .../>` should be a child of `PathFigure`. It represents an elliptical arc between two instances of `Point` (Figure 9-2). `ArcSegment` does not contain its start point location because the start point is assumed to be the current `Point` of the parent `PathFigure`.

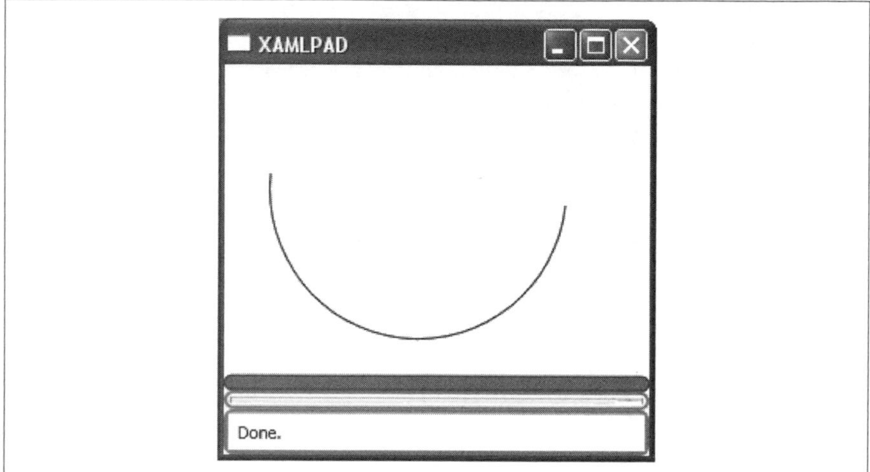

Figure 9-2. ArcSegment

Attributes

`LargeArc` *(optional)*

This `Boolean` value determines whether the arc should be drawn with an angle of 180 degrees or greater.

`true`

The arc will be drawn with an angle greater than 180 degrees.

`false`

The arc will be drawn with an angle less than 180 degrees.

`Point` *(required)*

This attribute describes the end point of the arc. This attribute can be described as a `Point` either explicitly or using abbreviated markup syntax.

`Size` *(required)*

This attribute describes the x- and y-radius of the arc as a `Size`.

`SweepFlag` *(optional)*

This `Boolean` value determines whether the angle of the arc is drawn in a positive-angle or negative-angle direction.

`true`

The angle is drawn in a positive-angle direction.

`false`

The angle is drawn in a negative-angle direction.

`XRotation` *(optional)*

This `Double` value indicates how the arc should be rotated relative to the current coordinate system.

BezierSegment

Type: Geometry

Hierarchy: Freezable → Animatable → PathSegment

```
<BezierSegment
    Point1="1,1"
```

```
    Point2="150,50"
    Point3="140,10" />
```

<BezierSegment .../> describes a Bezier curve between two points. Like ArcSegment, BezierSegment must be the child of a PathFigure. Point1 affects the beginning segment of the curve, while Point2 affects the ending segment of the curve. Control points act like magnets, pulling the curve toward them. Figure 9-3 shows the BezierSegment described above.

Figure 9-3. BezierSegment

Attributes

Point1 *(required)*
: Describes the first control point on the curve

Point2 *(required)*
: Describes the second control point on the curve

Point3 *(required)*
: Describes the end point of the curve

CloseSegment

Type: Geometry

Hierarchy: Freezable → Animatable → PathSegment

```
<CloseSegment />
```

<CloseSegment .../> represents the final line of a PathFigure, which joins the figure's last Point to its first Point.

CombinedGeometry

Type: Geometry

Hierarchy: Freezable → Animatable → Geometry

```
<CombinedGeometry
    CombineMode="Union|Xor|Exclude|Intersect" />
```

<CombinedGeometry .../> combines two Geometry elements as specified by the CombineMode attribute.

Attributes

CombineMode *(optional)*

Determines how the two child Geometry elements will be combined

Exclude

The two regions described by the child elements will be combined by excluding the area in the second geometry from the area in the first geometry. The result is Geometry A – Geometry B.

Intersect

The two regions described by the child elements will be combined by taking the area that exists in both regions. This is the opposite of Xor mode. The result is (Geometry A – Geometry B) – ((Geometry B – Geometry A) + (Geometry A – Geometry B)).

Union

The two regions described by the child elements will be combined by including the union of both regions. The result is Geometry A + Geometry B.

Xor

The two regions described by the child elements will be combined by including the area that exists in the first region but not the second and the area that exists in the second region but not the first. The result is (Geometry A – Geometry B) + (Geometry B – Geometry A). This is the opposite of the Intersect mode.

DrawingBrush

Hierarchy: Freezeable → Animatable → Brush → TileBrush

```
<DrawingBrush>
    <Drawing>
    </Drawing>
</DrawingBrush>
```

<DrawingBrush .../> paints an area with a Drawing. It derives from TileBrush.

Attributes

Drawing *(optional)*

A collection of elements to be drawn. It can comprise images, shapes, video, text, and other instances of Drawing. The default value is null.

DrawingGroup

Hierarchy: Freezable → Animatable → Drawing

```
<DrawingGroup>
    <Drawing .../>
    <Drawing .../>
</DrawingGroup>
```

<DrawingGroup .../> comprises one or more Drawing elements that are drawn as a group.

Ellipse

Type: Shape

Hierarchy: UIElement → FrameworkElement → Shape

```
<Ellipse
    Height="50"
    Width="100" />
```

<Ellipse ...> is used to draw ellipses and circles on a Canvas. The radii of an ellipse are specified using the Height and Width properties. Using equivalent Height/Width combinations will result in a circle. Figure 9-4 shows an example of an Ellipse with a longer width (x-radius) than height (y-radius).

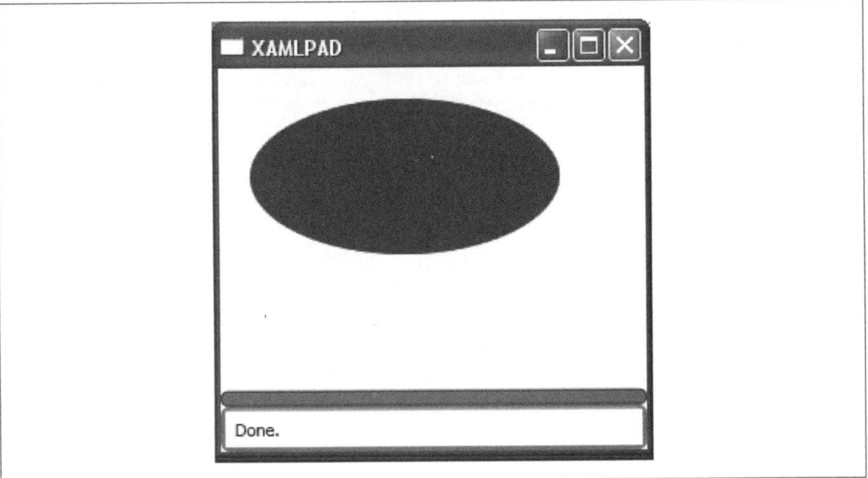

Figure 9-4. Ellipse

EllipseGeometry

Type: Simple Geometry

Hierarchy: Freezable → Animatable → Geometry

```
<EllipseGeometry
    Center="50,50"
    RadiusX="20"
    RadiusY="20" />
```

or:

```
<EllipseGeometry
    RadiusX="20"
    RadiusY="20">
    <EllipseGeometry.Center>
        <Point
            X="50"
            Y="50" />
    </EllipseGeometry.Center>
</EllipseGeometry>
```

<EllipseGeometry ...> represents the geometry of an ellipse or a circle. The Center attribute can be specified either as inline markup or by declaring a Point. A circle can be defined with equivalent values in RadiusX and RadiusY (Figure 9-5).

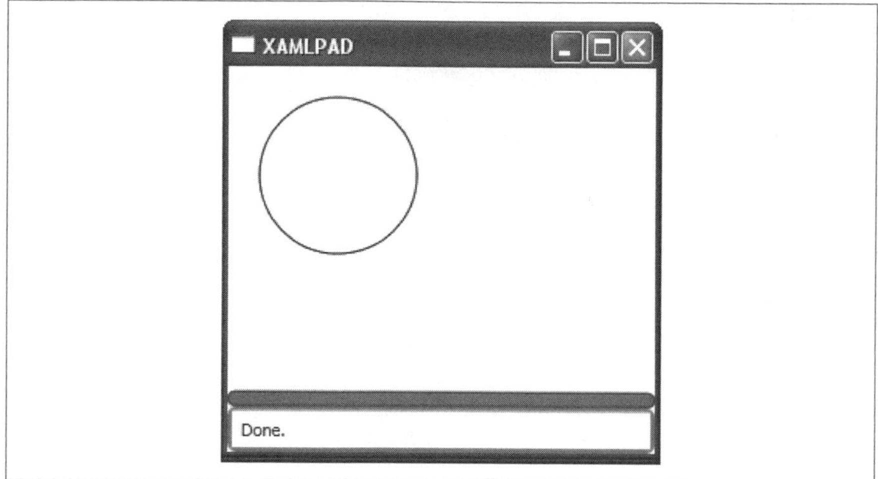

Figure 9-5. Drawing a circle with EllipseGeometry

Attributes

`Center` *(required)*
: Describes the center of the ellipse using inline markup as a comma-separated x-, y-coordinate pair or by explicitly declaring a `Point` element

`RadiusX` *(required)*
: A `Double` value representing the x-radius of the ellipse

`RadiusY` *(required)*
: A `Double` value representing the y-radius of the ellipse

GeometryDrawing

Hierarchy: Freezable → Animatable → Drawing

```
<GeometryDrawing
    Brush="Blue"
    <GeometryDrawing.Pen>
        <Pen Thickness="1" Brush="Black" />
    </GeometryDrawing.Pen>
    <GeometryDrawing.Geometry>
        <GeometryGroup>
            <EllipseGeometry RadiusX="0.2" RadiusY="0.45" Center="0.5,0.5" />
            <EllipseGeometry RadiusX="0.45" RadiusY="0.2" Center="0.5,0.5" />
        </GeometryGroup>
    </GeometryDrawing.Geometry>
</GeometryDrawing>
```

`<GeometryDrawing .../>` draws a `Geometry` with the specified `Brush` and `Pen`.

Attributes

`Brush` *(optional)*
: Specifies the `Brush` used to paint the `Geometry`.

`Pen` *(optional)*
: Specifies the `Pen` used to outline the `Geometry`.

`Geometry` *(required)*
: Specifies the `Geometry` to be drawn. This attribute may be a single `Geometry` or a `GeometryGroup`.

GeometryGroup

Hierarchy: Freezable → Animatable → Geometry

```
<GeometryGroup>
    <LineGeometry StartPoint="50,50" EndPoint="100,100" />
    <EllipseGeometry Center="40,80" RadiusX="20" RadiusY="20" />
    <RectangleGeometry Rect="20,20 100 50" />
</GeometryGroup>
```

`<GeometryGroup .../>` describes a group of geometric shapes used to render a `Path` or that will be drawn by a `GeometryDrawing`. `GeometryGroup` is a container for one or more geometries.

Attributes

`Children` *(required)*
: A collection of `Geometry` elements. This attribute is generally not set directly but is created by adding nested instances of varying `Geometry` elements.

ImageDrawing

Hierarchy: Freezable → Animatable → Drawing

```
<ImageDrawing
    ImageSource="c:\\r.gif"
    Rect="0,0 50 50" />
```

`<ImageDrawing .../>` draws an image in the region specified by `Rect`.

Attributes

`ImageSource` *(optional)*
: The source of the image used for the drawing

`Rect` *(optional)*
: The dimensions of the drawing area in terms of top-left corner, width, and height

Line

Type: Shape

Hierarchy: UIElement → FrameworkElement → Shape → StretchableShape

```
<Line
    X1="10"
    Y1="10"
    X2="50"
    Y2="50"
```

```
        Stroke="Red"
        StrokeThickness="2" />
```

<Line .../> represents a geometric line drawn between two distinct points (Figure 9-6). If you do not specify a Stroke, the line will not be visible to the end user.

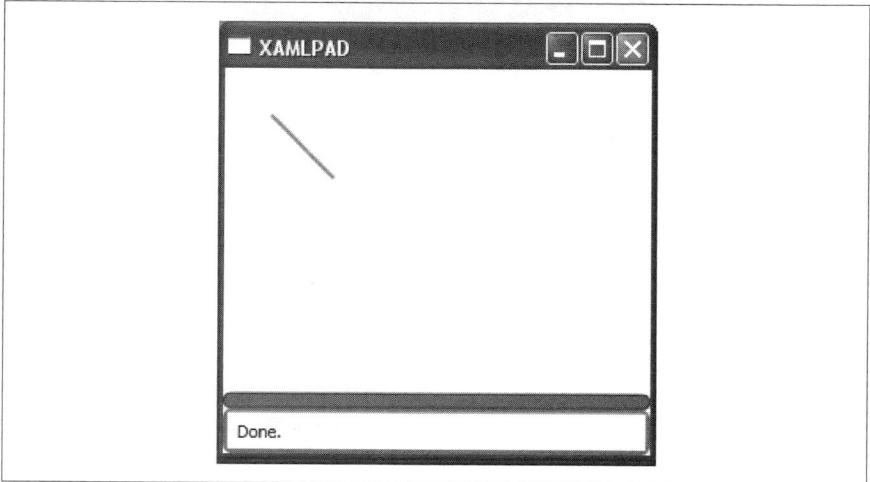

Figure 9-6. Line

Attributes

X1 *(required)*
: A Double value representing the x-coordinate of the start point

X2 *(required)*
: A Double value representing the x-coordinate of the end point

Y1 *(required)*
: A Double value representing the y-coordinate of the start point

Y2 *(required)*
: A Double value representing the y-coordinate of the end point

LineGeometry

Type: Simple Geometry

Hierarchy: Freezable → Animatable → Geometry

```
<LineGeometry
    StartPoint="50,50"
    EndPoint="100,100" />
```

or:

```
<LineGeometry>
    <LineGeometry.StartPoint>
        <Point X="50" Y="50" />
    </LineGeometry.StartPoint>
    <LineGeometry.EndPoint>
        <Point X="100" Y="100" />
    </LineGeometry.EndPoint>
</LineGeometry>
```

`<LineGeometry .../>` represents the geometry of a line (Figure 9-7). The `StartPoint` and `EndPoint` properties can be specified either as inline markup or by declaring `Point` elements.

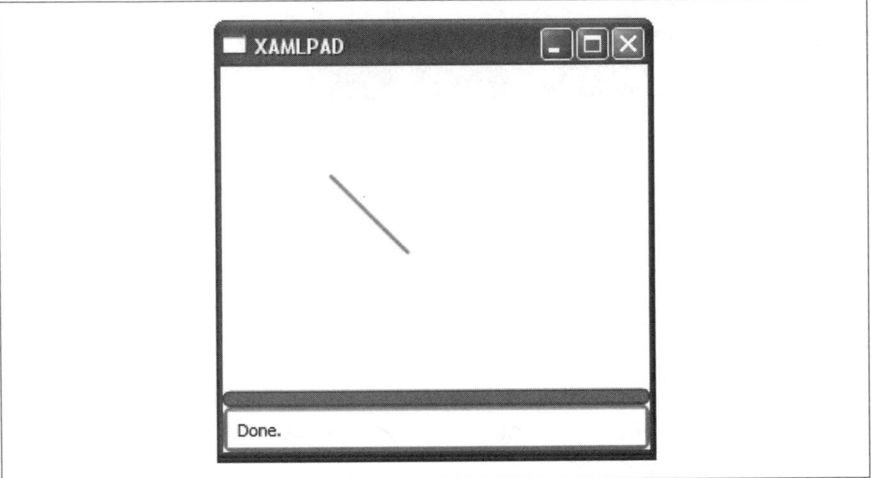

Figure 9-7. LineGeometry

Attributes

`EndPoint` *(required)*
: Describes the end point of the line using inline markup as a comma-separated x-, y-coordinate pair or by explicitly declaring a `Point` element

`StartPoint` *(required)*
: Describes the starting point of the line using inline markup as a comma-separated x-, y-coordinate pair or by explicitly declaring a `Point` element

LineSegment

Type: Path Geometry

Hierarchy: Freezable → Animatable → PathSegment

```
<LineSegment
    Point="5,5" />
```

or:

```
<LineSegment>
    <LineSegment.Point>
        <Point X="5" Y="5" />
    </LineSegment.Point>
</LineSegment>
```

`<LineSegment .../>` represents a line between two instances of `Point` (Figure 9-8). It must be contained within a `PathFigure`. `LineSegment` describes the end point, assuming that the start point is the last point added before the `LineSegment` in the `PathFigure`.

Attributes

`Point` *(required)*
: Describes the end point of the line segment

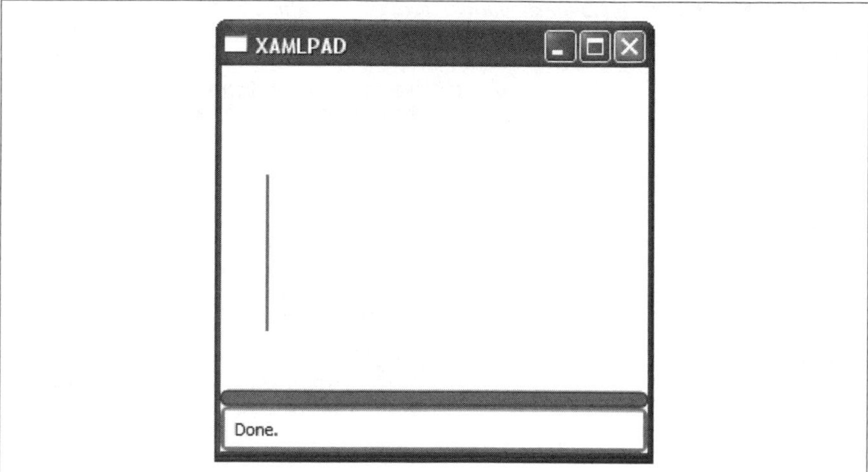

Figure 9-8. LineSegment

Path

Hierarchy: UIElement → FrameworkElement → Shape → StretchableShape

```
<Path
    Stroke="Black"
    Data="M 100 100 L 300 100 L 200 300 z"></Path>
```

or:

```
<Path
    Stroke="Black">
    <Path.Data>
        <GeometryGroup>
            <LineGeometry StartPoint="100,100" EndPoint="300,100"/>
            <LineGeometry StartPoint="300,100" EndPoint="200,300"/>
            <LineGeometry StartPoint="200,300" EndPoint="100,100"/>
        </GeometryGroup>
    </Path.Data>
</Path>
```

`<Path .../>` is used to draw a series of lines and curves. `Path` can use abbreviated inline markup commands (described in Table 9-2) to designate the geometry used when drawing the path, or the geometry can be explicitly declared using a `GeometryGroup`.

Table 9-2. Abbreviated syntax for subpath declarations

Command	Syntax	Description
`Move`	M x,y or m x,y	Establishes a new current point. Each path segment must begin with a move command; subsequent move commands indicate the start of a new subpath.
`Line`	L x,y or l x,y	Draws a straight line from the current point to the specified point.

Shapes and Geometry

Table 9-2. Abbreviated syntax for subpath declarations (continued)

Command	Syntax	Description
`Horizontal Line`	H x or h x	Draws a horizontal line from the current point to the specified x-coordinate.
`Vertical Line`	V y or v y	Draws a vertical line from the current point to the specified y-coordinate.
`Cubic Bezier Curve`	C x1,y1 x2,y2 x3,y3 or c x1,y1 x2,y2 x3,y3	Draws a cubic Bezier curve from the current point to the specified point (x3,y3) using the two specified control points (x1,y1 and x2,y2). The first control point determines the beginning of the curve, and the second control point determines the end of the curve.
`Quadratic Bezier Curve`	Q x1,y1 x2,y2 or q x1,y1 x2,y2	Draws a quadratic Bezier curve from the current point to the specified point (x2,y2) using the specified control point (x1,y1).
`Smooth Cubic Bezier Curve`	S x1,y1 x2,y2 or s x1,y1 x2,y2	Draws a cubic Bezier curve from the current point to the specified point (x2,y2). The first control point is assumed to be the reflection (relative to the current point) of the previous command's second control point. If there is no previous command or if the previous command was neither a cubic Bezier curve command nor a smooth cubic Bezier curve command, assume the first control point coincides with the current point. The second control point—the control point for the end of the curve—is specified by x1,y1.
`Elliptical Arc`	A xr,yr rx flag1 flag2 x,y or a xr,yr rx flag1 flag2 x,y	Draws an elliptical arc from the current point to the specified point (x,y). The size and orientation of the ellipse are defined by xr, yr, and rx. xr defines the x-radius, yr defines the y-radius, and rx defines the x-axis rotation in degrees, which indicates how the ellipse is rotated relative to the current coordinate system. The center of the ellipse is calculated automatically. In most situations, four different arcs satisfy the specified constraints; flag1 and flag2 indicate which arc to use. Of the four candidate arc sweeps, two represent large arcs with sweeps of 180 degrees or greater, and two represent smaller arcs with sweeps of 180 degrees or less. If flag1 is 1, one of the two larger arc sweeps is chosen; if flag1 is 0, one of the smaller arc sweeps is chosen. If flag2 is 1, the arc is drawn in a positive-angle direction. If flag2 is 0, the arc is drawn in a negative-angle direction.
`Close Path`	Z or z	Ends the current subpath and draws a straight line from the current point to the initial point of the current subpath. If a `Move` command (an M or an m) follows the `Close Path` command, the `Move` command identifies the next subpath's start point. Otherwise, the next subpath starts at the same initial point as the current subpath.

Attributes

Data *(required)*

Describes the path to be drawn. In XAML, Data can be declared either by declaring instances of specific Geometry types or by using abbreviated syntax to describe subpaths.

PathFigure

Hierarchy: Freezable → Animatable

```
<PathFigure
    IsFilled="true|false">
    <PathFigure.Segments>
        <PathSegmentCollection />
    </PathFigure.Segments>
</PathFigure>
```

<PathFigure .../> represents a single interconnected series of 2-D figures. Example 9-2 shows a PathFigure that combines multiple segments to form the 2-D figure in Figure 9-9. The starting point of each segment element is the last point of the previous segment.

Example 9-2. A PathFigure

```
<StackPanel
    xmlns="http://schemas.microsoft.com/winfx/avalon/2005"
    Margin="20">
    <Path Stroke="Black" StrokeThickness="1">
    <Path.Data>
        <PathGeometry>
          <PathGeometry.Figures>
            <PathFigureCollection>
              <PathFigure>
                <PathFigure.Segments>
                  <PathSegmentCollection>
                     <StartSegment Point="10,50" />
                     <LineSegment Point="10,150"/>
                     <BezierSegment Point1="20,20" Point2="30,30" Point3="40,40" />
                     <LineSegment Point="50,50" />
                     <ArcSegment Size="40,50" XRotation="50" />
                  </PathSegmentCollection>
                </PathFigure.Segments>
              </PathFigure>
            </PathFigureCollection>
          </PathGeometry.Figures>
        </PathGeometry>
    </Path.Data>
</Path>
</StackPanel>
```

Shapes and Geometry

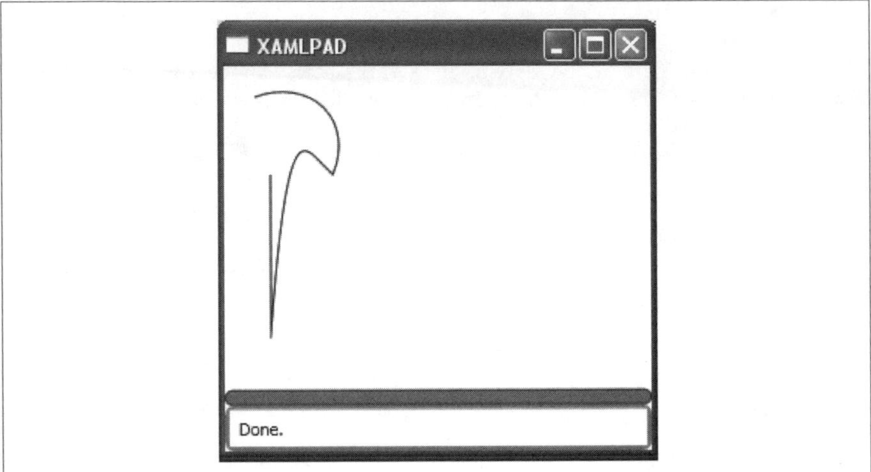

Figure 9-9. PathFigure

Attributes

`IsFilled` *(optional)*

This `Boolean` determines whether the region contained by the `PathFigure` should be used for rendering, hit-testing, and clipping.

`true`
: The region will be used.

`false`
: The region will not be used; only the outline of the `PathFigure` will be considered.

`Segments` *(required)*

This attribute describes a `PathSegmentCollection`.

PathFigureCollection

Hierarchy: Freezable → Animatable

```
<PathFigureCollection>
    <PathFigure ... />
    ...
    <PathFigure ... />
</PathFigureCollection>
```

`<PathFigureCollection .../>` is a container for one or more instances of `PathFigure`.

PathGeometry

Hierarchy: Freezable → Animatable → Geometry

```
<PathGeometry FillRule="NonZero|EvenOdd" >
    <PathGeometry.Figures>
        <PathFigureCollection>
            <PathFigure>
                <PathFigure.Segments>
```

```
                <PathSegmentCollection>
                </PathSegmentCollection>
            </PathFigure.Segments>
        </PathFigure>
    </PathFigureCollection>
  </PathGeometry.Figures>
</PathGeometry>
```

<PathGeometry .../> describes a series of connected ellipses, arcs, line segments, curves, and rectangles.

Attributes

Figures *(optional)*
: A PathFigureCollection

FillRule *(optional)*
: Describes the rule used to determine if a Point is inside the shape and should therefore be painted according to the Fill attribute value

  EvenOdd
  : After the Point is examined, a ray is drawn from it to infinity in any direction. If the number of path segments the ray crosses is even, the Point is outside the shape. If the number of path segments the ray crosses is odd, the Point is inside the shape and is painted according to the Fill attribute value.

  NonZero
  : After the Point is examined, a ray is drawn from it to infinity in any direction. Starting from zero, the count increases by one every time a path segment crosses the ray from left to right and decreases by one every time a path segment crosses the ray from right to left. If the resulting value is 0, then the Point is outside the shape; otherwise, it is inside the shape and will be painted accordingly.

PathSegmentCollection

Hierarchy: Freezable → Animatable

```
<PathSegmentCollection>
    ...
</PathSegmentCollection>
```

<PathSegmentCollection .../> is a container for segments. It may contain LineSegment, EllipseSegment, BezierSegment, PolyBezierSegment, PolyQuadraticBezierSegment, QuadraticBezierSegment, StartSegment, or CloseSegment.

Point

Point is a structure and has no class hierarchy.

```
<Point X="50" Y="100" />
```

<Point .../> describes a point in x- and y-coordinates. Point is used primarily to describe more complex shapes such as Polygon and Polyline.

Point is often declared through the use of abbreviated markup syntax. Wherever an attribute is specified as a Point, it can be declared as a comma-separated pair of Double values representing the x-coordinate and the y-coordinate, respectively:

```
<Element SomePointAttribute="0,0" />
```

Attributes

X *(required)*
: A Double value representing the x-coordinate of the point

Y *(required)*
: A Double value representing the y-coordinate of the point

Point3D

Point3D is a structure and has no class hierarchy.

```
<Point X="50" Y="100" Z="50" />
```

<Point3D .../> describes a point in x-, y-, and z-coordinates. Point3D is used primarily to describe more complex 3-D shapes.

Point3D is often declared through the use of abbreviated markup syntax. Wherever an attribute is specified as a Point, it can be declared as a comma-separated triplet of Double values representing the x-coordinate, y-coordinate, and z-coordinate, respectively:

```
<Element SomePoint3DAttribute="0,0,0" />
```

Attributes

X *(required)*
: A Double value representing the x-coordinate of the point

Y *(required)*
: A Double value representing the y-coordinate of the point

Z *(required)*
: A Double value representing the z-coordinate of the point

PointCollection

Hierarchy: Freezable

```
<PointCollection>
...
</PointCollection>
```

<PointCollection .../> is a container for Point.

PolyBezierSegment

Type: Path Geometry

Hierarchy: Freezable → Animatable → PathSegment

```
<PolyBezierSegment>
    <PolyBezierSegment.Points>
        <PointCollection>
       ...
        </PointCollection>
    </PolyBezierSegment.Points>
</PolyBezierSegment>
```

or:

```
<PolyBezierSegment
    Points="10,100 50,110 100,200" />
```

<PolyBezierSegment .../> represents a series of Bezier lines (Figure 9-10).

Figure 9-10. PolyBezierSegment

Attributes

Points *(optional)*

An ordered PointCollection

Polygon

Type: Shape

Hierarchy: UIElement → FrameworkElement → Shape → StretchableShape

```
<Polygon
    Points="10,110 60,10 110,110"
    Fill="Red"
    FillRule="EvenOdd|NonZero" />
```

or:

```
<Polygon
   Fill="Red"
   FillRule="EvenOdd|NonZero" >
   <Polygon.Points>
      <Point X="10" Y="110" />
      <Point X="60" Y="10" />
      <Point X="110" Y="110" />
   </Polygon.Points>
</Polygon>
```

<Polygon .../> draws a series of connected lines as a closed shape (Figure 9-11). If you do not specify a value for the Fill attribute, the shape will be filled with the default color, Transparent.

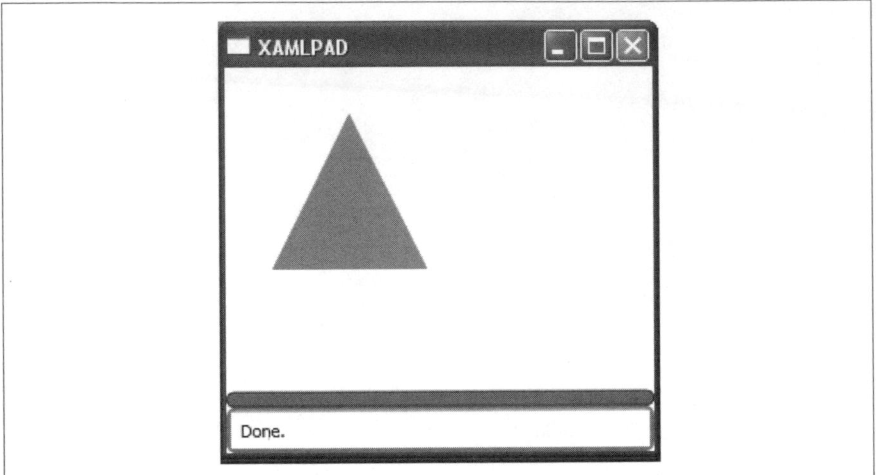

Figure 9-11. Polygon

Attributes

`FillRule` *(optional)*

Describes the rule used to determine if a `Point` is inside the shape and should therefore be painted according to the `Fill` attribute value.

`EvenOdd`

After the `Point` is examined, a ray is drawn from it to infinity in any direction. If the number of path segments the ray crosses is even, the `Point` is outside the shape. If the number of path segments the ray crosses is odd, the `Point` is inside the shape and is painted according to the `Fill` attribute value.

`NonZero`

After the `Point` is examined, a ray is drawn from the point to infinity in any direction. Starting from zero, the count increases by one every time a path segment crosses the ray from left to right and decreases by one every time a path segment crosses the ray from right to left. If the resulting value is 0, then the `Point` is outside the shape; otherwise, it is inside the shape and will be painted accordingly.

`Points` *(required)*

A series of points describing the vertices of the `Polygon`. In XAML, `Points` can be described as a space-delimited list of comma-separated x- and y-coordinate pairs using inline markup or as a series of `Point` elements.

Polyline — Type: Shape

Hierarchy: UIElement → FrameworkElement → Shape → StretchableShape

```
<Polyline
    Points="10,100 50,10 100,150"
    Stroke="Black"
    StrokeThickness="4" />
```

or:

```
<Polyline
    Stroke="Black"
    StrokeThickness="4">
    <Polyline.Points>
        <Point X="10" Y="100" />
        <Point X="50" Y="10" />
        <Point X="100" Y="50" />
    </Polyline.Points>
</Polyline>
```

`<Polyline .../>` draws a series of connected lines (Figure 9-12). Because `Polyline` is not a closed shape, the `Fill` attribute has no effect, even if you close the shape. To draw a closed series of lines you can fill, use the `Polygon` shape.

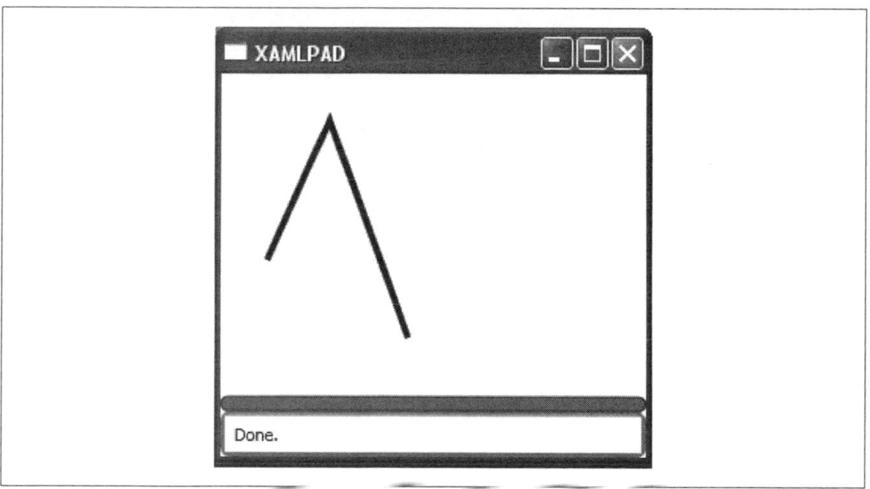

Figure 9-12. Polyline

Attributes

`Points` *(required)*

A series of points describing the vertices of the `Polyline`. `Points` can be described in XAML as a space-delimited list of comma-separated x- and y-coordinate pairs as inline markup or as a series of `Point` elements.

PolyLineSegment

Type: Path Geometry

Hierarchy: Freezable → Animatable → PathSegment

```
<PolyLineSegment>
    <PolyLineSegment.Points>
        <PointCollection>
        </PointCollection>
    </PolyLineSegment.Points>
</PolyLineSegment>
```

`<PolyLineSegment .../>` describes a `Polyline` comprised of an ordered list of `Points`, each of which represents the end point in a `LineTo` operation (Figure 9-13).

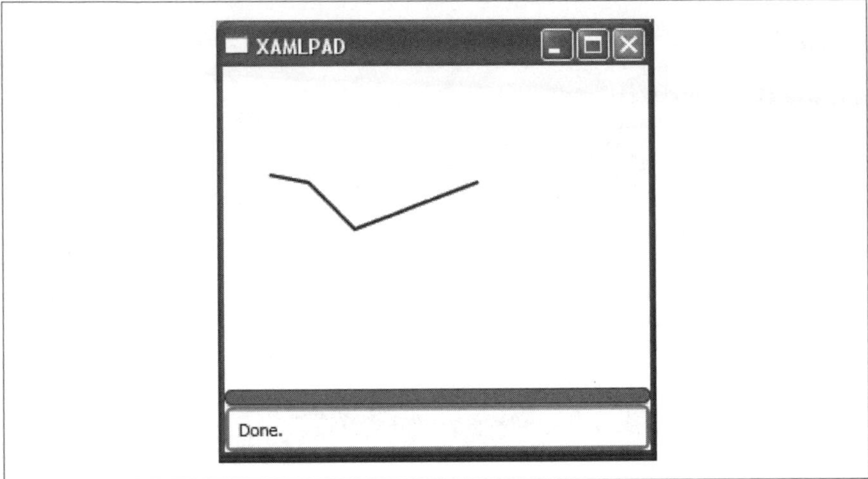

Figure 9-13. PolyLineSegment

Attributes

`Points` *(optional)*
: A `PointCollection` comprising an ordered collection of `Point` elements

PolyQuadraticBezierSegment

Type: Path Geometry

Hierarchy: Freezable → Animatable → PathSegment

```
<PolyQuadraticBezierSegment
    Points="10,10 50,50 100,100" />
```

or:

```
<PolyQuadraticBezierSegment>
    <PolyQuadraticBezierSegment.Points>
        <PointCollection>
        </PointCollection>
    </PolyQuadraticBezierSegment>
</PolyQuadraticBezierSegment>
```

`<PolyQuadraticBezierSegment .../>` defines a series of quadratic Bezier segments (Figure 9-14).

Attributes

`Points` *(optional)*
: A `PointCollection` containing the points used to generate the segment

QuadraticBezierSegment

Type: Path Geometry

Hierarchy: Freezable → Animatable → PathSegment

```
<QuadraticBezierSegment
    Point1="10,10"
    Point2="50,50" />
```

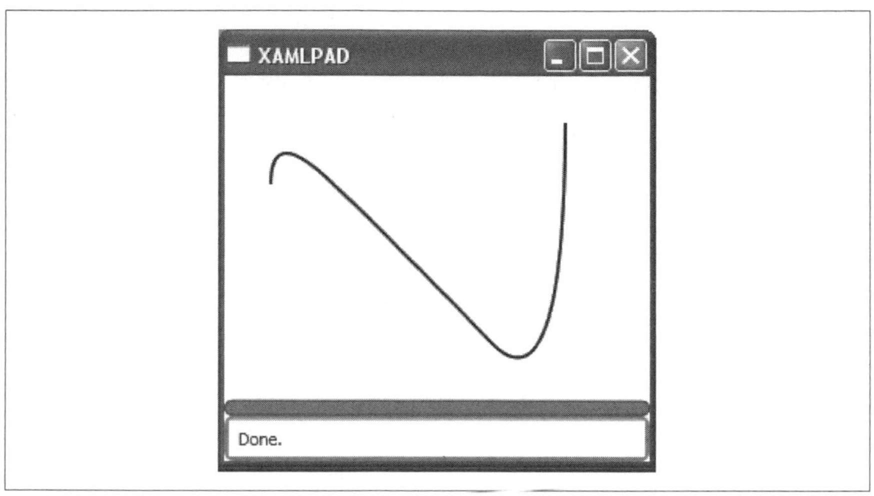

Figure 9-14. PolyQuadraticBezierSegment

or:

```
<QuadraticBezierSegment>
    <QuadraticBezierSegment.Point1>
        <Point X="10" Y="10" />
    </QuadraticBezierSegment.Point1>
    <QuadraticBezierSegment.Point2>
        <Point X="50" Y="50" />
    </QuadraticBezierSegment.Point2>
</QuadraticBezierSegment>
```

`<QuadraticBezierSegment .../>` draws a quadratic Bezier between two points (Figure 9-15).

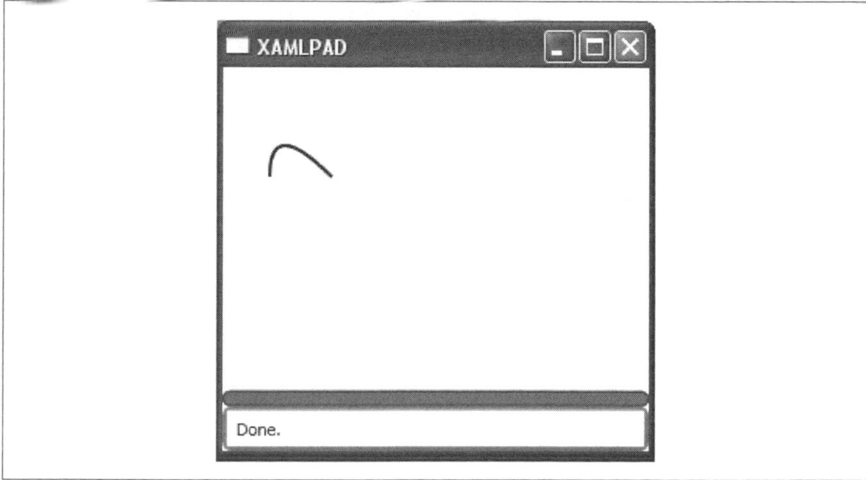

Figure 9-15. QuadraticBezierSegment

Attributes

`Point1` *(required)*
: The control point on the curve

`Point2` *(required)*
: The end point of the segment

Rect

Rect is a structure and has no class hierarchy.

```
<Rect
    Location="0,0"
    Width="100"
    Height="100" />
```

or:

```
<Rect
    X="0"
    Y="0"
    Width="100"
    Height="100" />
```

`<Rect .../>` represents a rectangle and is most commonly used in other elements to describe rectangular regions for hit-testing or filling a region. `Rect` is generally set through abbreviated markup syntax using a space-delimited list of parameters, beginning with the `Location` and followed by `Width` and `Height`:

```
<Element RectangleAttribute="0,0 100 100" />
```

Attributes

`Height` *(optional)*
: This `Double` value describes the height of the rectangle.

`Location` *(optional)*
: This `Point` describes the top-left corner of the rectangle. It can be described using abbreviated markup syntax or explicitly using the `X` and `Y` attributes.

`Width` *(optional)*
: This `Double` value describes the width of the rectangle.

`X` *(optional)*
: This `Double` value describes the x-coordinate of the top-left corner of the rectangle.

`Y` *(optional)*
: This `Double` value describes the y-coordinate of the top-left corner of the rectangle.

Rect3D

Rect3D is a structure and has no class hierarchy.

```
<Rect3D
    Location="0,0,0"
    Size="10 10 10"/>
```

or:

```
<Rect3D
    X="0"
    Y="0"
    Z="0"
    SizeX="10"
    SizeY="10"
    SizeZ="10" />
```

<Rect3D .../> represents a rectangle and is most commonly used in other elements to describe rectangular regions for hit-testing or filling a region.

Attributes

Location *(optional)*
: This Point3D describes the top-left corner of the rectangle. It can be described using abbreviated markup syntax or explicitly using the X, Y, and Z attributes.

SizeX *(optional)*
: This Double value describes the size of the rectangle in the x-dimension.

SizeY *(optional)*
: This Double value describes the size of the rectangle in the y-dimension.

SizeZ *(optional)*
: This Double value describes the size of the rectangle in the z-dimension.

X *(optional)*
: This Double value describes the x-coordinate of the top-left corner of the rectangle.

Y *(optional)*
: This Double value describes the y-coordinate of the top-left corner of the rectangle.

Z *(optional)*
: This Double value describes the z-coordinate of the top-left corner of the rectangle.

Rectangle

Type: Shape

Hierarchy: UIElement → FrameworkElement → Shape → StretchableShape

```
<Rectangle
    Fill="Blue"
    Height="50"
    Width="100"
    RadiusX="20"
    RadiusY="20" />
```

<Rectangle .../> draws a rectangle. The Width and Height properties inherited from FrameworkElement are necessary to describe the rectangle's geometry. Figure 9-16 shows the Rectangle defined above when evaluated in XamlPad.

Attributes

RadiusX *(optional)*
: Describes the x-radius of an ellipse used to round the Rectangle's corners

RadiusY *(optional)*
: Describes the y-radius of an ellipse used to round the Rectangle's corners

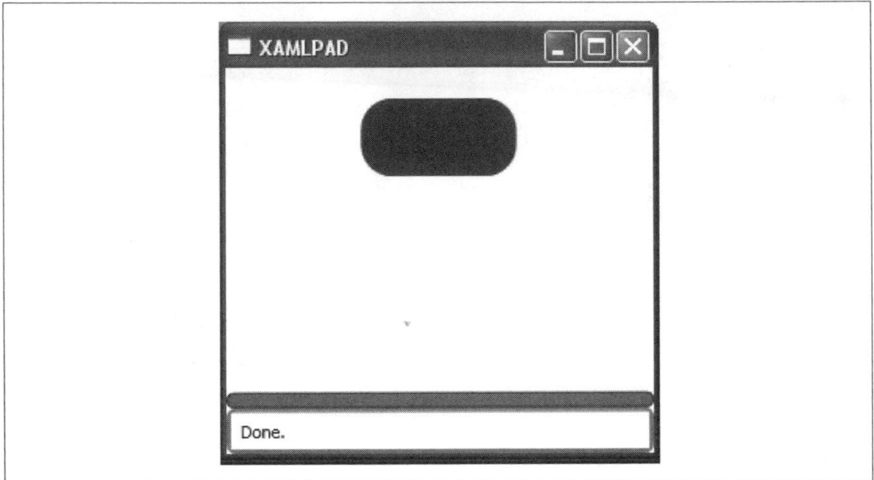

Figure 9-16. Rectangle

RectangleGeometry

Type: Simple Geometry

Hierarchy: Freezable → Animatable → Geometry

```
<RectangleGeometry
    Rect="50,50 100 50"
    RadiusX="20"
    RadiusY="20" />
```

`<RectangleGeometry .../>` represents the geometry of a rectangle. Figure 9-17 shows the result of evaluating the `RectangleGeometry` declared above in XamlPad.

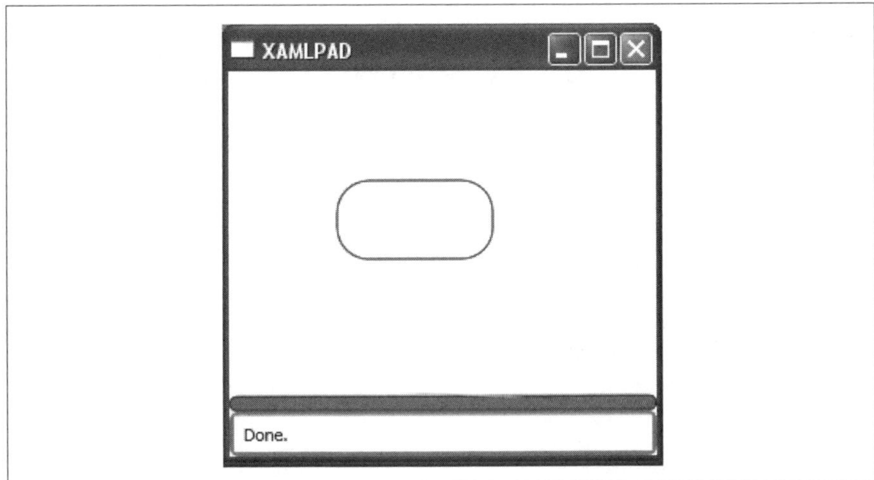

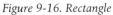

Figure 9-17. RectangleGeometry

Attributes

RadiusX *(optional)*
: Describes the x-radius of an ellipse that rounds the corners of the Rectangle described by the Rect attribute

RadiusY *(optional)*
: Describes the y-radius of an ellipse that rounds the corners of the Rectangle described by the Rect attribute

Rect *(required)*
: Describes the dimensions of the rectangle in terms of top-left corner, width, and height

StartSegment

Hierarchy: Freezable → Animatable → PathSegment

```
<StartSegment
    Point="10,10" />
```

or:

```
<StartSegment>
    <StartSegment.Point>
        <Point X="10" Y="10" />
    </StartSegment.Point>
</StartSegment>
```

<StartSegment ...> describes the start point for a PathFigure. Each PathFigure must begin with a StartSegment and cannot contain more than one.

Attributes

Point *(required)*
: The start Point of a path

10
Layout

The elements in this chapter are all used to position and decorate content on a page. Some elements are controls, such as `Grid` and `StackPanel`, while others are documents, such as `FixedDocument`. These elements have been grouped together because they are all focused on laying out the page, either by controlling the rendering and positioning of elements or by using it as a container of specific content types.

Border

Hierarchy: UIElement → FrameworkElement → Decorator

```
<Border
    Height="25"
    Background="White"
    BorderBrush="Black"
    BorderThickness="1"
    CornerRadius="20"
    Padding="2 2 2 2">
</Border>
```

`<Border .../>` draws a border, background, or both around an element (Figure 10-1). Only elements contained within a parent `Border` element can display a border.

`Border` can have only one child. To display multiple children, an additional `Panel` element needs to be placed within the parent `Border`. Child elements can then be placed within that `Panel` element.

Attributes

`Background` *(optional)*
: Describes the `Brush` used to fill the interior of the element.

`BorderBrush` *(optional)*
: Describes the `Brush` used to paint the border.

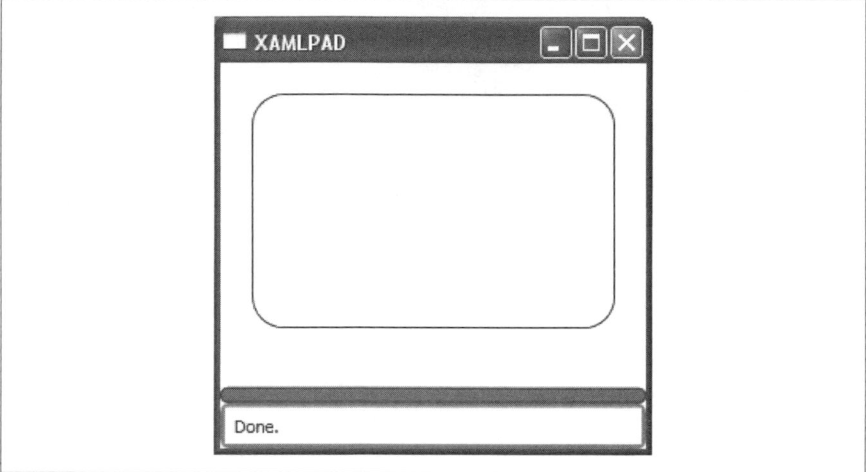

Figure 10-1. Border

`BorderThickness` *(optional)*
: Describes the thickness of the line used to draw the border. It is described in terms of `Left`, `Top`, `Right`, and `Bottom`, all of which are `Double` values representing a pixel value. It is most often described as a single value.

`CornerRadius` *(optional)*
: Describes the degree to which the corners of the `Border` are rounded. Though the name of the attribute implies a single value, non-uniform radii may be used.

`Padding` *(optional)*
: Describes how much the child element size is increased. It is described in terms of `Left`, `Top`, `Right`, and `Bottom`, all of which are `Double` values representing a pixel value.

Canvas

Hierarchy: UIElement → FrameworkElement → Panel

```
<Canvas />
```

`<Canvas .../>` allows content to be positioned according to absolute x- and y-coordinates. Elements are drawn in a unique location unless they occupy the same coordinates, in which case they're drawn in the order in which they appear in markup. The default `Height` and `Width` of a `Canvas` is 0, unless it has a parent that automatically sizes child elements.

`Canvas` has attached attributes, meaning they are used by child elements and defined as attributes of such. The following is an example of declaring the attached attributes of `Canvas` within a child element:

```
<Canvas>
    <TextBox
        Canvas.Top="20"
        Canvas.Left="20"
```

```
        Canvas.Right="20"
        Canvas.Bottom="20">My text
    </TextBox>
</Canvas>
```

Attached Attributes

`Canvas.Bottom` *(optional)*
: A `Double` value that describes the distance of the element from the bottom of the `Canvas`

`Canvas.Left` *(optional)*
: A `Double` value that describes the distance of the element from the left edge of the `Canvas`

`Canvas.Right` *(optional)*
: A `Double` value that describes the distance of the element from the right edge of the `Canvas`

`Canvas.Top` *(optional)*
: A `Double` value that describes the distance of the element from the top of the `Canvas`

ColumnDefinition

Hierarchy: DependencyObject → FrameworkContentElement → DefinitionBase

```
<ColumnDefinition
    MinWidth="20"
    MaxWidth="100"
    Width="50" />
```

`<ColumnDefinition .../>` defines column-specific properties in a `Grid`.

Attributes

`MinWidth` *(optional)*
: This `Double` value determines the minimum width of the column.

`MaxWidth` *(optional)*
: This `Double` value determines the maximum width of the column.

`Width` *(optional)*
: This `Double` value determines the initial width of the column.

DashStyle

Hierarchy: DependencyObject → Freezable → Animatable

```
<Element Dashes="2,3,2,5,2,3,2,5" />
```

`DashStyle` defines the series of dashes and gaps drawn by a `Pen` element. It is an array of `Double` elements interpreted as a pair of `dash`, `gap` values. The actual length of the dash or gap is determined by multiplying the declared size of the dash or gap by the `Pen`'s `Thickness`. `DashStyle` is rarely directly used; rather, it is used primarily to describe the `StrokeDashArray` attribute used by `Path` and other geometries when drawing `Path` elements.

Example 10-1 shows the use of a `DashStyle` when defining the `StrokeDashArray` attribute of a `Path`. This example (shown in Figure 10-2) draws a `Line` with a series of dashes of length 5*StrokeThickness (5*4), a gap of length 2*StrokeThickness (2*4), a dash of length 6*StrokeThickness (6*4), and so on, according to the StrokeDashArray attribute.

Example 10-1. Using DashStyle to describe a pattern for a line

```
<StackPanel
    xmlns="http://schemas.microsoft.com/winfx/avalon/2005"
    Margin="20">
    <Path
        Stroke="Blue"
        StrokeThickness="4"
        StrokeDashArray="5,2,6,2,7,2,6,2,5,2" />
        <Path.Data>
            <LineGeometry StartPoint="10,10" EndPoint="250,10" />
        </Path.Data>
    </Path>
</StackPanel>
```

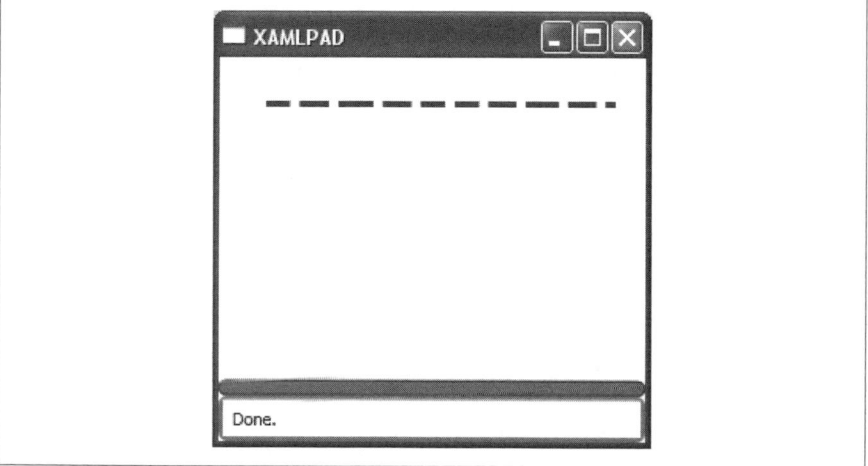

Figure 10-2. DashStyle

DockPanel

Hierarchy: UIElement → FrameworkElement → Panel

```
<DockPanel .../>
```

<DockPanel .../> uses the attached Dock attribute to position content along the edges of a container. When Dock is set to Top or Bottom, it stacks the child elements above or below each other. When Dock is set to Left or Right, it stacks the child elements to the left or right of each other. You can use DockPanel to position a group of related controls, such as a set of buttons.

As with the properties of Canvas, Dock is an attached attribute and is declared by child elements. The default value of Dock is Left. The following is an example of elements declaring the DockPanel.Dock attribute:

```
<DockPanel>
    <Button DockPanel.Dock="Top|Right|Bottom|Left" Content="Button 1" />
    <TextBox DockPanel.Dock="Top|Right|Bottom|Left" Content="This is my
content" />
</DockPanel>
```

Attached Attributes

DockPanel.Dock *(optional)*

Determines where a child element will be placed within the DockPanel

Bottom
: Element is positioned at the bottom of the DockPanel in the order in which it was declared.

Left
: Element is positioned at the left of the DockPanel in the order in which it was declared.

Right
: Element is positioned at the right of the DockPanel in the order in which it was declared.

Top
: Element is positioned at the top of the DockPanel in the order in which it was declared.

FixedDocument

Hierarchy: DependencyObject → FrameworkContentElement → Document

```
<FixedDocument
    xmlns="http://schemas.microsoft.com/metro/2005/02/rp"
    PageSize="8.5,11">
    <PageContent Source="FixedPage1.xaml"/>
    <PageContent Source="FixedPage2.xaml"/>
    <PageContent Source="FixedPage3.xaml"/>
</FixedDocument>
```

or:

```
<FixedDocument
    xmlns="http://schemas.microsoft.com/metro/2005/02/rp">
    <FixedDocument.PageSize>
        <Size Height="11" Width="8.5" />
    </FixedDocument.PageSize>
    <PageContent Source="FixedPage1.xaml"/>
</FixedDocument>
```

<FixedDocument .../> hosts a fixed-format document with read access for user text selection, keyboard navigation, and search. The only allowable child element of FixedDocument is PageContent.

Attributes

PageSize *(optional)*
: Sets the size of the page as described by a Size element or through inline markup of a Size

xmlns *(required)*
: The namespace for the document to be loaded

FlowDocument

Hierarchy: DependencyObject → FrameworkContentElement → Document

```
<FlowDocument
    ColumnGap="5"
    ColumnWidth="300"
    ColumnRuleWidth="15"
    ColumnRuleBrush="LightGray"
    IsColumnWidthFlexible="true|false"
    FlowDirection="LeftToRightThenTopToBottom|RightToLeftThenTopToBottom "
    LineHeight="12"
    MaxPageHeight="1000"
    MaxPageWidth="1000"
    MinPageHeight="400"
    MinPageWidth="400"
    PageHeight="700"
    PageWidth="700"
    PagePadding="5,10,5,10"
    TextAlignment="Center|End|Justify|Left|Right|Start"
    TextTrimming="CharacterEllipsis|WordEllipsis|None"
    TextWrap="Wrap|NoWrap|Emergency" />
```

<FlowDocument .../> provides a mechanism for displaying and formatting text with advanced features such as pagination and columns.

Attributes

ColumnGap *(optional)*
: This Double value describes the distance between columns. If ColumnWidth is null, this value has no effect. The value of this attribute cannot exceed the page Width minus the PagePadding.

ColumnRuleBrush *(optional)*
: This attribute describes the Brush used to paint the column rule. If ColumnRuleWidth is 0, this attribute has no effect. Exposed predefined colors from the Color class, listed in Appendix G, may be used to describe this attribute.

ColumnRuleWidth *(optional)*
: This Double value describes the width of the rule between columns. The default is 0.

ColumnWidth *(optional)*
: This Double value describes the width of the columns.

FlowDirection *(optional)*
: Determines the direction that text flows within the document:

- LeftToRightThenTopToBottom
- RightToLeftThenTopToBottom

`IsColumnWidthFlexible` *(optional)*

This `Boolean` determines whether `ColumnWidth` is flexible.

`true`

Column widths will frequently be larger than specified.

`false`

Column widths will always be exactly the width specified.

`LineHeight` *(optional)*

This `Double` describes the height of each generated line of text. It does not affect the font size.

`MaxPageHeight` *(optional)*

This `Double` describes the maximum height of a page of content.

`MaxPageWidth` *(optional)*

This `Double` describes the maximum width of a page of content.

`MinPageHeight` *(optional)*

This `Double` describes the minimum height of a page of content.

`MinPageWidth` *(optional)*

This `Double` describes the minimum width of a page of content.

`PageHeight` *(optional)*

This `Double` describes the height of a page of content.

`PagePadding` *(optional)*

This `Thickness` describes the amount of padding to apply. It can be described as a uniform value (`PagePadding="10"`) or as individual values (`PagePadding="0,5,10,5"`).

`PageWidth` *(optional)*

This `Double` describes the width of a page of content.

`TextAlignment` *(optional)*

This attribute describes the horizontal alignment of text.

`Center`

The text is center-aligned.

`End`

The text is aligned on the end of the inline progression, as determined by the current text-advance direction.

`Justify`

Text is justified. This will increase spacing between words if necessary to keep text justified across the width of the `FlowDocument`.

`Left`

In horizontal inline progression, the text is aligned on the left.

`Right`

In horizontal inline progression, the text is aligned on the right.

`Start`

The text is aligned on the start of the inline progression, as determined by the current text-advance direction.

`TextTrimming` *(optional)*

Determines how to treat text that flows past the end of the element.

`CharacterEllipsis`
: Text is trimmed at a character boundary. Remaining text is replaced with an ellipsis (...).

`None`
: Text is not trimmed.

`WordEllipsis`
: Text is trimmed at a word boundary. Remaining text is replaced with an ellipsis (...).

`TextWrap` *(optional)*
: Determines the behavior of text when it reaches the boundary of its containing box.

  `Emergency`
  : Text is wrapped even if the line-breaking algorithm cannot determine an optimal wrapping opportunity. This is the default behavior.

  `NoWrap`
  : Text is not wrapped.

  `Wrap`
  : Text is wrapped.

Grid

Hierarchy: UIElement → FrameworkElement → Panel

```
<Grid ShowGridLines="true|false" />
```

`<Grid .../>` is similar to a `Table` but is more flexible than its traditional counterpart. `Grid` allows layering of content, including multiple elements in a single cell, whereas `Table` does not. Child elements in a `Grid` can be absolutely positioned relative to the upper-left corner of their cell boundaries. Finally, child elements are added to `Grid` based on row and column index, while child elements in a `Table` are declared within its parent cell.

`Grid` is a container for `ColumnDefinition`, `RowDefinition`, and elements that are placed by specifying their desired row and column attributes.

An example of a `Grid` with content follows and is evaluated in XamlPad in Figure 10-3:

```
<Grid ShowGridLines="true">
    <ColumnDefinition Width="100"/>
    <ColumnDefinition Width="100"/>
    <RowDefinition Height="100" />
    <RowDefinition Height="25" />
    <RowDefinition Height="25" />
    <TextBlock Grid.Column="0" Grid.Row="0">Col 0, Row 0</TextBlock>
    <TextBlock Grid.Column="1" Grid.Row="0">Col 1, Row 0</TextBlock>
    <TextBlock Grid.Column="0" Grid.Row="1">Col 0, Row 1</TextBlock>
    <TextBlock Grid.Column="1" Grid.Row="1">Col 1, Row 1</TextBlock>
    <TextBlock Grid.Column="0" Grid.Row="2">Col 0, Row 2</TextBlock>
    <TextBlock Grid.Column="1" Grid.Row="2">Col 1, Row 2</TextBlock>
</Grid>
```

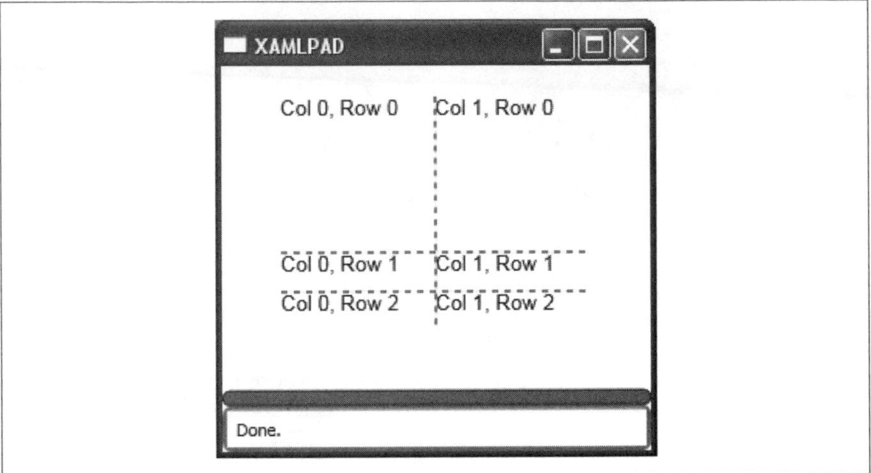

Figure 10-3. Grid with content and ShowGridLines=true

Attributes

`ShowGridLines` *(optional)*
: This attribute determines whether the grid will be lined.

  `true`
  : The gridlines will be displayed.

  `false`
  : No gridlines will be displayed.

Attached Attributes

`Grid.Column`
: A zero-based integer representing the column of the `Grid` into which the element should be placed

`Grid.Row`
: A zero-based integer representing the row of the `Grid` into which the element should be placed

PageContent

Hierarchy: UIElement → FrameworkElement

```
<PageContent
    Source="filename.xaml" />
```

`<PageContent .../>` provides the content data stream for `FlowDocument` and `FixedDocument`.

Attributes

`Source` *(required)*
: Describes the URI that points to the data stream

Panel

Hierarchy: UIElement → FrameworkElement

Panel is the base element for all Avalon elements defining layout characteristics. Panel elements are used to position and lay out child elements. Avalon includes a healthy number of predefined elements derived from Panel. The four derived elements useful for UI design are:

- Canvas
- Grid
- DockPanel
- StackPanel

All elements derived from Panel share a common set of properties, as described in Table 10-1.

Table 10-1. Common properties of elements derived from Panel

Property	Data type	Description
Height	Double	The height of the element.
Width	Double	The width of the element.
IsItemsHost	Boolean	Specifies whether the Panel is a container for elements generated for an ItemHost. true If the element is an item host false If the element is not an item host
HorizontalAlignment	Enumeration	Specifies how the Panel should align horizontally when placed within a parent Panel or ItemHost. Left Align the element on the left of its parent's layout area. Right Align the element on the right of its parent's layout area. Center Align the element in the center of its parent's layout area. Stretch Stretch the element to fill its parent's horizontal layout area.
VerticalAlignment	Enumeration	Specifies how the Panel should align vertically when placed within a parent Panel or ItemHost. Bottom Align the element on the bottom of its parent's layout area. Center Align the element in the center of its parent's layout area. Top Align the element at the top of its parent's layout area. Stretch Stretch the element to fill its parent's vertical layout area.

Table 10-1. Common properties of elements derived from Panel (continued)

Property	Data type	Description

`Visibility`	`Enumeration`	Determines the visibility of the element.
		`Visible`
		The element is displayed.
		`Hidden`
		The element is not displayed but does occupy layout space.
		`Collapsed`
		The element is not displayed and does not occupy layout space.

`FlowDirection`	`Enumeration`	Describes how text and other child elements flow within a parent. The enumerations are self-explanatory. The default is `LeftToRightThenTopToBottom`. • `LeftToRightThenTopToBottom` • `RightToLeftThenTopToBottom` • `TopToBottomThenLeftToRight` • `TopToBottomThenRightToLeft`
`LayoutTransform`	`UIElement`	The name of the `Transform` to be applied during layout of this element.
`Margin`	`Thickness`	Represents the margin around the element.
`Background`	`Fill`	Describes how to fill the area between the boundaries.
`MinWidth`	`Double`	Describes the minimum width of this element.
`MinHeight`	`Double`	Describes the minimum height of this element.

RowDefinition

Hierarchy: DependencyObject → FrameworkContentElement → DefinitionBase

```
<RowDefinition />
```

`<RowDefinition .../>` is used within a `Grid` to define a row.

Setter

Hierarchy: Object → SetterBase

```
<Setter
    Property="PropertyBeingSet"
    TargetName="{x:Type NameOfTheTarget}"
    Value="ValueBeingSet"|{"DynamicResource ResourceName"} |
          {"StaticResource ResourceName"} />
```

`<Setter .../>` defines a property for a specific element. It is used to apply a `Style` or `Trigger` to multiple elements of a specific type, e.g., all `Buttons`, all `TextBlocks`, etc. The element declares the attribute (property) to be set, the target element type, and the value to which to set the attribute. For example, `Setter` could be used to set the `Background` of all `Button` elements to a specific `Color` (Example 10-2) or to set the width of all `Button` elements to the same size (Example 10-3).

Example 10-2. Using Setter to define the Background of all Button elements

```
<StackPanel
    xmlns="http://schemas.microsoft.com/winfx/avalon/2005"
    xmlns:x="http://schemas.microsoft.com/winfx/xaml/2005"
    Margin="20">
    <StackPanel.Resources>
        <Style TargetType="{x:Type Button}">
            <Setter Property="Background" Value="Blue"/>
        </Style>
    </StackPanel.Resources>
    <Button Content="Button 1" />
    <Button Content="Button 2" />
</StackPanel>
```

Example 10-3. Using Setter to define the Width of all Button elements

```
<StackPanel
    xmlns="http://schemas.microsoft.com/winfx/avalon/2005"
    xmlns:x="http://schemas.microsoft.com/winfx/xaml/2005"
    Margin="20">
    <StackPanel.Resources>
        <Style TargetType="{x:Type Button}">
            <Setter Property="Width" Value="100"/>
        </Style>
    </StackPanel.Resources>
    <Button Content="Button 1" />
    <Button Content="Button 2" />
</StackPanel>
```

Attributes

`Property` *(required)*
: The name of the attribute being set. Examples include `Font`, `Height`, and `Background`.

`TargetName` *(required)*
: The type of the child node the `Setter` will target, if any (Example 10-4).

`Value` *(required)*
: The value for the attribute. The value may be a literal representation (`"Blue"`, `"2"`) or a reference to a `DynamicResource` or a `StaticResource`.

Example 10-4. Example of setting the TargetName of the Setter to a child node

```
TargetName="{x:Type ComboBoxItem}"

TargetName="{x:Type Button}"
```

StackPanel

Hierarchy: UIElement → FrameworkElement → Panel

```
    <StackPanel
        Orientation="Horizontal|Vertical" />
```

<StackPanel .../> stacks elements in the direction specified by the Orientation attribute. Specifying Horizontal as the Orientation causes child elements to flow left to right. If the Orientation is declared as Vertical, elements will flow top to bottom.

Attributes

Orientation *(optional)*
: Determines how child elements are stacked in the panel.

  Horizontal
  : Child elements are stacked from left to right. This is the default behavior.

  Vertical
  : Child elements are stacked from top to bottom.

Style

Hierarchy: Object

```
<Style
    BasedOn="StyleName"
    TargetType="{x:Type NameOfElementOrControl}"
    x:Key="Name" />
```

Note that *x* is replaceable for both the TargetType value and the Key attribute. It refers to the XAML namespace (http://schemas.microsoft.com/winfx/xaml/2005), which must be included in your document when using this method of reference.

<Style .../> describes the visual presentation of elements. A style contains a collection of Setter, Storyboard, and Trigger. Style is explored in depth in Chapter 5.

Attributes

BasedOn *(optional)*
: Describes the Style this Style attribute is based on.

TargetType *(required)*
: Describes the element or control that is targeted by this Style (Example 10-5).

x:Key *(optional)*
: Names the Style so that it can be referenced by the Style attribute of elements and controls. If this attribute is not set, the style will be applied to all elements of TargetType.

Example 10-5. Examples of targeting an element with a Style

```
TargetType="{x:Type MenuItem}"

TargetType="{x:Type RadioButton}"
```

Table

Hierarchy: DependencyObject → FrameworkContentElement → TextElement → Block

```
<TextFlow>
    <Table
        CellSpacing="5">
        <TableRowGroup>
            <TableRow>
                <TableCell>Cell 1</TableCell>
                <TableCell>Cell 2</TableCell>
                <TableCell>Cell 3/TableCell>
            </TableRow>
        </TableRowGroup>
    </Table>
</TextFlow>
```

`<Table .../>` is a typographic element comprising `TableRowGroup`. The `Table` element must be nested either within a parent `TextFlow` or within another element nested within a `TextFlow` (Example 10-6).

Example 10-6. Example of a full Table declaration

```
<TextFlow>
    <Table CellSpacing="5">
        <TableRowGroup>
            <TableRow>
                <TableCell><TextBlock>Header Text</TextBlock></TableCell>
            </TableRow>
            <TableRow>
                <TableCell><TextBlock>Body Text</TextBlock></TableCell>
            </TableRow>
            <TableRow>
                <TableCell><TextBlock>Footer Text</TextBlock></TableCell>
            </TableRow>
        </TableRowGroup>
    </Table>
</TextFlow>
```

Attributes

`CellSpacing` *(optional)*
: Sets the amount of spacing between `TableCell` elements

TableCell

Hierarchy: DependencyObject → FrameworkContentElement → TextElement → Block

```
<TableCell
    ColumnSpan="4"
    RowSpan="3"
    BreakPageBefore="true|false"
    BreakColumnBefore="true|false"
    KeepTogether="true|false"
    KeepWithNext="true|false" />
```

<TableCell .../> defines a content cell for a Table object. TableCell elements must be contained within a TableRow element. TableCell elements can only contain elements derived from Block.

Attributes

ColumnSpan *(optional)*
: Determines how many TableColumn elements the TableCell spans

RowSpan *(optional)*
: Determines how many TableRow elements the TableCell occupies

TableColumn

Hierarchy: DependencyObject → FrameworkContentElement

```
<TableColumn Width="20" />
```

<TableColumn .../> is used to apportion a Table element. The Width attribute is used to describe its width.

TableRow

Hierarchy: DependencyObject → FrameworkContentElement → TextElement

```
<TableRow Height="30" />
```

<TableRow .../> defines rows within a Table element. The Height attribute is used to describe the height of the row.

Trigger

Hierarchy: Object → TriggerBase

```
<Trigger
    Property="PropertyName"
    Value="Value" />
```

<Trigger .../> is used to conditionally style targets (Example 10-7). It contains one or more Setter elements that describe what to apply when the Trigger is active.

Example 10-7. Using a Trigger to conditionally style a Button

```
<Page
    xmlns="http://schemas.microsoft.com/winfx/avalon/2005"
    xmlns:x="http://schemas.microsoft.com/winfx/xaml/2005">
    <Page.Resources>
        <Style
            TargetType="{x:Type Button}">
            <Style.Triggers>
                <Trigger
                    Property="Button.IsMouseOver"
                    Value="true">
                    <Setter
                        Property = "Foreground"
                        Value="Green"/>
                    <Setter
                        Property = "Background"
```

Example 10-7. Using a Trigger to conditionally style a Button (continued)

```
                    Value="Red"/>
            </Trigger>
        </Style.Triggers>
    </Style>
</Page.Resources>
<StackPanel>
    <Button
        Content="My Button" />
</StackPanel>
</Page>
```

Attributes

`Property` *(required)*
: The attribute name examined by `Value` to determine whether to execute the `Trigger` (Example 10-8).

`Value` *(required)*
: The value of the attribute. If the value of the target attribute matches this value, the `Trigger` fires.

Example 10-8. Setting the Value attribute for a Trigger

```
<Trigger Property="ComboBoxItem.IsMouseOver" Value="true" >
```

11

Animations and Transformations

Animations and transformations provide a way to modify an element's attributes over time without requiring code. The concepts behind animation and transformations are explored more deeply in Chapter 6.

AnimationTimeline

Hierarchy: DependencyObject → Freezable → Animatable → Timeline

`<AnimationTimeline .../>` is a base class for a number of other abstract classes that can animate specific types of data. All the derived classes are the same, except for the type of data they are intended to animate. A few derived classes specifically implement a separate `Animation`, such as `ColorAnimation` and `DoubleAnimation`.

All of the *Type*`AnimationBase` elements have at least one subclass that can animate the data type supported by using a collection of `KeyFrame` elements. Each subclass is appropriately named *Type*`AnimationUsingKeyFrames`. These elements are identical to each other in functionality; they simply require the use of a data type–specific `KeyFrame`, which is named using the format *Type*`KeyFrame`. Each *Type*`KeyFrame` element is detailed in this chapter. For example, the `BooleanAnimationBase` element has one subclass, `BooleanAnimationUsingKeyFrames`, which requires a collection of `BooleanKeyFrame` elements as its children.

Example 11-1 offers a `DoubleAnimationUsingKeyFrames` as a template for how to use the classes derived from `AnimationTimeline`.

Example 11-1. A DoubleAnimationUsingKeyFrames definition

```
<DoubleAnimationUsingKeyFrames
    Duration="0:0:15"
    FillBehavior="HoldEnd">
    <DoubleAnimationUsingKeyFrames.KeyFrames>
        <LinearDoubleKeyFrame
            Value="500"
            KeyTime="0:0:7|Uniform|Paced|30%" />
```

Example 11-1. A DoubleAnimationUsingKeyFrames definition (continued)

```
        <LinearDoubleKeyFrame
            Value="200"
            KeyTime="0:0:10|Uniform|Paced|30%" />
        <LinearDoubleKeyFrame
            Value="350"
            KeyTime="0:0:15|Uniform|Paced|30%" />
    </DoubleAnimationUsingKeyFrames.KeyFrames>
</DoubleAnimationUsingKeyFrames>
```

Animating Elements

Similarly, a majority of the *Type*AnimationBase elements have *Type*Animation subclasses. These predefined animations offer a way to animate specific types of data in an easy-to-define element. Each of the elements utilizes the same attributes: From, To, By, and Duration. The only difference between them is that the From, To, and By attributes are specific to the type of the animation. From, To, and By are of type Color for a ColorAnimation; for a DoubleAnimation, they are of type Double (Example 11-2).

Example 11-2. A DoubleAnimation definition

```
<DoubleAnimation
    From="2.0"
    To="5.0"
    By="1.0"
    Duration="0:0:10" />
```

All of the *Type*Animation elements are declared in a similar manner, substituting the appropriate *Type* with From, To, or By. These elements are not further documented because they are declared exactly the same way and with the same attributes, differentiated only by their data type. The elements are listed in this chapter but refer back to AnimationTimeline as their main reference.

Do not specify both the To and the By attribute in a *Type*Animation.

The AnimationTimeline-derived elements are:

BooleanAnimationBase →
    BooleanAnimationUsingKeyFrames

CharAnimationBase →
    CharAnimationUsingKeyFrames

ColorAnimationBase →
    ColorAnimationUsingKeyFrames
    ColorAnimation

DecimalAnimationBase →
    DecimalAnimationUsingKeyFrames
    DecimalAnimation

DoubleAnimationBase →
    DoubleAnimationUsingKeyFrames
    DoubleAnimation

```
Int16AnimationBase →
    Int16AnimationUsingKeyFrames
    Int16Animation
Int32AnimationBase →
    Int32AnimationUsingKeyFrames
    Int32Animation
Int64AnimationBase →
    Int64AnimationUsingKeyFrames
    Int64Animation
MatrixAnimationBase →
    MatrixAnimationUsingKeyFrames
Point3DAnimationBase →
    Point3DAnimationUsingKeyFrames
    Point3DAnimation
PointAnimationBase →
    PointAnimationUsingKeyFrames
    PointAnimation
Rect3DAnimationBase →
    Rect3DAnimationUsingKeyFrames
    Rect3DAnimation
RectAnimationBase →
    RectAnimationUsingKeyFrames
    RectAnimation
Rotation3DAnimationBase →
    Rotation3DAnimationUsingKeyFrames
    RotationAnimation
SingleAnimationBase →
    SingleAnimationUsingKeyFrames
    SingleAnimation
Size3DAnimationBase →
    Size3DAnimationUsingKeyFrames
    Size3DAnimation
SizeAnimationBase →
    SizeAnimationUsingKeyFrames
    SizeAnimation
StringAnimationBase →
    StringAnimationUsingKeyFrames
ThicknessAnimationBase →
    ThicknessAnimationUsingKeyFrames
    ThicknessAnimation
Vector3DAnimationBase →
    Vector3DAnimationUsingKeyFrames
    Vector3DAnimation
VectorAnimationBase →
    VectorAnimationUsingKeyFrames
    VectorAnimation
```

BooleanKeyFrame

Hierarchy: DependencyObject → Freezable

BooleanKeyFrame is the base class for only one subclass, DiscreteBooleanKeyFrame:

```
<DiscreteBooleanKeyFrame
    KeyTime="0:0:10|Uniform|Paced|30%"
    Value="true|false" />
```

<DiscreteBooleanKeyFrame .../> animates a Boolean from a previous value to its own at KeyTime.

Attributes

KeyTime *(required)*
: The time, relative to the animation, that Value will be reached:

- A time period specified in hours:minutes:seconds.
- Uniform: The Duration will be split evenly among all key frames.
- Paced: The Duration will be split among key frames in a way that ensures the speed of the animation remains relatively constant.
- A percentage of the total duration.

Value *(required)*
: The Boolean value destination

CharKeyFrame

Hierarchy: DependencyObject → Freezable

CharKeyFrame is the base class for only one subclass, DiscreteCharKeyFrame:

```
<DiscreteCharKeyFrame
    KeyTime="0:0:10"
    Value="t" />
```

<DiscreteCharKeyFrame .../> animates a Char from a previous value to its own at KeyTime.

Attributes

KeyTime *(required)*
: The time, relative to the animation, that Value will be reached:

- A time period specified in hours:minutes:seconds.
- Uniform: The Duration will be split evenly among all key frames.
- Paced: The Duration will be split among key frames in a way that ensures the speed of the animation remains relatively constant.
- A percentage of the total duration.

Value *(required)*
: The Char value destination

ColorAnimation

See AnimationTimeline.

ColorKeyFrame

Hierarchy: DependencyObject → Freezable

ColorKeyFrame is the base class for three types of color key frames: discrete, linear, and spline. Each of the three subclasses of ColorKeyFrame represents a key frame with a distinct interpolation technique, indicated by its name:

```
<LinearColorKeyFrame
    KeyTime="0:0:10|Uniform|Paced|30%"
    Value="Red" />

<DiscreteColorKeyFrame
    KeyTime="0:0:10|Uniform|Paced|30%"
    Value="Blue" />

<SplineColorKeyFrame
    KeyTime="0:0:10|Uniform|Paced|30%"
    Value="Green" >
    <SplineColorKeyFrame.KeySpline>
        <KeySpline ControlPoint1="5,5" ControlPoint2="10,10" />
    </SplineColorKeyFrame.KeySpline>
</SplineColorKeyFrame>
```

All three ColorKeyFrame subclasses determine when (KeyTime) the frame will reach the designated value (Value). KeyTime is specified in terms of hours:minutes:seconds. The Value attribute of all ColorKeyFrame subclasses is a Color.

DiscreteColorKeyFrame
: Skips from one value to the desired value without interpolation. Thus, the Value will not be reached until KeyTime (relative to the beginning of the animation).

LinearColorKeyFrame
: Utilizes linear interpolation to reach the desired value. Linear interpolation progresses the animation at a steady rate for its duration.

SplineColorKeyFrame
: Uses a concept similar to Bezier curves to interpolate values until Value has been reached. This subclass requires an additional attribute, KeySpline, which is used to interpolate the value in much the same way as control points are used to interpolate a line when declaring a Bezier curve.

Attributes

KeySpline *(required)* (SplineColorKeyFrame *only)*
: This KeySpline describes how the key frame will be altered during animation.

KeyTime *(required)*
: This attribute specifies when, relative to the animation, this key frame takes place:

- A time period specified in hours:minutes:seconds.
- Uniform: The Duration will be split evenly among all key frames.
- Paced: The Duration will be split among key frames in a way that ensures the speed of the animation remains relatively constant.
- A percentage of the total duration.

Value *(required)*
: This Color describes the destination value of the key frame.

DecimalAnimation

See AnimationTimeline.

DecimalKeyFrame

Hierarchy: DependencyObject → Freezable

DecimalKeyFrame is the base class for three types of decimal key frames: discrete, linear, and spline. Each of the three subclasses of DecimalKeyFrame represents a key frame with a distinct interpolation technique, indicated by its name:

```
<LinearDecimalKeyFrame
    KeyTime="0:0:10|Uniform|Paced|30%"
    Value="1.2" />

<DiscreteDecimalKeyFrame
    KeyTime="0:0:10|Uniform|Paced|30%"
    Value="1.2" />

<SplineDecimalKeyFrame
    KeyTime="0:0:10|Uniform|Paced|30%"
    Value="1.2">
    <SplineDecimalKeyFrame.KeySpline>
        <KeySpline ControlPoint1="5,5" ControlPoint2="10,10" />
    </SplineDecimalKeyFrame.KeySpline>
</SplineInt64KeyFrame>
```

All three DecimalKeyFrame subclasses determine when (KeyTime) the frame will reach the designated value (Value). KeyTime is specified in terms of hours:minutes:seconds. The Value attribute of all DecimalKeyFrame subclasses is a Decimal.

DiscreteDecimalKeyFrame
: Skips from one value to the desired value without interpolation. Thus, the Value will not be reached until KeyTime (relative to the beginning of the animation).

LinearDecimalKeyFrame
: Utilizes linear interpolation to reach the desired value. Linear interpolation progresses the animation at a steady rate for its duration.

SplineDecimalKeyFrame
: Uses a concept similar to Bezier curves to interpolate values until Value has been reached. This subclass requires an additional attribute, KeySpline, which is used to interpolate the value in much the same way as control points are used to interpolate a line when declaring a Bezier curve.

Attributes

KeySpline *(required)* (SplineDecimalKeyFrame *only)*
: This KeySpline describes how the key frame will be altered during animation.

KeyTime *(required)*
: This attribute specifies when, relative to the animation, this key frame takes place:

    - A time period specified in hours:minutes:seconds.
    - Uniform: The Duration will be split evenly among all key frames.

- Paced: The Duration will be split among key frames in a way that ensures the speed of the animation remains relatively constant.
- A percentage of the total duration.

Value *(required)*
: This Decimal describes the destination value of the key frame.

DoubleAnimation

See AnimationTimeline.

DoubleAnimationUsingPath

Hierarchy: DependencyObject → Freezable → Animatable → Timeline → AnimationTimeline → DoubleAnimationBase

```
<DoubleAnimationUsingPath
    Duration="0:0:10"
    Source="Angle|X|Y">
    <DoubleAnimationUsingPath.PathGeometry>
        <PathGeometry>
            <PathGeometry.Figures>
                <PathFigureCollection>
                    <PathFigure>
                        <PathFigure.Segments>
                            <PathSegmentCollection>
                                <StartSegment Point="10,50" />
                                <LineSegment Point="200,70"/>
                            </PathSegmentCollection>
                        </PathFigure.Segments>
                    </PathFigure>
                </PathFigureCollection>
            </PathGeometry.Figures>
        </PathGeometry>
    </DoubleAnimationUsingPath.PathGeometry>
</DoubleAnimationUsingPath>
```

<DoubleAnimationUsingPath .../> animates a visual object along a path.

Attributes

PathGeometry *(required)*
: This PathGeometry element represents the path of the animation.

Source (required)
: This attribute specifies which output property of the path this animation will represent.

DoubleKeyFrame

Hierarchy: DependencyObject → Freezable

DoubleKeyFrame is the base class for three types of double key frames: discrete, linear, and spline. Each of the three subclasses of DoubleKeyFrame represents a key frame with a distinct interpolation technique, indicated by its name:

```
<LinearDoubleKeyFrame
    KeyTime="0:0:5|Uniform|Paced|30%"
    Value="3.0" />

<DiscreteDoubleKeyFrame
    KeyTime="0:0:5|Uniform|Paced|30%"
    Value="3.0" />

<SplineDoubleKeyFrame
    KeyTime="0:0:5|Uniform|Paced|30%"
    Value="3.0" >
    <SplineDoubleKeyFrame.KeySpline>
        <KeySpline ControlPoint1="5,5" ControlPoint2="10,10" />
    </SplineDoubleKeyFrame.KeySpline>
</SplineDoubleKeyFrame>
```

All three DoubleKeyFrame subclasses determine when (KeyTime) the frame will reach the designated value (Value). KeyTime is specified in terms of hours:minutes:seconds. The Value attribute of all DoubleKeyFrame subclasses is a Double.

DiscreteDoubleKeyFrame
: Skips from one value to the desired value without interpolation. Thus, the Value will not be reached until KeyTime (relative to the beginning of the animation).

LinearDoubleKeyFrame
: Utilizes linear interpolation to reach the desired value. Linear interpolation progresses the animation at a steady rate for its duration.

SplineDoubleKeyFrame
: Uses a concept similar to Bezier curves to interpolate values until Value has been reached. This subclass requires an additional attribute, KeySpline, which is used to interpolate the value in much the same way as control points are used to interpolate a line when declaring a Bezier curve.

Attributes

KeySpline *(required)* (SplineDoubleKeyFrame *only)*
: This KeySpline describes how the key frame will be altered during animation.

KeyTime *(required)*
: This attribute specifies when, relative to the animation, this key frame takes place:

- A time period specified in hours:minutes:seconds.
- Uniform: The Duration will be split evenly among all key frames.
- Paced: The Duration will be split among key frames in a way that ensures the speed of the animation remains relatively constant.
- A percentage of the total duration.

Value *(required)*
: This Double describes the destination value of the key frame.

Int16KeyFrame

Hierarchy: DependencyObject → Freezable

`Int16KeyFrame` is the base class for three types of short key frames: discrete, linear, and spline. Each of the three subclasses of `Int16KeyFrame` represents a key frame with a distinct interpolation technique, indicated by its name:

```
<LinearInt16KeyFrame
    KeyTime="0:0:10|Uniform|Paced|30%"
    Value="1" />

<DiscreteInt16KeyFrame
    KeyTime="0:0:10|Uniform|Paced|30%"
    Value="1" />

<SplineInt16KeyFrame
    KeyTime="0:0:10|Uniform|Paced|30%"
    Value="1" >
    <SplineInt16KeyFrame.KeySpline>
        <KeySpline ControlPoint1="5,5" ControlPoint2="10,10" />
    </SplineInt16KeyFrame.KeySpline>
</SplineInt16KeyFrame>
```

All three `Int16KeyFrame` subclasses determine when (`KeyTime`) the frame will reach the designated value (`Value`). `KeyTime` is specified in terms of hours:minutes:seconds. The `Value` attribute of all `Int16KeyFrame` subclasses is a `short`.

`DiscreteInt16KeyFrame`
: Skips from one value to the desired value without interpolation. Thus, the `Value` will not be reached until `KeyTime` (relative to the beginning of the animation).

`LinearInt16KeyFrame`
: Utilizes linear interpolation to reach the desired value. Linear interpolation progresses the animation at a steady rate for its duration.

`SplineInt16KeyFrame`
: Uses a concept similar to Bezier curves to interpolate values until `Value` has been reached. This subclass requires an additional attribute, `KeySpline`, which is used to interpolate the value in much the same way as control points are used to interpolate a line when declaring a Bezier curve.

Attributes

`KeySpline` *(required)* (`SplineInt16KeyFrame` *only)*
: This `KeySpline` describes how the key frame will be altered during animation.

`KeyTime` *(required)*
: This attribute specifies when, relative to the animation, this key frame takes place:

- A time period specified in hours:minutes:seconds.
- `Uniform`: The `Duration` will be split evenly among all key frames.
- `Paced`: The `Duration` will be split among key frames in a way that ensures the speed of the animation remains relatively constant.
- A percentage of the total duration.

`Value` *(required)*
: This `short` describes the destination value of the key frame.

Int32KeyFrame

Hierarchy: DependencyObject → Freezable

Int32KeyFrame is the base class for three types of integer key frames: discrete, linear, and spline. Each of the three subclasses of Int32KeyFrame represents a key frame with a distinct interpolation technique, indicated by its name:

```
<LinearInt32KeyFrame
    KeyTime="0:0:10|Uniform|Paced|30%"
    Value="1" />

<DiscreteInt32KeyFrame
    KeyTime="0:0:10|Uniform|Paced|30%"
    Value="1" />

<SplineInt32KeyFrame
    KeyTime="0:0:10|Uniform|Paced|30%"
    Value="1"
     <SplineInt32KeyFrame.KeySpline>
        <KeySpline ControlPoint1="5,5" ControlPoint2="10,10" />
    </SplineInt32KeyFrame.KeySpline>
</SplineInt32KeyFrame>
```

All three Int32KeyFrame subclasses determine when (KeyTime) the frame will reach the designated value (Value). KeyTime is specified in terms of hours:minutes:seconds. The Value attribute of all Int32KeyFrame subclasses is an Integer.

DiscreteInt32KeyFrame
: Skips from one value to the desired value without interpolation. Thus, the Value will not be reached until KeyTime (relative to the beginning of the animation).

LinearInt32KeyFrame
: Utilizes linear interpolation to reach the desired value. Linear interpolation progresses the animation at a steady rate for its duration.

SplineInt32KeyFrame
: Uses a concept similar to Bezier curves to interpolate values until Value has been reached. This subclass requires an additional attribute, KeySpline, which is used to interpolate the value in much the same way as control points are used to interpolate a line when declaring a Bezier curve.

Attributes

KeySpline *(required)* (SplineInt32KeyFrame *only)*
: This KeySpline describes how the key frame will be altered during animation.

KeyTime *(required)*
: This attribute specifies when, relative to the animation, this key frame takes place:

- A time period specified in hours:minutes:seconds.
- Uniform: The Duration will be split evenly among all key frames.
- Paced: The Duration will be split among key frames in a way that ensures the speed of the animation remains relatively constant.
- A percentage of the total duration.

Value *(required)*
: This Integer describes the destination value of the key frame.

Int64KeyFrame

Hierarchy: DependencyObject → Freezable

Int64KeyFrame is the base class for three types of long key frames: discrete, linear, and spline. Each of the three subclasses of Int64KeyFrame represents a key frame with a distinct interpolation technique, indicated by its name:

```
<Linearint64KeyFrame
    KeyTime="0:0:10|Uniform|Paced|30%"
    Value="1" />

<DiscreteInt64KeyFrame
    KeyTime="0:0:10|Uniform|Paced|30%"
    Value="1" />

<SplineInt64KeyFrame
    KeyTime="0:0:10|Uniform|Paced|30%"
    Value="1" >
    <SplineInt64KeyFrame.KeySpline>
        <KeySpline ControlPoint1="5,5" ControlPoint2="10,10" />
    </SplineInt64KeyFrame.KeySpline>
</SplineInt64KeyFrame>
```

All three Int64KeyFrame subclasses determine when (KeyTime) the frame will reach the designated value (Value). KeyTime is specified in terms of hours:minutes:seconds. The Value attribute of all Int64KeyFrame subclasses is a Long.

DiscreteInt64KeyFrame
: Skips from one value to the desired value without interpolation. Thus, the Value will not be reached until KeyTime (relative to the beginning of the animation).

LinearInt64KeyFrame
: Utilizes linear interpolation to reach the desired value. Linear interpolation progresses the animation at a steady rate for its duration.

SplineInt64KeyFrame
: Uses a concept similar to Bezier curves to interpolate values until Value has been reached. This subclass requires an additional attribute, KeySpline, which is used to interpolate the value in much the same way as control points are used to interpolate a line when declaring a Bezier curve.

Attributes

KeySpline *(required)* (SplineInt64KeyFrame *only)*
: This KeySpline describes how the key frame will be altered during animation.

KeyTime *(required)*
: This attribute specifies when, relative to the animation, this key frame takes place:

- A time period specified in hours:minutes:seconds.
- Uniform: The Duration will be split evenly among all key frames.
- Paced: The Duration will be split among key frames in a way that ensures the speed of the animation remains relatively constant.
- A percentage of the total duration.

Value *(required)*
: This Long describes the destination value of the key frame.

KeySpline

Hierarchy: DependencyObject → Freezable

```
<KeySpline
    ControlPoint1="5,5"
    ControlPoint2="10,10" />
```

pr:

```
<KeySpline>
    <KeySpline.ControlPoint1>
        <Point X="5" Y="5" />
    </KeySpline.ControlPoint1>
    <KeySpline.ControlPoint2>
        <Point X="10" Y="10" />
    </KeySpline.ControlPoint2>
</KeySpline>
```

`<KeySpline .../>` defines the control points used to modify the transition of a spline-based key frame. Both control points can be declared using abbreviated markup syntax or explicitly as `Point` elements.

Attributes

`ControlPoint1` *(required)*
: Represents the first control point

`ControlPoint2` *(required)*
: Represents the second control point

Matrix

Matrix is a structure and has no class hierarchy.

```
<Matrix
    M11="2.0"
    M12="3.0"
    M21="2.0"
    M22="3.0"
    OffsetX="1.0"
    OffsetY="1.0" />
```

`<Matrix .../>` represents a 3×3 matrix used for transformations. Avalon supports only *affine transformations*—linear transformations followed by a translation—so the matrix has only six entries instead of nine. The final three entries in the matrix are predefined, as shown in Table 11-1.

Table 11-1. The Avalon Matrix structure

M11	M12	0
M21	M22	0
M11	M12	0

Attributes

`M11` *(required)*
: A `Double` value representing the value in the first row and first column of the `Matrix`

`M12` *(required)*
: A `Double` value representing the value in the first row and second column of the `Matrix`

`M21` *(required)*
: A `Double` value representing the value in the second row and first column of the `Matrix`

`M22` *(required)*
: A `Double` value representing the value in the second row and second column of the `Matrix`

`OffsetX` *(optional)*
: A `Double` value representing the amount of the x-offset in the translation following the transformation

`OffsetY` *(optional)*
: A `Double` value representing the amount of the y-offset in the translation following the transformation

MatrixAnimationUsingPath

Hierarchy: DependencyObject → Freezable → Animatable → Timeline → AnimationTimeline → MatrixAnimationBase

```
<MatrixAnimationUsingPath
    Duration="0:0:10" >
    <MatrixAnimationUsingPath.PathGeometry>
        <PathGeometry>
            <PathGeometry.Figures>
                <PathFigureCollection>
                    <PathFigure>
                        <PathFigure.Segments>
                            <PathSegmentCollection>
                                <StartSegment Point="10,50" />
                                <LineSegment Point="200,70"/>
                            </PathSegmentCollection>
                        </PathFigure.Segments>
                    </PathFigure>
                </PathFigureCollection>
            </PathGeometry.Figures>
        </PathGeometry>
    </MatrixAnimationUsingPath.PathGeometry>
</MatrixAnimationUsingPath>
```

`<MatrixAnimationUsingPath .../>` animates a visual object along a path.

Attributes

`PathGeometry` *(required)*
: This `PathGeometry` element represents the path of the animation.

MatrixKeyFrame

Hierarchy: DependencyObject → Freezable

MatrixKeyFrame is the base class for only one subclass, DiscreteMatrixKeyFrame:

```
<DiscreteMatrixKeyFrame
    KeyTime="0:0:10|Uniform|Paced|30%"
    Value="0 0 0 0 0 0" />
```

<DiscreteMatrixKeyFrame .../> animates a Matrix from a previous value to its own at KeyTime. The Matrix can be declared using abbreviated markup syntax or by explicitly declaring a Matrix element.

Attributes

KeyTime *(required)*

The time, relative to the animation, that Value will be reached:

- A time period specified in hours:minutes:seconds.
- Uniform: The Duration will be split evenly among all key frames.
- Paced: The Duration will be split among key frames in a way that ensures the speed of the animation remains relatively constant.
- A percentage of the total duration.

Value *(required)*

The Matrix value destination

MediaTimeline

Hierarchy: DependencyObject → Freezable → Animatable → Timeline

```
<MediaTimeline
    IsMuted="true|false"
    Source="c:\\beehive.wmv"
    VolumeRatio="2.0" />
```

<MediaTimeline .../> describes a Timeline specifically for a MediaElement.

Attributes

IsMuted *(optional)*

This Boolean value determines whether the media source is initially muted.

true

The source is muted.

false

The source is not muted.

Source *(required)*

This attribute determines the absolute URI to the media being displayed.

VolumeRatio *(optional)*

This Double value describes the initial volume of the timeline

ParallelTimeline

Hierarchy: DependencyObject → Freezable → Animatable → Timeline → TimelineGroup

```
<ParallelTimeline />
```

<ParallelTimeline .../> represents a group of Timeline elements capable of running at the same time. Timeline elements in a ParallelTimeline become active according to the value specified by their BeginTime attribute rather than the order in which they are declared.

PointAnimationUsingPath

Hierarchy: DependencyObject → Freezable → Animatable → Timeline → AnimationTimeline → PointAnimationBase

```
<PointAnimationUsingPath
    Duration="0:0:10"
    <PointAnimationUsingPath.PathGeometry>
        <PathGeometry>
            <PathGeometry.Figures>
                <PathFigureCollection>
                    <PathFigure>
                        <PathFigure.Segments>
                            <PathSegmentCollection>
                                <StartSegment Point="10,50" />
                                <LineSegment Point="200,70"/>
                            </PathSegmentCollection>
                        </PathFigure.Segments>
                    </PathFigure>
                </PathFigureCollection>
            </PathGeometry.Figures>
        </PathGeometry>
    </PointAnimationUsingPath.PathGeometry>
</PointAnimationUsingPath>
```

<PointAnimationUsingPath .../> animates a visual object along a path.

Attributes

PathGeometry *(required)*
This PathGeometry element represents the path of the animation.

Point3DKeyFrame

Hierarchy: DependencyObject → Freezable

Point3DKeyFrame is the base class for three types of long key frames: discrete, linear, and spline. Each of the three subclasses of Point3DKeyFrame represents a key frame with a distinct interpolation technique, indicated by its name:

```
<LinearPoint3DKeyFrame
    KeyTime="0:0:10|Uniform|Paced|30%"
    Value="1,1,1" />
```

```
<DiscretePoint3DKeyFrame
    KeyTime="0:0:10|Uniform|Paced|30%"
    Value="1,1,1" />

<SplinePoint3DKeyFrame
    KeyTime="0:0:10|Uniform|Paced|30%"
    Value="1,1,1" >
    <SplinePoint3DKeyFrame.KeySpline>
        <KeySpline ControlPoint1="5,5" ControlPoint2="10,10" />
    </SplinePoint3DKeyFrame.KeySpline>
</SplinePoint3DKeyFrame>
```


All three Point3DKeyFrame subclasses determine when (KeyTime) the frame will reach the designated value (Value). KeyTime is specified in terms of hours:minutes:seconds. The Value attribute of all Point3DKeyFrame subclasses is a Point3D.

DiscretePoint3DKeyFrame
: Skips from one value to the desired value without interpolation. Thus, the Value will not be reached until KeyTime (relative to the beginning of the animation).

LinearPoint3DKeyFrame
: Utilizes linear interpolation to reach the desired value. Linear interpolation progresses the animation at a steady rate for its duration.

SplinePoint3DKeyFrame
: Uses a concept similar to Bezier curves to interpolate values until Value has been reached. This subclass requires an additional attribute, KeySpline, which is used to interpolate the value in much the same way as control points are used to interpolate a line when declaring a Bezier curve.

The Point3D value may be specified using abbreviated markup syntax or explicitly declared as a Point3D element.

Attributes

KeySpline *(required)* (SplinePoint3DKeyFrame *only)*
: This KeySpline describes how the key frame will be altered during animation.

KeyTime *(required)*
: This attribute specifies when, relative to the animation, this key frame takes place:

- A time period specified in hours:minutes:seconds.
- Uniform: The Duration will be split evenly among all key frames.
- Paced: The Duration will be split among key frames in a way that ensures the speed of the animation remains relatively constant.
- A percentage of the total duration.

Value *(required)*
: This Point3D describes the destination value of the key frame.

PointKeyFrame

Hierarchy: DependencyObject → Freezable

IntPointFrame is the base class for three types of long key frames: discrete, linear, and spline. Each of the three subclasses of PointKeyFrame represents a key frame with a distinct interpolation technique, indicated by its name:

```
<LinearPointKeyFrame
    KeyTime="0:0:10|Uniform|Paced|30%"
    Value="1,1" />

<DiscretePointKeyFrame
    KeyTime="0:0:10|Uniform|Paced|30%"
    Value="1,1" />

<SplinePointKeyFrame
    KeyTime="0:0:10|Uniform|Paced|30%"
    Value="1,1" >
    <SplinePointKeyFrame.KeySpline>
        <KeySpline ControlPoint1="5,5" ControlPoint2="10,10" />
    </SplinePointKeyFrame.KeySpline>
</SplinePointKeyFrame>
```

All three PointKeyFrame subclasses determine when (KeyTime) the frame will reach the designated value (Value). KeyTime is specified in terms of hours:minutes:seconds. The Value attribute of all PointKeyFrame subclasses is a Point.

DiscretePointKeyFrame
: Skips from one value to the desired value without interpolation. Thus, the Value will not be reached until KeyTime (relative to the beginning of the animation).

LinearPointKeyFrame
: Utilizes linear interpolation to reach the desired value. Linear interpolation progresses the animation at a steady rate for its duration.

SplinePointKeyFrame
: Uses a concept similar to Bezier curves to interpolate values until Value has been reached. This subclass requires an additional attribute, KeySpline, which is used to interpolate the value in much the same way as control points are used to interpolate a line when declaring a Bezier curve.

The Point value may be specified using abbreviated markup syntax or explicitly declared as a Point element.

Attributes

KeySpline *(required)* (SplinePointKeyFrame *only)*
: This KeySpline describes how the key frame will be altered during animation.

KeyTime *(required)*
: This attribute specifies when, relative to the animation, this key frame takes place:

- A time period specified in hours:minutes:seconds.
- Uniform: The Duration will be split evenly among all key frames.

- Paced: The Duration will be split among key frames in a way that ensures the speed of the animation remains relatively constant.
- A percentage of the total duration.

Value *(required)*
: This Point describes the destination value of the key frame.

RectAnimation

See AnimationTimeline.

Rect3DKeyFrame

Hierarchy: DependencyObject → Freezable

Rect3DPointFrame is the base class for three types of Rect3D key frames: discrete, linear, and spline. Each of the three subclasses of Rect3DKeyFrame represents a key frame with a distinct interpolation technique, indicated by its name:

```
<LinearRect3DKeyFrame
    KeyTime="0:0:10|Uniform|Paced|30%"
    Value="1,1,1 10 10 10" />

<DiscreteRect3DKeyFrame
    KeyTime="0:0:10|Uniform|Paced|30%"
    Value="1,1,1 10 10 10" />

<SplineRect3DKeyFrame
    KeyTime="0:0:10|Uniform|Paced|30%"
    Value="1,1,1 10 10 10" >
    <SplineRect3DKeyFrame.KeySpline>
        <KeySpline ControlPoint1="5,5" ControlPoint2="10,10" />
    </SplineRect3DKeyFrame.KeySpline>
</SplineRect3DKeyFrame>
```

All three Rect3DKeyFrame subclasses determine when (KeyTime) the frame will reach the designated value (Value). KeyTime is specified in terms of hours:minutes:seconds. The Value attribute of all Rect3DKeyFrame subclasses is a Rect3D.

DiscreteRect3DKeyFrame
: Skips from one value to the desired value without interpolation. Thus, the Value will not be reached until KeyTime (relative to the beginning of the animation).

LinearRect3DKeyFrame
: Utilizes linear interpolation to reach the desired value. Linear interpolation progresses the animation at a steady rate for its duration.

SplineRect3DKeyFrame
: Uses a concept similar to Bezier curves to interpolate values until Value has been reached. This subclass requires an additional attribute, KeySpline, which is used to interpolate the value in much the same way as control points are used to interpolate a line when declaring a Bezier curve.

The Rect3D value may be specified using abbreviated markup syntax or explicitly declared as a Rect3D element.

Attributes

KeySpline *(required)* (SplineRect3DKeyFrame *only)*
: This KeySpline describes how the key frame will be altered during animation.

KeyTime *(required)*
: This attribute specifies when, relative to the animation, this key frame takes place:
  - A time period specified in hours:minutes:seconds.
  - Uniform: The Duration will be split evenly among all key frames.
  - Paced: The Duration will be split among key frames in a way that ensures the speed of the animation remains relatively constant.
  - A percentage of the total duration.

Value *(required)*
: This Rect3D describes the destination value of the key frame.

RectKeyFrame

Hierarchy: DependencyObject → Freezable

RectPointFrame is the base class for three types of Rect key frames: discrete, linear, and spline. Each of the three subclasses of RectKeyFrame represents a key frame with a distinct interpolation technique, indicated by its name:

```
<LinearRectKeyFrame
    KeyTime="0:0:10|Uniform|Paced|30%"
    Value="1,1 10 10" />

<DiscreteRectKeyFrame
    KeyTime="0:0:10|Uniform|Paced|30%"
    Value="1,1 10 10" />

<SplineRectKeyFrame
    KeyTime="0:0:10|Uniform|Paced|30%"
    Value="1,1 10 10" >
    <SplineRectKeyFrame.KeySpline>
        <KeySpline ControlPoint1="5,5" ControlPoint2="10,10" />
    </SplineRectKeyFrame.KeySpline>
</SplineRectKeyFrame>
```

All three RectKeyFrame subclasses determine when (KeyTime) the frame will reach the designated value (Value). KeyTime is specified in terms of hours:minutes:seconds. The Value attribute of all RectKeyFrame subclasses is a Rect.

DiscreteRectKeyFrame
: Skips from one value to the desired value without interpolation. Thus, the Value will not be reached until KeyTime (relative to the beginning of the animation).

LinearRectKeyFrame
: Utilizes linear interpolation to reach the desired value. Linear interpolation progresses the animation at a steady rate for its duration.

SplineRectKeyFrame
: Uses a concept similar to Bezier curves to interpolate values until Value has been reached. This subclass requires an additional attribute, KeySpline, which is used to interpolate the value in much the same way as control points are used to interpolate a line when declaring a Bezier curve.

The Rect value may be specified using abbreviated markup syntax or explicitly declared as a Rect element.

Attributes

KeySpline *(required)* (SplineRectKeyFrame *only)*
: This KeySpline describes how the key frame will be altered during animation.

KeyTime *(required)*
: This attribute specifies when, relative to the animation, this key frame takes place:

- A time period specified in hours:minutes:seconds.
- Uniform: The Duration will be split evenly among all key frames.
- Paced: The Duration will be split among key frames in a way that ensures the speed of the animation remains relatively constant.
- A percentage of the total duration.

Value *(required)*
: This Rect describes the destination value of the key frame.

RotateTransform

Hierarchy: DependencyObject → Freezable → Animatable → Transform

```
<RotateTransform
    Center="0,0"
    Angle="45" />
```

or:

```
<RotateTransform
    Angle="45" >
    <RotateTransform.Center>
        <Point X="0" Y="0" />
    </RotateTransform.Center>
</RotateTransform>
```

<RotateTransform .../> describes a rotation around a point, based on the specified angle. Figure 11-1 shows the result of applying a 45-degree rotation to a Rectangle (Example 11-3).

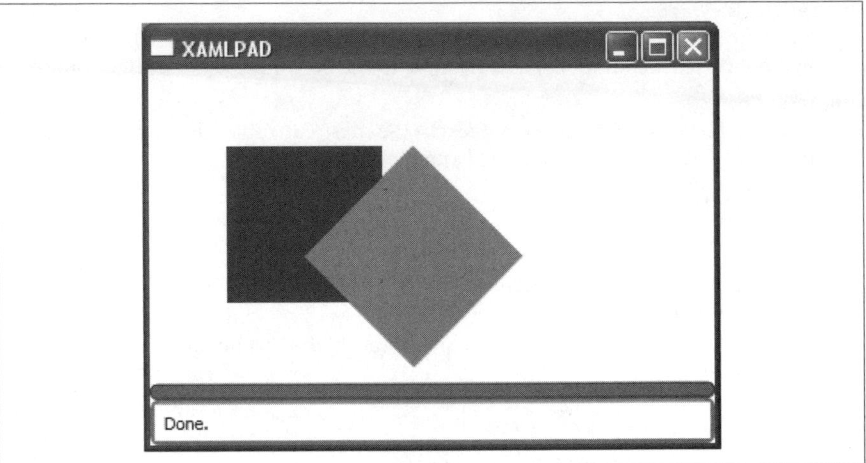

Figure 11-1. Rectangle and rotated rectangle comparison

Example 11-3. Applying a RotateTransform to a Rectangle

```
<Page
    xmlns="http://schemas.microsoft.com/winfx/avalon/2005"
    xmlns:x="http://schemas.microsoft.com/winfx/xaml/2005">
<Canvas>
    <Rectangle
        Canvas.Top="50"
        Canvas.Left="50"
        Height="100"
        Width="100"
        Fill="Blue" />
    <Rectangle
        Canvas.Top="50"
        Canvas.Left="170"
        Height="100"
        Width="100"
        Fill="Red" >
        <Rectangle.RenderTransform>
            <RotateTransform
                Angle="45"
                Center="0,0" />
       </Rectangle.RenderTransform>
    </Rectangle>
</Canvas>
</Page>
```

Attributes

`Angle` *(optional)*
: This `Double` value describes the angle of rotation.

`Center` *(optional)*
: This `Point` describes the point around which the element is rotated.

Rotation3D

Hierarchy: DependencyObject → Freezable → Animatable

```
<Rotation3D
    Angle="45"
    Axis="0,0,0" />
```

or:

```
<Rotation3D
    Angle="45" >
    <Rotation3D.Axis>
        <Vector3D
            X="5"
            Y="5"
            Z="5" />
    </Rotation3D.Axis>
</Rotation3D>
```

`<Rotation3D .../>` rotates a 3-D model around the specified `Axis` at the specified `Angle`.

Attributes

`Angle` *(required)*

This `Double` represents the spherical orientation of a transformed 3-D model as an angle between 0 and 360 degrees.

`Axis` *(required)*

This `Vector3D` represents the axis around which the rotation should occur.

Rotation3DKeyFrame

Hierarchy: DependencyObject → Freezable

`Rotation3DPointFrame` is the base class for three types of `Rotation3D` key frames: discrete, linear, and spline. Each of the three subclasses of `Rotation3DKeyFrame` represents a key frame with a distinct interpolation technique, indicated by its name:

```
<LinearRotation3DKeyFrame
    KeyTime="0:0:10|Uniform|Paced|30%"
    Value="1,1,1" />

<DiscreteRotation3DKeyFrame
    KeyTime="0:0:10|Uniform|Paced|30%"
    Value="1,1,1" />

<SplineRotation3DKeyFrame
    KeyTime="0:0:10|Uniform|Paced|30%"
    Value="1,1,1" >
    <SplineRotation3DKeyFrame.KeySpline>
        <KeySpline ControlPoint1="5,5" ControlPoint2="10,10" />
    </SplineRotation3DKeyFrame.KeySpline>
</SplineRotation3DKeyFrame>
```

All three Rotation3DKeyFrame subclasses determine when (KeyTime) the frame will reach the designated value (Value). KeyTime is specified in terms of hours:minutes:seconds. The Value attribute of all Rotation3DKeyFrame subclasses is a Rotation3D.

DiscreteRotation3DKeyFrame
: Skips from one value to the desired value without interpolation. Thus, the Value will not be reached until KeyTime (relative to the beginning of the animation).

LinearRotation3DKeyFrame
: Utilizes linear interpolation to reach the desired value. Linear interpolation progresses the animation at a steady rate for its duration.

SplineRotation3DKeyFrame
: Uses a concept similar to Bezier curves to interpolate values until Value has been reached. This subclass requires an additional attribute, KeySpline, which is used to interpolate the value in much the same way as control points are used to interpolate a line when declaring a Bezier curve.

The Rotation3D value may be specified using abbreviated markup syntax or explicitly declared as a Rotation3D element.

Attributes

KeySpline *(required)* (SplineRotation3DKeyFrame *only)*
: This KeySpline describes how the key frame will be altered during animation.

KeyTime *(required)*
: This attribute specifies when, relative to the animation, this key frame takes place:

  - A time period specified in hours:minutes:seconds.
  - Uniform: The Duration will be split evenly among all key frames.
  - Paced: The Duration will be split among key frames in a way that ensures the speed of the animation remains relatively constant.
  - A percentage of the total duration.

Value *(required)*
: This Rotation3D describes the destination value of the key frame.

ScaleTransform

Hierarchy: DependencyObject → Freezable → Animatable → Transform

```
<ScaleTransform
    Center="0,0"
    ScaleX="2"
    ScaleY="2" />
```

or:

```
<ScaleTransform
    ScaleX="2"
    ScaleY="2" >
    <ScaleTransform.Center>
        <Point X="0" Y="0" />
    </ScaleTransform.Center>
</ScaleTransform>
```

<ScaleTransform .../> scales an element by the specified factor. The scaling can be applied in both the x- and y-directions. Example 11-4 applies a scaling transformation to a Rectangle, effectively doubling its size (Figure 11-2).

Example 11-4. Applying a ScaleTransform to a Rectangle

```
<Page
    xmlns="http://schemas.microsoft.com/winfx/avalon/2005"
    xmlns:x="http://schemas.microsoft.com/winfx/xaml/2005">
<Canvas>
    <Rectangle
         Canvas.Top="50"
         Canvas.Left="50"
         Height="100"
         Width="100"
         Fill="Blue" />
    <Rectangle
         Canvas.Top="50"
         Canvas.Left="170"
         Height="100"
         Width="100"
         Fill="Red" >
        <Rectangle.RenderTransform>
            <ScaleTransform
                ScaleX="2"
                ScaleY="2"
                Center="0,0" />
        </Rectangle.RenderTransform>
    </Rectangle>
</Canvas>
</Page>
```

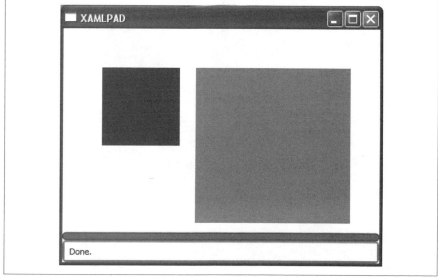

Figure 11-2. Scaling a Rectangle using ScaleTransform

Attributes

`Center` *(optional)*
: This attribute represents the center point of the scaling operation. The default is a `Point` at (0,0).

`ScaleX` *(optional)*
: This `Double` value represents the factor by which to scale the width of the element. 1.0 is equivalent to the original size, or 100 percent. A factor of 0.5 would reduce the width by 50 percent, and a factor of 1.5 would increase the width by 150 percent.

`ScaleY` *(optional)*
: This `Double` value represents the factor by which to scale the height of the element. 1.0 is equivalent to the original size, or 100 percent. A factor of 0.5 would reduce the height by 50 percent, and a factor of 1.5 would increase the height by 150 percent.

SetterTimeline

Hierarchy: DependencyObject → Freezable → Animatable → Timeline → TimelineGroup → ParallelTimeline

```
<SetterTimeline
    Path="(Button.Width)"
    TargetName="MyButton" />
```

`<SetterTimeline .../>` objects are used inside storyboards to apply animations to framework elements. A `SetterTimeline`'s `TargetName` property specifies the name of the element to target and its `Path` property specifies the property to animate.

To apply animations to the targeted element, add them as children of the `SetterTimeline`. When the storyboard is processed, clocks are created for the animations and connected to the targeted properties.

Attributes

`Path` *(required)*
: This attribute describes where the value will be set, according to the timeline specifications.

`TargetName` *(required)*
: This `String` attribute represents the name of the element whose value is set according to the `Path` attribute.

SkewTransform

Hierarchy: DependencyObject → Freezable → Animatable → Transform

```
<SkewTransform
    AngleX="45"
    AngleY="30"
    Center="0,0" />
```

or:

```
<SkewTransform
    AngleX="45"
    AngleY="30" >
```

```
        <SkewTransform.Center>
            <Point X="0" Y="0" />
        </SkewTransform.Center>
    </SkewTransform>
```

<SkewTransform .../> describes a skew, or shear, transformation. SkewTransform stretches the coordinate space in a non-uniform manner, as seen in Figure 11-3. The code to produce the transformation is found in Example 11-5.

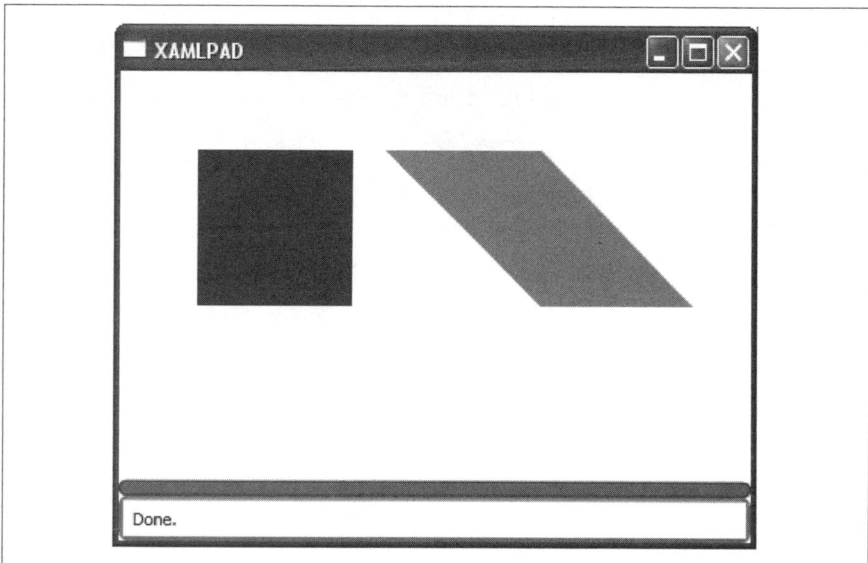

Figure 11-3. Modifying a Rectangle using SkewTransform

Example 11-5. Applying a SkewTransform to a Rectangle

```
<Page
    xmlns="http://schemas.microsoft.com/winfx/avalon/2005"
    xmlns:x="http://schemas.microsoft.com/winfx/xaml/2005">
<Canvas>
    <Rectangle
        Canvas.Top="50"
        Canvas.Left-"50"
        Height="100"
        Width="100"
        Fill="Blue" />
    <Rectangle
        Canvas.Top="50"
        Canvas.Left="170"
        Height="100"
        Width="100"
        Fill="Red" >
        <Rectangle.RenderTransform>
            <SkewTransform
                AngleX="45"
                Center="0,0" />
```

Example 11-5. Applying a SkewTransform to a Rectangle (continued)

```
        </Rectangle.RenderTransform>
    </Rectangle>
</Canvas>
</Page>
```

Attributes

`Center` *(optional)*
: This `Point` specifies the center of the transformation.

`AngleX` *(optional)*
: This `Double` value determines the skew of the x-axis values relative to the current coordinate system.

`AngleY` *(optional)*
: This `Double` value determines the skew of the y-axis values relative to the current coordinate system.

SizeAnimation

See `AnimationTimeline`.

Size3D

Size3D is a structure and has no class hierarchy.

```
<Size3D
    X="5"
    Y="5"
    Z="5" />
```

`<Size3D .../>` describes a size in three dimensions.

Attributes

`X` *(required)*
: This `Double` value describes the size of the x-dimension.

`Y` *(required)*
: This `Double` value describes the size of the y-dimension.

`Z` *(required)*
: This `Double` value describes the size of the z-dimension.

Size3DKeyFrame

Hierarchy: DependencyObject → Freezable

`Size3DPointFrame` is the base class for three types of `Size3D` key frames: discrete, linear, and spline. Each of the three subclasses of `Size3DKeyFrame` represents a key frame with a distinct interpolation technique, indicated by its name:

```
<LinearSize3DKeyFrame
    KeyTime="0:0:10|Uniform|Paced|30%"
    Value="1 1 1" />
```

```
<DiscreteSize3DKeyFrame
    KeyTime="0:0:10|Uniform|Paced|30%"
    Value="1 1 1" />

<SplineSize3DKeyFrame
    KeyTime="0:0:10|Uniform|Paced|30%"
    Value="1 1 1" >
    <SplineSize3DKeyFrame.KeySpline>
        <KeySpline ControlPoint1="5,5" ControlPoint2="10,10" />
    </SplineSize3DKeyFrame.KeySpline>
</SplineSize3DKeyFrame>
```

All three `Size3DKeyFrame` subclasses determine when (`KeyTime`) the frame will reach the designated value (`Value`). `KeyTime` is specified in terms of hours:minutes:seconds. The `Value` attribute of all `Size3DKeyFrame` subclasses is a `Size3D`.

`DiscreteSize3DKeyFrame`
: Skips from one value to the desired value without interpolation. Thus, the `Value` will not be reached until `KeyTime` (relative to the beginning of the animation).

`LinearSize3DKeyFrame`
: Utilizes linear interpolation to reach the desired value. Linear interpolation progresses the animation at a steady rate for its duration.

`SplineSize3DKeyFrame`
: Uses a concept similar to Bezier curves to interpolate values until `Value` has been reached. This subclass requires an additional attribute, `KeySpline`, which is used to interpolate the value in much the same way as control points are used to interpolate a line when declaring a Bezier curve.

The `Size3D`value may be specified using abbreviated markup syntax or explicitly declared as a `Size3D` element.

Attributes

`KeySpline` *(required)* (`SplineSize3DKeyFrame` *only)*
: This `KeySpline` describes how the key frame will be altered during animation.

`KeyTime` *(required)*
: This attribute specifies when, relative to the animation, this key frame takes place:

- A time period specified in hours:minutes:seconds.
- `Uniform`: The `Duration` will be split evenly among all key frames.
- `Paced`: The `Duration` will be split among key frames in a way that ensures the speed of the animation remains relatively constant.
- A percentage of the total duration.

`Value` *(required)*
: This `Size3D` describes the destination value of the key frame.

SizeKeyFrame

Hierarchy: DependencyObject → Freezable

SizeKeyFrame is the base class for three types of Size key frames: discrete, linear, and spline. Each of the three subclasses of SizeKeyFrame represents a key frame with a distinct interpolation technique, indicated by its name:

```
<LinearSizeKeyFrame
    KeyTime="0:0:10|Uniform|Paced|30%"
    Value="1 1" />

<DiscreteSizeKeyFrame
    KeyTime="0:0:10|Uniform|Paced|30%"
    Value="1 1" />

<SplineSizeKeyFrame
    KeyTime="0:0:10|Uniform|Paced|30%"
    Value="1 1" >
    <SplineSizeKeyFrame.KeySpline>
        <KeySpline ControlPoint1="5,5" ControlPoint2="10,10" />
    </SplineSizeKeyFrame.KeySpline>
</SplineSizeKeyFrame>
```

All three SizeKeyFrame subclasses determine when (KeyTime) the frame will reach the designated value (Value). KeyTime is specified in terms of hours:minutes:seconds. The Value attribute of all SizeKeyFrame subclasses is a Size.

DiscreteSizeKeyFrame
: Skips from one value to the desired value without interpolation. Thus, the Value will not be reached until KeyTime (relative to the beginning of the animation).

LinearSizeKeyFrame
: Utilizes linear interpolation to reach the desired value. Linear interpolation progresses the animation at a steady rate for its duration.

SplineSizeKeyFrame
: Uses a concept similar to Bezier curves to interpolate values until Value has been reached. This subclass requires an additional attribute, KeySpline, which is used to interpolate the value in much the same way as control points are used to interpolate a line when declaring a Bezier curve.

The Size value may be specified using abbreviated markup syntax or explicitly declared as a Size element.

Attributes

KeySpline *(required)* (SplineSizeKeyFrame *only)*
: This KeySpline describes how the key frame will be altered during animation.

KeyTime *(required)*
: This attribute specifies when, relative to the animation, this key frame takes place:

- A time period specified in hours:minutes:seconds.
- Uniform: The Duration will be split evenly among all key frames.

- Paced: The Duration will be split among key frames in a way that ensures the speed of the animation remains relatively constant.
- A percentage of the total duration.

Value *(required)*
: This Size describes the destination value of the key frame.

StringKeyFrame

Hierarchy: DependencyObject → Freezable

StringKeyFrame is the base class for only one subclass, DiscreteStringKeyFrame:

```
<DiscreteStringKeyFrame
    KeyTime="0:0:10|Uniform|Paced|30%"
    Value="String" />
```

<DiscreteStringKeyFrame .../> animates a string from a previous value to its own at KeyTime.

Attributes

KeyTime *(required)*
: This attribute specifies the time, relative to the animation, when Value will be reached:
  - A time period specified in hours:minutes:seconds.
  - Uniform: The Duration will be split evenly among all key frames.
  - Paced: The Duration will be split among key frames in a way that ensures the speed of the animation remains relatively constant.
  - A percentage of the total duration.

Value *(required)*
: This String describes the destination value of the key frame.

ThicknessKeyFrame

Hierarchy: DependencyObject → Freezable

ThicknessKeyFrame is the base class for three types of Thickness key frames: discrete, linear, and spline. Each of the three subclasses of ThicknessKeyFrame represents a key frame with a distinct interpolation technique, indicated by its name:

```
<LinearThicknessKeyFrame
    KeyTime="0:0:10|Uniform|Paced|30%"
    Value="1,1,1,1" />

<DiscreteThicknessKeyFrame
    KeyTime="0:0:10|Uniform|Paced|30%"
    Value="1,1,1,1" />

<SplineThicknessKeyFrame
    KeyTime="0:0:10|Uniform|Paced|30%"
    Value="1,1,1,1" >
```

```
        <SplineThicknessKeyFrame.KeySpline>
            <KeySpline ControlPoint1="5,5" ControlPoint2="10,10" />
        </SplineThicknessKeyFrame.KeySpline>
    </SplineThicknessKeyFrame>
```

All three ThicknessKeyFrame subclasses determine when (KeyTime) the frame will reach the designated value (Value). KeyTime is specified in terms of hours:minutes:seconds. The Value attribute of all ThicknessKeyFrame subclasses is a Thickness.

DiscreteThicknessKeyFrame
: Skips from one value to the desired value without interpolation. Thus, the Value will not be reached until KeyTime (relative to the beginning of the animation).

LinearThicknessKeyFrame
: Utilizes linear interpolation to reach the desired value. Linear interpolation progresses the animation at a steady rate for its duration.

SplineThicknessKeyFrame
: Uses a concept similar to Bezier curves to interpolate values until Value has been reached. This subclass requires an additional attribute, KeySpline, which is used to interpolate the value in much the same way as control points are used to interpolate a line when declaring a Bezier curve.

The Thickness value may be specified using abbreviated markup syntax or explicitly declared as a Thickness element.

Attributes

KeySpline *(required)* (SplineThicknessKeyFrame *only)*
: This KeySpline describes how the key frame will be altered during animation.

KeyTime *(required)*
: This attribute specifies when, relative to the animation, this key frame takes place:

- A time period specified in hours:minutes:seconds.
- Uniform: The Duration will be split evenly among all key frames.
- Paced: The Duration will be split among key frames in a way that ensures the speed of the animation remains relatively constant.
- A percentage of the total duration.

Value *(required)*
: This Thickness describes the destination value of the key frame.

Timeline

Hierarchy: DependencyObject → Freezable → Animatable

```
<Timeline
    AccelerationRatio="1"
    AutoReverse="true|false"
    BeginTime="100"
    CutOffTime="300"
    FillBehavior="Deactivate|HoldEnd"
    DecelerationRatio="1"
    Duration="Automatic|Forever|100"
    RepeatBehavior="IterationCount|RepeatDuration|Forever"
    SpeedRatio="0.5" />
```

<Timeline .../> is an abstract element that represents a time period. Timeline makes use of the TimeSpan structure, which is represented textually as "d:h:s," where "d" is the number of days, "h" is the number of hours, and "s" is the number of seconds.

Attributes

AccelerationRatio *(optional)*
: This Double value represents the percentage of the Duration spent accelerating from zero to its maximum rate. This attribute must be set to a value between 0 and 1, inclusive. The default value is 0.

AutoReverse *(optional)*
: This Boolean value determines whether the timeline will play in reverse after it has completed a forward iteration.

  true
  : The timeline will play in reverse at the end of each forward iteration.

  false
  : The timeline will not play in reverse. This is the default value.

BeginTime *(optional)*
: This TimeSpan attribute determines when the timeline will begin. The default value is 0.

CutOffTime *(optional)*
: This TimeSpan attribute determines when the timeline should end, relative to BeginTime.

DecelerationRatio *(optional)*
: This Double value represents the percentage of the Duration spent decelerating from its maximum rate to zero. This attribute must be set to a value between 0 and 1, inclusive. The default value is 0.

Duration *(optional)*
: This attribute determines how long the timeline should continue, not counting repetitions.

  Automatic
  : The timeline automatically ends when its last child stops playing.

  Forever
  : The timeline will continue playing indefinitely.

  TimeSpan
  : The value of this attribute is a time span.

FillBehavior *(optional)*
: This value determines how the animation will behave once it has completed but while its parent is still active.

  Deactivate
  : The Timeline is turned off when its parent is no longer active.

  HoldEnd
  : The Timeline holds its progress until the end of its parent's active and hold periods.

RepeatBehavior *(optional)*
: This attribute determines how the timeline will repeat its Duration, if at all.

`Forever`
: The timeline will repeat indefinitely.

`IterationCount`
: The timeline's behavior is determined by this value. A value of 1.0 means that the timeline will execute exactly once. A value of 2.0 means that the timeline will execute twice. A value of 0.5 means that the timeline will execute only half of its intended duration. An `IterationCount` is specified using the following syntax: `RepeatBehavior="2x"`, where *2* is the desired iteration count and *x* is a keyword that indicates the type of `RepeatBehavior` being declared.

`RepeatDuration`
: The timeline will repeat for the amount of time specified by this value. A `RepeatDuration` is specified by declaring the `RepeatBehavior` as a `TimeSpan`, e.g., "0:0:5" specifies a `RepeatDuration` time of five seconds.

`SpeedRatio` *(optional)*
: This `Double` value specifies the rate of movement over the `Duration`. The default value is 1.0.

TranslateTransform

Hierarchy: DependencyObject → Freezable → Animatable → Transform

```
<TranslateTransform
    X="5"
    Y="5" />
```

`<TranslateTransform .../>` defines an axis-aligned transition in the x- and y-directions. It moves an element the specified number of 1/96" units in the x- and y-direction. Example 11-6 shows the original `Rectangle` and then the same `Rectangle` translated along the x- and y-axis. Figure 11-4 shows the result of evaluating the code in XamlPad.

Example 11-6. Applying a TranslateTransform to a Rectangle

```
<Page
    xmlns="http://schemas.microsoft.com/winfx/avalon/2005"
    xmlns:x="http://schemas.microsoft.com/winfx/xaml/2005">
<Canvas>
    <Rectangle
        Canvas.Top="50"
        Canvas.Left="50"
        Height="100"
        Width="100"
        Fill="Blue" />
    <Rectangle
        Canvas.Top="50"
        Canvas.Left="50"
        Height="100"
        Width="100"
        Fill="Red" >
        <Rectangle.RenderTransform>
            <TranslateTransform
                X="20" Y="10" />
       </Rectangle.RenderTransform>
```

Example 11-6. Applying a TranslateTransform to a Rectangle (continued)

```
    </Rectangle>
</Canvas>
</Page>
```

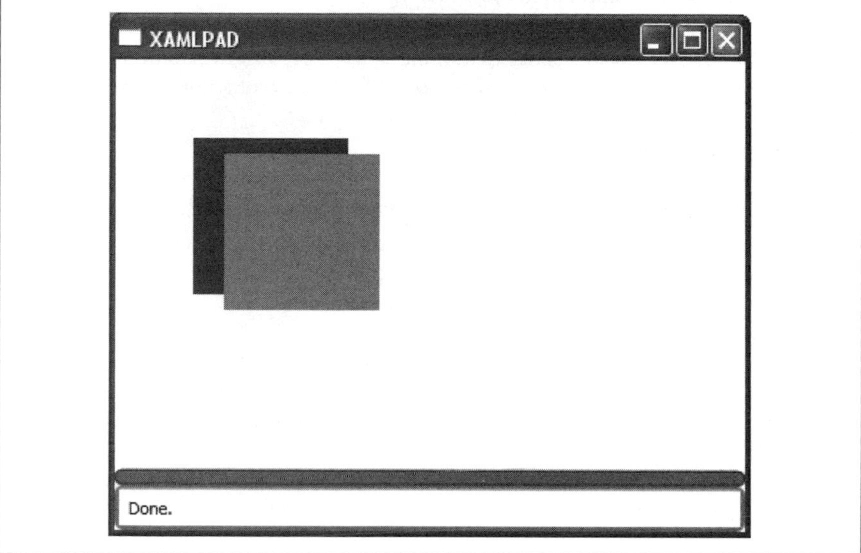

Figure 11-4. TranslateTransform applied to a Rectangle

Attributes

`X` *(optional)*
: This `Double` value determines the distance along the x-axis to move the element.

`Y` *(optional)*
: This `Double` value determines the distance along the y-axis to move the element.

VectorAnimation

See `AnimationTimeline`.

VectorKeyFrame

Hierarchy: DependencyObject → Freezable

`VectorPointFrame` is the base class for three types of `Vector` key frames: discrete, linear, and spline. Each of the three subclasses of `VectorKeyFrame` represents a key frame with a distinct interpolation technique, indicated by its name:

```
<LinearVectorKeyFrame
    KeyTime="0:0:10|Uniform|Paced|30%"
    Value="1,1" />

<DiscreteVectorKeyFrame
    KeyTime="0:0:10|Uniform|Paced|30%"
    Value="1,1" />
```

```
<SplineVectorKeyFrame
    KeyTime="0:0:10|Uniform|Paced|30%"
    Value="1,1" >
    <SplineVectorKeyFrame.KeySpline>
        <KeySpline ControlPoint1="5,5" ControlPoint2="10,10" />
    </SplineVectorKeyFrame.KeySpline>
</SplineVectorKeyFrame>
```

All three `VectorKeyFrame` subclasses determine when (`KeyTime`) the frame will reach the designated value (`Value`). `KeyTime` is specified in terms of hours:minutes:seconds. The `Value` attribute of all `VectorKeyFrame` subclasses is a `Vector`.

`DiscreteVectorKeyFrame`
: Skips from one value to the desired value without interpolation. Thus, the `Value` will not be reached until `KeyTime` (relative to the beginning of the animation).

`LinearVectorKeyFrame`
: Utilizes linear interpolation to reach the desired value. Linear interpolation progresses the animation at a steady rate for its duration.

`SplineVectorKeyFrame`
: Uses a concept similar to Bezier curves to interpolate values until `Value` has been reached. This subclass requires an additional attribute, `KeySpline`, which is used to interpolate the value in much the same way as control points are used to interpolate a line when declaring a Bezier curve.

The `Vector` value may be specified using abbreviated markup syntax or explicitly declared as a `Vector` element.

Attributes

`KeySpline` *(required)* (`SplineVectorKeyFrame` *only)*
: This `KeySpline` describes how the key frame will be altered during animation.

`KeyTime` *(required)*
: This attribute specifies when, relative to the animation, this key frame takes place:

- A time period specified in hours:minutes:seconds.
- `Uniform`: The `Duration` will be split evenly among all key frames.
- `Paced`: The `Duration` will be split among key frames in a way that ensures the speed of the animation remains relatively constant.
- A percentage of the total duration.

`Value` *(required)*
: This `Vector` describes the destination value of the key frame.

Vector3DKeyFrame

Hierarchy: DependencyObject → Freezable

`Vector3DPointFrame` is the base class for three types of `Vector3D` key frames: discrete, linear, and spline. Each of the three subclasses of `Vector3DKeyFrame` represents a key frame with a distinct interpolation technique, indicated by its name:

```
<LinearVector3DKeyFrame
    KeyTime="0:0:10|Uniform|Paced|30%"
    Value="1,1,1" />
```

```
<DiscreteVector3DKeyFrame
    KeyTime="0:0:10|Uniform|Paced|30%"
    Value="1,1,1" />

<SplineVector3DKeyFrame
    KeyTime="0:0:10|Uniform|Paced|30%"
    Value="1,1,1" >
    <SplineVector3DKeyFrame.KeySpline>
        <KeySpline ControlPoint1="5,5" ControlPoint2="10,10" />
    </SplineVector3DKeyFrame.KeySpline>
</SplineVector3DKeyFrame>
```


All three `Vector3DKeyFrame` subclasses determine when (`KeyTime`) the frame will reach the designated value (`Value`). `KeyTime` is specified in terms of hours:minutes:seconds. The `Value` attribute of all `Vector3DKeyFrame` subclasses is a `Vector3D`.

`DiscreteVector3DKeyFrame`
: Skips from one value to the desired value without interpolation. Thus, the `Value` will not be reached until `KeyTime` (relative to the beginning of the animation).

`LinearVector3DKeyFrame`
: Utilizes linear interpolation to reach the desired value. Linear interpolation progresses the animation at a steady rate for its duration.

`SplineVector3DKeyFrame`
: Uses a concept similar to Bezier curves to interpolate values until `Value` has been reached. This subclass requires an additional attribute, `KeySpline`, which is used to interpolate the value in much the same way as control points are used to interpolate a line when declaring a Bezier curve.

The `Vector3D` value may be specified using abbreviated markup syntax or explicitly declared as a `Vector3D` element.

Attributes

`KeySpline` *(required)* (`SplineVector3DKeyFrame` *only)*
: This `KeySpline` describes how the key frame will be altered during animation.

`KeyTime` *(required)*
: This attribute specifies when, relative to the animation, this key frame takes place:

  - A time period specified in hours:minutes:seconds.
  - `Uniform`: The `Duration` will be split evenly among all key frames.
  - `Paced`: The `Duration` will be split among key frames in a way that ensures the speed of the animation remains relatively constant.
  - A percentage of the total duration.

`Value` *(required)*
: This `Vector3D` describes the destination value of the key frame.

Vector

Vector is a structure and has no hierarchy.

```
<Vector
    X="5"
    Y="5" />
```

`<Vector .../>` represents the direction and magnitude of a line segment. It describes the movement of the x- and y-coordinates of a point along the x- and y-axes. If a line has start point (0,0) and end point (5,5), then the `Vector` describing the line segment is (5,5)—essentially, the difference between the start and end points. `Vector` is a transformation mechanism; specifically, it is used to transform lines within a 2-D space.

Attributes

`X` *(optional)*
: This `Double` value represents the x-component of the `Vector`. The default value is 0.

`Y` *(optional)*
: This `Double` value represents the y-component of the `Vector`. The default value is 0.

Vector3D

Vector3D is a structure and has no hierarchy.

```
<Vector3D
    X="5"
    Y="5"
    Z="5" />
```

`<Vector3D .../>` represents a displacement in 3-D space. It describes the movement of all three coordinates of a 3-D point along the x-, y-, and z-axes. If a three-dimensional line has start point (0,0,0) and end point (5,5,5), then the `Vector` describing the line segment is (5,5,5)—essentially, the difference between the start and end points. `Vector3D` is a transformation mechanism; specifically, it is used to transform lines within a 3-D space.

Attributes

`X` *(required)*
: This `Double` value represents the x-component of the `Vector3D`.

`Y` *(required)*
: This `Double` value represents the y-component of the `Vector3D`.

`Z` *(required)*
: This `Double` value represents the z-component of the `Vector3D`.

12
Events

In a typical application, UI elements will contain other elements as children. A Page contains a Button and a Label; a StackPanel might contain multiple Button elements as well as text-based and Image elements. UI elements and their children are designed with user interaction in mind. When a user interacts with an element, a corresponding event is raised and—if declared—an event handler is executed. When a Button is clicked, the Click event is raised; when the selection in a ComboBox changes, the SelectionChanged event is raised; and so on. Chapter 8 notes the events raised by controls along with each element and lists the common events for all controls.

While this material is likely familiar to developers, there is a fundamental difference in how Avalon elements deal with events. In a typical Windows Forms or other Microsoft .NET application, only the element that raised the event responds to the event. If a Button is clicked by a user, the Button element receives the corresponding event indicating that the button has been clicked. In a XAML application, the parent element of the Button may handle the event instead, or any other element in the tree in which the Button is declared.

Consider the following XAML application (Figure 12-1) and its XAML code (Example 12-1).

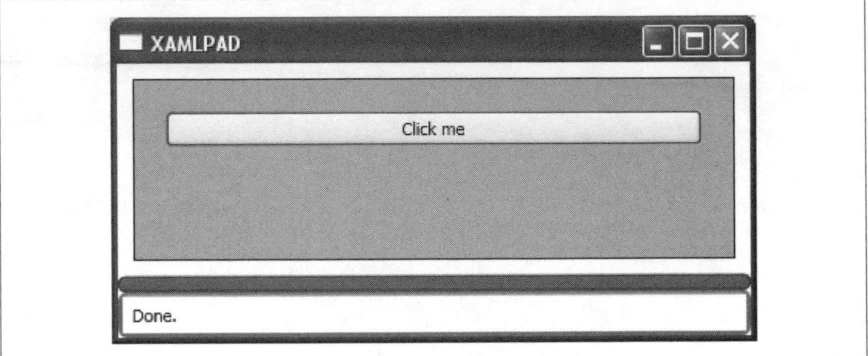

Figure 12-1. A simple XAML application

Example 12-1. A simple XAML application

```
<Page
    xmlns="http://schemas.microsoft.com/winfx/avalon/2005"
    xmlns:x="http://schemas.microsoft.com/winfx/xaml/2005">
    <Border
        Margin="10"
        Padding="10"
        BorderBrush="Black"
        Background="SkyBlue"
        BorderThickness="1">
        <StackPanel
            Margin="10">
            <Button
                Content="Click me" />
        </StackPanel>
    </Border>
</Page>
```

The application consists of four elements: `Page`, `Border`, `StackPanel`, and `Button`. `Button` is a child of `StackPanel`, `StackPanel` is a child of `Border`, and `Border` is a child of `Page`. Just as your grandparent is a kind of "parent," so too are the parent elements of a XAML element's parent. This is illustrated by the formatting of the examples in this book; using indentation to nest elements within their parent helps to visualize their relationship.

Usually, the event handler for the `Button` element's `Click` event would be defined with the `Button` element and handled by the `Button`. However, Avalon does not require that `Button` handle its own `Click` event. In Example 12-1, `StackPanel` or `Border` can just as easily handle the `Click` event by declaring it as through it were an attached attribute:

```
<StackPanel Margin="10" Button.Click="MyButtonHandler" />
```

Avalon allows parent elements to participate in many events directed at its children through *event routing*. An event can be routed through multiple elements in a parent/child relationship (the "tree") until it is marked as `Handled` by one of the elements in the tree.

This might be useful to group together controls that should use the same event handler when any one of them raises a particular event (Example 12-2). For example, a "Yes" and a "No" button might be grouped together in a StackPanel. The same application logic will likely be executed when either button is clicked, but there will probably be some differences to account for.

Example 12-2. Grouping Buttons together to use a common event handler

```
<StackPanel Button.Click="ButtonWasClicked">
    <Button Name="YesButton" Content="Yes" />
    <Button Name="NoButton" Content="No" />
</StackPanel>
```


A single event handler (Example 12-3) can then be defined to handle both cases and to execute common application logic.

Example 12-3. Common event code in C#

```
public void ButtonWasClicked(object sender, RoutedArgs e)
{
    FrameworkElement source = e.Source as FrameworkElement;
    switch (source Name)
    {
        case "YesButton":
            // yes specific code
        break;
        case "NoButton":
            // no specific code
        break;
    }
    // common application logic
}
```

Avalon uses three distinct types of routing, which will be discussed further in the next section.

Routing Strategies

There are three types of routed event strategies in Avalon: bubble, direct, and tunnel:

Bubble
: A bottom-up routing strategy. The target element is first notified, then its parent, then *its* parent, and so on. If the event is marked Handled, then no other event handlers will be invoked. Microsoft suggests marking an event as Handled as soon as you know that there are no further elements along the route because there are performance advantages to keeping the codepath as short as possible.

Direct
: The type of routing strategy used by Windows Forms and other Microsoft .NET libraries. Direct routing means that only the event source element is notified. If

the event was raised by a Button, then only the Button in question will receive notification. Very few UI events in Avalon use the direct-routing strategy.

Tunnel
: Works in the opposite direction as bubble; it starts at the root of the tree and works down, stopping with the target element. Tunneling events are prefixed in Avalon with the word Preview. Generally, there is a corresponding bubble event for each tunnel event. If the tunnel event is named PreviewKeyDown, then the bubble event is called KeyDown. Similarly, if there is a bubble event called KeyUp, then there is likely a tunneling event called PreviewKeyUp.

Because of tunneling and bubbling, parent elements often receive events when the source is one of their child elements. If necessary, the source of the event can be determined programmatically by accessing the Source property of the EventArgs parameter passed to the event handler, as in Example 12-3.

Not all events are routed. The XAML designer will need to know whether they are, because routed events can be used within styles to created triggers; non-routed events cannot. Events are specifically marked as routed or non-routed to assist the XAML designer with trigger creation.

Event Argument Reference

The signature for event handlers is primarily the same for all events; only the event argument changes for different types of events. The syntax for all event handlers is:

```
C#:
    public void HandlerName(Object sender, EventArgs e)
Visual Basic:
    Sub HandlerName(ByVal sender As Object, ByVal e As EventArgs)
```

Each event argument type holds values specific to the event as well as general data such as the source element and the original source element. This section details the event argument types.

RoutedEventArgs

RoutedEventArgs is the base class for many other routed event argument types and is also the argument type passed to the event handler for events such as Click and Closed.

Properties

Handled
: This Boolean designates whether the event has been handled. If it is set to true, then no other event handlers will be invoked.

OriginalSource
: OriginalSource is stored as an Object and is generally cast to FrameworkElement in order to determine its true type. OriginalSource is the original element that raised the event.

RoutedEvent
: This RoutedEvent type indicates the associated routed event. This value can never be null.

Source
: Source is stored as an Object, and is generally cast to FrameworkElement in order to determine its true type. Because of routing strategies, Source may not be the original source of the event.

DependencyPropertyChangedEventArgs

DependencyPropertyChangedEventArgs is passed to handlers that are raised when a dependency property changes. It is not associated with routed events. DependencyPropertyChangedEventArgs has properties that help to determine both the old value and new attribute values. This class also allows you to programmatically determine the state of a selector, such as CheckBox or RadioButton, as well as handle changes in other properties.

Events

Properties

NewValue
: NewValue is an Object that can be cast to the appropriate type. NewValue holds the new value of the property.

OldValue
: OldValue is an Object that can be cast to the appropriate type. OldValue holds the previous value of the property.

Property
: This field returns the actual property that has been changed, allowing you to programmatically manipulate it.

PropertyName
: This String represents the name of the property that has been changed.

KeyEventArgs

KeyEventArgs describes the arguments passed to a handler for a key-based event, such as KeyUp or KeyDown.

Properties

Device
: This property gets or sets the InputDevice that raised the event.

Handled
: This Boolean designates whether the event has been handled. If it is set to true, then no other event handlers will be invoked.

InputSource
: This property is the PresentationSource that raised the event. At this time, there is only one implementation of a presentation source: the Windows standard HwndSource.

IsDown
: This Boolean indicates whether the key referenced by the event is down.

`IsRepeat`
: This `Boolean` indicates whether the key referenced by the event is a repeated key.

`IsToggled`
: This `Boolean` indicates whether the key referenced by the event is toggled.

`IsUp`
: This `Boolean` indicates whether the key referenced by the event is up.

`Key`
: This `Key` (enumeration) indicates the key referenced by the event. See Microsoft's documentation for `Key` enumeration values.

`KeyboardDevice`
: `KeyboardDevice` contains the logical `KeyboardDevice`.

`KeyState`
: This `KeyState` (enumeration containing `Down`, `None`, `Toggled`) indicates the state of the key associated with the event.

`OriginalSource`
: `OriginalSource` is stored as an `Object` and is generally cast to `FrameworkElement` in order to determine its true type. `OriginalSource` is the original element that raised the event.

`RoutedEvent`
: This property indicates the associated routed event. This value can never be `null`.

`Source`
: `Source` is stored as an `Object` and is generally cast to `FrameworkElement` in order to determine its true type. Because of routing strategies, `Source` may not be the original source of the event.

`SystemKey`
: This property indicates the `Key` associated with this event if the event is going to be processed by the system.

`TimeStamp`
: This property is an `Integer` representing the time the event occurred.

ScrollChangedEventArgs

`ScrollChangedEventArgs` is derived from `RoutedEventArgs` and extends the class with properties specific to scrollbars.

Properties

`HorizontalChange`
: A `Double` value indicating the amount of horizontal change in the scrolled content

`HorizontalOffset`
: A `Double` value indicating the updated horizontal position of the content

`VerticalChange`
: A `Double` value indicating the amount of vertical change in the scrolled content

`VerticalOffset`
: A `Double` value indicating the updated vertical position of the content

TextChangedEventArgs

TextChangedEventArgs is derived from RoutedEventArgs and adds properties specific to the TextChanged event.

Properties

UndoAction
: UndoAction is an enumeration indicating how the change in text will affect the undo stack.

  Clear
  : The action will clear the undo stack.

  Create
  : The action will create a new undo stack.

  Merge
  : This change will merge into the previous undo stack.

  None
  : This change will not affect the undo stack.

  Redo
  : This change is the result of a call to Redo( ).

  Undo
  : This change is the result of a call to Undo( ).

MouseEventArgs

MouseEventArgs provide access to the mouse and its various states.

Properties

Device
: This property gets or sets the InputDevice that raised the event.

Handled
: This Boolean designates whether the event has been handled. If it is set to true, then no other event handlers will be invoked.

LeftButton
: This MouseButtonState (an enumeration containing Pressed and Released) indicates the state of the left button of the mouse.

MiddleButton
: This MouseButtonState (an enumeration containing Pressed and Released) indicates the state of the middle button of the mouse.

MouseDevice
: This property gets the MouseDevice associated with the event.

OriginalSource
: OriginalSource is stored as an Object and is generally cast to FrameworkElement in order to determine its true type. OriginalSource is the original element that raised the event.

RightButton
: This MouseButtonState (an enumeration containing Pressed and Released) indicates the state of the right button of the mouse.

`RoutedEvent`
: This property indicates the associated routed event. This value can never be `null`.

`Source`
: `Source` is stored as an `Object` and is generally cast to type `FrameworkElement` in order to determine its true type. Because of routing strategies, `Source` may not be the original source of the event.

`StylusPointer`
: This `Object` represents the stylus mouse associated with the event.

`TimeStamp`
: This `Integer` represents the time the event occurred.

`XButton1`
: This `MouseButtonState` (an enumeration containing `Pressed` and `Released`) indicates the state of the first extended button of the mouse.

`XButton2`
: This `MouseButtonState` (an enumeration containing `Pressed` and `Released`) indicates the state of the second extended button of the mouse.

MouseButtonEventArgs

`MouseButtonEventArgs` extends `MouseEventArgs` and adds several properties dealing specifically with the mouse buttons. It is generally used by non-routed mouse button events such as `MouseLeftButtonDown` and `MouseLeftButtonUp`.

Properties

`ButtonState`
: This property is read-only and indicates the `MouseButtonState` (`Pressed` or `Released`) of the mouse button associated with the event.

`ChangedButton`
: This property is read-only and indicates which `MouseButton` (an enumeration containing `Left`, `Middle`, `Right`, `XButton1`, or `XButton2`) has changed.

`ClickCount`
: This `Integer` indicates the click count of the button associated with the event.

SelectionChangedEventArgs

`SelectionChangedEventArgs` is derived from `RoutedEventArgs` and adds properties specific to the `SelectionChanged` event.

Properties

`SelectedItems`
: `SelectedItems` is an `IList` (a non-generic collection of objects that can be accessed by index) of all items selected as a result of this event.

`UnselectedItems`
: `UnselectedItems` is an `IList` (a non-generic collection of objects that can be accessed by index) of all items unselected as a result of this event.

Event Reference

Click

Routed Event

Yes

Elements

`MenuItem`
`Hyperlink`
`ButtonBase`

Description

`Click` is raised on an element's `MouseLeftButtonDown` and `MouseRightButtonDown` events.

Event Argument Type

`RoutedEventArgs`

Closed

Routed Event

Yes

Elements

`ContextMenu`
`ToolTip`
`Popup`
`Pag`
`Windo`
`NavigationWindow`

Description

`Closed` is raised when the element has closed.

Event Argument Type

`RoutedEventArgs`

DragEnter

Routed Event

Yes

Elements

`UIElement`

Description

`DragEnter` is raised when an underlying system drag event is raised, with either this element or a child element along the route as the target. The corresponding event is `PreviewDragEnter`.

Event Argument Type

`RoutedEventArgs`

DragLeave

Routed event

Yes

Elements

`UIElement`

Description

`DragLeave` is raised when an underlying system drag event is raised, with either this element or a child element along the route identified as the origin. The corresponding event is `PreviewDragLeave`.

Event Argument Type

`RoutedEventArgs`

DragOver

Routed Event

Yes

Elements

`UIElement`

Description

`DragOver` is raised when an underlying system drag event is raised, with either this element or a child element along the route as the target. The corresponding event is `PreviewDragOver`. This event is raised even if the origin of the drag event is within the boundaries of the element.

Event Argument Type

`RoutedEventArgs`

Drop

Routed Event

Yes

Elements

`UIElement`

Description

`Drop` is raised when an underlying system drop event is raised, with either this element or a child element along the route as the target. The corresponding event is `PreviewDrop`.

Event Argument Type

`RoutedEventArgs`

GotFocus

Routed Event

Yes

Elements

`UIElement`

Description

`GotFocus` is a routed event that occurs when the element receives focus. The corresponding event is `PreviewGotFocus`. It uses a bubbling event strategy.

Event Argument Type

`RoutedEventArgs`

IsCheckedChanged

Routed event

Yes

Elements

`ToggleButton`
`MenuItem`

Description

`IsCheckedChanged` is raised when the `IsChecked` attribute of an element changes state.

Event Argument Type

`RoutedEventArgs`

IsEnabledChanged

Routed event

No

Elements
`UIElement`

Description
`IsEnabledChanged` is raised when the `IsEnabled` attribute of an element changes state.

Event Argument Type
`DependencyPropertyChangedEventArgs`

IsFocusChanged

Routed event
No

Elements
`UIElement`

Description
`IsFocusChanged` is raised when the `IsFocused` attribute of an element changes state.

Event Argument Type
`DependencyPropertyChangedEventArgs`

IsMouseDirectlyOverChanged

Routed event
No

Elements
`UIElement`

Description
`IsMouseDirectlyOverChanged` is raised when the `IsMouseDirectlyOver` attribute of an element changes state.

Event Argument Type
`DependencyPropertyChangedEventArgs`

IsVisibleChanged

Routed event
No

Elements
`UIElement`

Description

`IsVisibleChanged` is raised when the `IsVisible` attribute of an element changes state.

Event Argument Type

`DependencyPropertyChangedEventArgs`

KeyDown

Routed Event

Yes

Elements

`UIElement`

Description

`KeyDown` is raised when a key is pressed while the element or a child element has focus. `KeyDown` uses a bubbling event strategy. The corresponding event is `PreviewKeyDown`.

Event Argument Type

`KeyEventArgs`

KeyUp

Routed Event

Yes

Elements

`UIElement`

Description

`KeyUp` is raised when a key is released while the element or a child element has focus. `KeyUp` uses a bubbling event strategy. The corresponding event is `PreviewKeyUp`.

Event Argument Type

`KeyEventArgs`

LayoutUpdated

Routed event

No

Elements

`UIElement`

Description

`LayoutUpdated` is raised when the layout of the element has been altered because a property, such as `Width` or `Content`, was changed; because a window was resized; or because the user specifically requested the layout update.

Event Argument Type

`DependencyPropertyChangedEventArgs`

LostFocus

Routed Event

Yes

Elements

`UIElement`

Description

`LostFocus` is a routed event that occurs when the element loses focus. The corresponding event is `PreviewLostFocus`. It uses a bubbling event strategy.

Event Argument Type

`RoutedEventArgs`

MouseEnter

Routed Event

Yes

Elements

`UIElement`

Description

`MouseEnter` is raised when the mouse pointer enters the boundaries of the element to which it is attached. It uses a direct routing strategy, so it is handled only in the element in which it was raised, but it does enable other routed event behaviors (such as event triggers in styles).

Event Argument Type

`RoutedEventArgs`

MouseLeave

Routed Event

Yes

Elements

`UIElement`

Description

`MouseLeave` is raised when the mouse pointer leaves the boundaries of the element to which it is attached. It uses a direct routing strategy, so it is handled only in the element in which it was raised, but it does enable other routed event behaviors (such as event triggers in styles).

Event Argument Type

`MouseEventArgs`

MouseMove

Routed Event

Yes

Elements

`UIElement`

Description

`MouseMove` is raised when the mouse pointer moves over the element or a child element along the route. It uses a bubbling strategy. The corresponding event is `PreviewMouseMove`.

Event Argument Type

`MouseEventArgs`

MouseLeftButtonDown

Routed Event

No

Elements

`UIElement`

Description

`MouseLeftButtonDown` is raised when the left mouse button is clicked over an element.

Event Argument Type

`MouseButtonEventArgs`

MouseLeftButtonUp

Routed Event

No

Elements

`UIElement`

Description

`MouseLeftButtonUp` is raised when the left mouse button is released while it is over the element.

Event Argument Type

`MouseButtonEventArgs`

MouseRightButtonDown

Routed Event

No

Elements

`UIElement`

Description

`MouseRightButtonDown` is raised when the right mouse button is clicked while it is over the element.

Event Argument Type

`MouseButtonEventArgs`

MouseRightButtonUp

Routed Event

No

Elements

`UIElement`

Description

`MouseRightButtonUp` is raised when the right mouse button is released while it is over an element.

Event Argument Type

`MouseButtonEventArgs`

Opened

Routed Event

Yes

Elements

`ContextMenu`
`Popup`
`Tooltip`

Description

`Opened` is raised when the element opens.

Event Argument Type

`RoutedEventArgs`

SelectionChanged

Routed event

Yes

Elements

`TextBoxBase`
`Selector`

Description

`SelectionChanged` is raised whenever a selection is changed, whether through binding, user interaction, or programmatically. It uses a bubble routing strategy.

Event Argument Type

`SelectionChangedEventArgs`

ScrollChanged

Routed Event

Yes

Elements

`ScrollViewer`

Description

`ScrollChanged` is raised when the scroll state has changed.

Event Argument Type

`ScrollChangedEventArgs`

TextChanged

Routed Event

Yes

Elements

`TextBoxBase`

Description

`TextChanged` is raised when the text in the element changes either through user interaction or programmatically. This is raised even when the element is initially created and the text is populated.

Event Argument Type

`TextChangedEventArgs`

IV

Appendixes

A
System.Windows.Controls

When writing code for event handlers, it is sometimes necessary to include the namespace in which specific elements reside. Here are the elements found in the `System.Windows.Controls` namespace:

- `Border`
- `Button`
- `Canvas`
- `CheckBox`
- `ColumnDefinition`
- `ColumnDefinitionsCollection`
- `ComboBox`
- `ComboBoxItem`
- `ContextMenu`
- `DockPanel`
- `DocumentViewer`
- `Expander`
- `Frame`
- `Grid`
- `HorizontalSlider`
- `Image`
- `Label`
- `ListBox`
- `ListBoxItem`
- `MediaElement`
- `Menu`

- MenuItem
- Page
- Panel
- PasswordBox
- RadioButton
- RadioButtonList
- RichTextBox
- RowDefinition
- ScrollViewer
- TabControl
- TabItem
- TextBlock
- TextBox
- TextSearch
- ToolBar
- ToolBarOverflowPanel
- ToolBarPanel
- ToolBarTray
- ToolTip
- VerticalSlider
- Viewbox
- Viewport3D

B
System.Windows.Documents

When writing code for event handlers, it is sometimes necessary to include the namespace in which specific elements reside. Here are the elements found in the `System.Windows.Documents` namespace:

- `Bold`
- `Figure`
- `FixedDocument`
- `FixedPage`
- `Floater`
- `FlowDocument`
- `Hyperlink`
- `Inline`
- `Italic`
- `LineBreak`
- `List`
- `ListItem`
- `PageContent`
- `Paragraph`
- `Section`
- `Subscript`
- `Superscript`
- `Table`
- `TableFooter`
- `TableBody`
- `TableCell`

- `TableColumn`
- `TableFooter`
- `TableHeader`
- `TableRow`
- `TableRowGroup`
- `Underline`

C
System.Windows.Shapes

When writing code for event handlers, it is sometimes necessary to include the namespace in which specific elements reside. Here are the elements found in the `System.Windows.Shapes` namespace:

- `Ellipse`
- `Line`
- `Path`
- `Polygon`
- `Polyline`
- `Rectangle`

D
System.Windows

When writing code for event handlers, it is sometimes necessary to include the namespace in which specific elements reside. Here are the elements found in the `System.Windows` namespace:

- `Application`
- `DataTemplate`
- `Setter`
- `Style`
- `TextDecoration`
- `Trigger`
- `Window`

E
System.Windows.Media

When writing code for event handlers, it is sometimes necessary to include the namespace in which specific elements reside. Here are the elements found in the `System.Windows.Media` namespace:

- `ArcSegment`
- `BezierSegment`
- `Brush`
- `CloseSegment`
- `Colors`
- `CombinedGeometry`
- `DashStyle`
- `Drawing`
- `DrawingBrush`
- `DrawingCollection`
- `DrawingGroup`
- `EllipseGeometry`
- `Geometry`
- `GeometryCollection`
- `GeometryDrawing`
- `GeometryGroup`
- `GradientBrush`
- `GradientStop`
- `ImageBrush`
- `LinearGradientBrush`
- `LineGeometry`

- LineSegment
- MatrixTransform
- MediaTimeline
- PathFigure
- PathFigureCollection
- PathGeometry
- PathSegment
- PathSegmentCollection
- Pen
- PointCollection
- PolyBezierSegment
- PolyLineSegment
- PolyQuadraticBezierSegment
- QuadraticBezierSegment
- RadialGradientBrush
- RectangleGeometry
- RotateTransform
- ScaleTransform
- SkewTransform
- SolidColorBrush
- StartSegment
- TextEffect
- TextEffectCollection
- TileBrush
- Transform
- TransformCollection
- TransformGroup
- TranslateTransform

F
System.Windows.Input.ApplicationCommands

In XAML, MenuItem can be assigned to any one of the common commands provided by Windows. Here are the commands found in the namespace System.Windows.Input.ApplicationCommands and descriptions of what each command represents:

Close
: Represents the Close command

ContextMenu
: Represents the Context Menu command

Copy
: Represents the Copy command

CorrectionList
: Represents the Correction List command

Cut
: Represents the Cut command

Delete
: Represents the Delete command

Find
: Represents the Find command

Help
: Represents the Help command

New
: Represents the New command

Open
: Represents the Open command

Paste
: Represents the Paste command

`Print`
: Represents the `Print` command

`PrintPreview`
: Represents the `Print Preview` command

`Properties`
: Represents the `Properties` command

`Redo`
: Represents the `Redo` command

`Replace`
: Represents the `Replace` command

`Save`
: Represents the `Save` command

`SaveAs`
: Represents the `Save As` command

`SelectAll`
: Represents the `Select All` command

`Stop`
: Represents the `Stop` command

`Undo`
: Represents the `Undo` command

G
Predefined Colors

The Brush element is often assigned by using a predefined color name such as Red or Blue. The following are the predefined colors supported in XAML for this purpose:

AliceBlue
AntiqueWhite
Aqua
Aquamarine
Azure
Beige
Bisque
Black
BlanchedAlmond
Blue
BlueViolet
Brown
BurlyWood
CadetBlue
Chartreuse
Chocolate
Coral
CornflowerBlue
Cornsilk
Crimson
Cyan
DarkBlue
DarkCyan
DarkGoldenrod
DarkGray
DarkGreen
DarkKhaki
DarkMagenta
DarkOliveGreen
DarkOrange
DarkOrchid
DarkRed
DarkSalmon
DarkSeaGreen
DarkSlateBlue
DarkSlateGray
DarkTurquoise
DarkViolet
DeepPink
DeepSkyBlue
DimGray
DodgerBlue
Firebrick
FloralWhite
ForestGreen
Fuchsia
Gainsboro
GhostWhite
Gold
Goldenrod
Gray
Green
GreenYellow
HoneyDew
HotPink
IndianRed
Indigo
Ivory
Khaki
Lavender
LavenderBlush
LawnGreen
LemonChiffon
LightBlue
LightCoral
LightCyan
LightGoldenrodYellow
LightGray
LightGreen
LightPink
LightSalmon
LightSeaGreen
LightSkyBlue
LightSlateGray
LightSteelBlue
LightYellow
Lime
LimeGreen

```
Linen                Orange              SeaShell
Magenta              OrangeRed           Sienna
Maroon               Orchid              Silver
MediumAquamarine     PaleGoldenrod       SkyBlue
MediumBlue           PaleGreen           SlateBlue
MediumOrchid         PaleTurquoise       SlateGray
MediumPurple         PaleVioletRed       Snow
MediumSeaGreen       PapayaWhip          SpringGreen
MediumSlateBlue      PeachPuff           SteelBlue
MediumSpringGreen    Peru                Tan
MediumTurquoise      Pink                Teal
MediumVioletRed      Plum                Thistle
MidnightBlue         PowderBlue          Tomato
MintCream            Purple              Transparent
MistyRose            Red                 Turquoise
Moccasin             RosyBrown           Violet
NavajoWhite          RoyalBlue           Wheat
Navy                 SaddleBrown         White
OldLace              Salmon              WhiteSmoke
Olive                SandyBrown          Yellow
OliveDrab            SeaGreen            YellowGreen
```

XAML Interface in Code

Anything in XAML can be done programmatically, due to the fact that XAML elements represent classes in WPF. Consider the following XAML declaration of a simple application:

```
<Page
    xmlns="http://schemas.microsoft.com/winfx/avalon/2005"
    xmlns:x="http://schemas.microsoft.com/winfx/xaml/2005" >
    <StackPanel>
    <StackPanel
        Orientation="Vertical"
        Width="100"
        HorizontalAlignment="Left" >
           <TextBlock>First Block of Text</TextBlock>
           <Button
            Content="Button 1" />
       </StackPanel>
    <StackPanel
        Orientation="Vertical"
        Width="100"
        HorizontalAlignment="Left" >
           <TextBlock>Second Block of Text</TextBlock>
           <Button
            Content="Button 2" />
       </StackPanel>
    </StackPanel>
</Page>
```

The following C# code declares the same controls and elements described in the preceding XAML declaration. Note that the C# code requires many more lines than the XAML representation, and the XAML representation is much clearer in terms of the hierarchy of elements. These are two of the advantages of using XAML over procedural code to declare a user interface.

```
using System;
using System.Collections;
using System.Text;
using System.Windows;
using System.Windows.Controls;
using System.Windows.Documents;
using System.Windows.Navigation;
using System.Windows.Media;
using System.Windows.Media.Imaging;
using System.IO;
using System.Threading;


namespace SimpleApplication
{
  public class MyApplication : Application
  {
    TextBlock txtElement1;
    TextBlock txtElement2;
    StackPanel rootPanel;
    Button btnElement1;
    StackPanel panel1;
    StackPanel panel2;
    Button btnElement2;
    Window win;

    protected override void OnStartup(StartupEventArgs e)
    {
       win = new System.Windows.Window( );
       rootPanel = new StackPanel( );

       panel1 = new StackPanel( );
       panel1.Orientation= System.Windows.Controls.Orientation.Vertical;
       panel1.HorizontalAlignment=System.Windows.HorizontalAlignment.Left;
       panel1.Width=100;
       txtElement1 = new TextBlock( );
       txtElement1.Text = "First Block of Text";
       btnElement1 = new Button( );
       btnElement1.Content = "Button 1";
       panel1.Children.Add(txtElement1);
       panel1.Children.Add(btnElement1);

       panel2 = new StackPanel( );
       panel2.Orientation= System.Windows.Controls.Orientation.Vertical;
       panel2.HorizontalAlignment=System.Windows.HorizontalAlignment.Left;
       panel2.Width=100;
       txtElement2 = new TextBlock( );
       txtElement2.Text = "Second Block of Text";
       btnElement2 = new Button( );
       btnElement2.Content = "Button 2";
       panel2.Children.Add(txtElement2);
       panel2.Children.Add(btnElement2);
```

```
            win.Content = rootPanel;
            rootPanel.Children.Add(panel1);
            rootPanel.Children.Add(panel2);
            win.Show( );
        }
    }

    internal sealed class Test
    {
        [System.STAThread( )]
        public static void Main( )
        {
            MyApplication app = new MyApplication( );
            app.Run( );
        }
    }
}
```

Index

We'd like to hear your suggestions for improving our indexes. Send email to *index@oreilly.com*.

B

C

D

E

F

G

H

I

K

Q

R

S

T

U

V

W

X

About the Author

Lori A. MacVittie is currently a Senior Technology Editor with *Network Computing Magazine*. In past lives, she has been a software developer, a network administrator, and an enterprise architect specializing in web-based technologies. Through the course of her career, she has nearly coded her way through the alphabet, starting with Apple BASIC, hitting "L" for LISP while consulting for Autodesk, and is currently on the letter "Y". Lori holds an M.S. in Computer Science from Nova Southeastern University and lives with her husband and children in the technological mecca of the Midwest, Green Bay, Wisconsin.

Colophon

The animal on the cover of *XAML in a Nutshell* is a kudu. Not to be confused with kudzu, a purple-flowered vine indigenous to East Asia, the kudu, native to East Africa, comprises 2 of the 90 species of antelope: Lesser Kudu and Greater Kudu. Both species have coats of a brownish hue that are adorned with white stripes. Males are easily distinguished from their distaff counterparts by their twisted horns, whose myriad traditional applications among African cultures include serving as musical instruments, honey receptacles, and ritual symbols of male potency.

The cover image is from the Dover Pictorial Archive. The cover font is Adobe ITC Garamond. The text font is Linotype Birka; the heading font is Adobe Myriad Condensed; and the code font is LucasFont's TheSans Mono Condensed.